SOUND TACTICS

RSA·STR
THE RSA SERIES IN TRANSDISCIPLINARY RHETORIC

Edited by
Michael Bernard-Donals *(University of Wisconsin)* and
Leah Ceccarelli *(University of Washington)*

Editorial Board:
Diane Davis, The University of Texas at Austin
Cara Finnegan, University of Illinois at Urbana-Champaign
Debra Hawhee, The Pennsylvania State University
John Lynch, University of Cincinnati
Steven Mailloux, Loyola Marymount University
Kendall Phillips, Syracuse University
Thomas Rickert, Purdue University

The RSA Series in Transdisciplinary Rhetoric is a collaboration with the Rhetoric Society of America to publish innovative and rigorously argued scholarship on the tremendous disciplinary breadth of rhetoric. Books in the series take a variety of approaches, including theoretical, historical, interpretive, critical, or ethnographic, and examine rhetorical action in a way that appeals, first, to scholars in communication studies and English or writing, and, second, to at least one other discipline or subject area.

A complete list of books in this series is located at the back of this volume.

Justin Eckstein

SOUND TACTICS

Auditory Power in Political Protests

THE PENNSYLVANIA STATE UNIVERSITY PRESS
UNIVERSITY PARK, PENNSYLVANIA

Library of Congress Cataloging-in-Publication Data

Names: Eckstein, Justin, 1984– author.
Title: Sound tactics : auditory power in political protests / Justin Eckstein.
Other titles: RSA series in transdisciplinary rhetoric.
Description: University Park, Pennsylvania : The Pennsylvania State University Press, [2025] | Series: The RSA series in transdisciplinary rhetoric | Includes bibliographical references and index.
Summary: "Explores how the use of sound in social movements not only involves simply hearing words at a protest, but embodies specific characteristics of sound to create meaning and inspire change"—Provided by publisher.
Identifiers: LCCN 2024055720 | ISBN 9780271099378 (hardback) | ISBN 9780271099385 (paperback)
Subjects: LCSH: Protest movements. | Social movements. | Sound—Political aspects.
Classification: LCC HM883 .E45 2025 | DDC 303.48/4—dc23/eng/20241204
LC record available at https://lccn.loc.gov/2024055720

Copyright © 2025 Justin Eckstein
All rights reserved
Printed in the United States of America
Published by The Pennsylvania State University Press, University Park, PA 16802–1003

© The Rhetoric Society of America, 2025

The Pennsylvania State University Press is a member of the Association of University Presses.

It is the policy of The Pennsylvania State University Press to use acid-free paper. Publications on uncoated stock satisfy the minimum requirements of American National Standard for Information Sciences—Permanence of Paper for Printed Library Material, ANSI Z39.48–1992.

A speech is not an essay on its hind legs.
—James A. Winans

To my wife, Lisa

Contents

Acknowledgments | ix

Introduction: The Sound of Resistance | 1

1 Acousmatic Rhetoric, a Transdisciplinary Exchange | 27

2 The Cut-Out and the Parkland Kid | 57

3 Heckling and HU Resist | 80

4 The Charivari and the Casseroles | 108

Conclusion: Unsound Tactics | 128

Notes | 149
Bibliography | 159
Index | 169

Acknowledgments

Creating this book has been an extensively collaborative endeavor, and I am profoundly grateful to those who have contributed their expertise, support, and encouragement throughout this process. I extend my heartfelt thanks to Leah Ceccarelli, the series editor whose meticulous attention and guidance shepherded this project through numerous revisions. Her dedication significantly enhanced the quality of this work. Josie DiKerby played an incremental role in guiding the book through production with finesse and professionalism. I want to thank Alex Ramos for carrying it over the finish line.

I am grateful to Amy Young, my chair, who not only read numerous articles but also provided relentless support throughout this journey. Thank you to Dean Cameron Bennett and Provost Joanna Gregson for the financial backing for my research (and the sabbatical to finish it!), and to Brian Galante and Greg Youtz for teaching me so much about music when I was writing the Parkland Kids chapter. I want to thank Peter Ehrenhaus and Marnie Ritche for listening to me ramble about social movements in the halls.

Thanks to my colleagues at UNLV who played crucial roles in the development of this book. Emma Bloomfield was instrumental in this journey. As a key member of the writing group where much of this book took shape, she patiently listened to numerous iterations of each chapter and reviewed countless drafts. Her feedback and support were invaluable. Donovan Conley deserves special recognition. Our relationship, which began at UNLV, has evolved into a lasting intellectual partnership. Donovan's influence on this work is profound; he not only inspired the title, *Sound Tactics*, during an early discussion of my research but also played a pivotal role following the Civic Wound conference. His insights were particularly crucial in shaping my work on the Parkland Kids. Donovan has been an unwavering advocate and thought partner throughout this process.

I owe a debt of gratitude to my normative pragmatics working group, which has been an invaluable space for developing and refining the case studies presented in this book. This collaborative environment has been crucial in shaping my understanding and definition of argumentation. Beth Innocenti has been a cornerstone of this intellectual journey. Her insights have been instrumental in refining the core ideas presented in this book. Through countless discussions, Beth has deepened my understanding of normative pragmatics from the project's inception to its completion. Her argumentation class at the University of Kansas provided a platform for me to present an early version of the Casseroles chapter, offering critical feedback that shaped its development. Jean Goodwin has been an equally influential mentor, guiding me through the nuances of argumentation theory. Her expertise and thoughtful advice have been constant throughout this project, significantly impacting the book's evolution. Jean's ability to challenge and expand my thinking has been invaluable in crafting a more robust and nuanced argument.

Bill Keith deserves a special mention for his assistance in crafting the first two chapters and the conclusion. His insights were crucial in crossing the finish line. My gratitude extends to Rob Asen for the opportunity to present the HU Resist case study in Wisconsin, which was a significant milestone for this project. Darrin Hicks has been encouraging and insightful, discussing case studies and broader impacts with me extensively. Trace Reddell has always been there to teach me about sound stuff, expanding my perspectives and enriching my understanding. Thank you, Christina Foust, for teaching me about social movements. Amanda Nell Edgar's influence in shaping and molding this project has been a beacon of guidance and inspiration. I am thankful for Lauren Moore, whose moral support, grammatical expertise, and friendship have been a constant source of comfort. Jamie Wright taught me that the magic is in the case studies—an invaluable lesson that has enriched this book immensely.

I owe a special debt of gratitude to my Tacoma writing crew, a group that has been indispensable in the crafting of this book. Special thanks to Nick Brody and Erik Tou, whose camaraderie and intellectual stimulation were crucial to my journey, and I am deeply thankful for their support. My gratitude extends to Amanda, Ben, and Betsy Myton for their generosity in letting me use their cabin (Camp Anawanna) for numerous writing retreats, providing me with a peaceful refuge to focus and write. I want to thank those who provided me friendship over the years and respite for the works of Tiffany Willink, Trevor Hamilton, Emma Hamilton, Will Taylor, and Ginny McClure.

I am profoundly grateful for the myriad friends, dinners, drinks, and conversations at conferences and panels that have sustained me through this endeavor. While there are far too many to name individually, I must highlight Nick Paliewicz, Stephen Llano, Constance Gordon, Katie Langford, and Damien

Pfister, whose camaraderie and intellectual exchanges have been delightful and immensely enriching. Each of these interactions, though sometimes informal, played a significant role in the creative and reflective processes behind this work. I would also like to express my gratitude to the exceptional group of students who worked with me over the years: Kate Hall, Matt Salzano, Vivian Shinall, Brooke Wolfe, Tate Adams, and Georgia Aust. I want to give a special shout-out to Brooke Wolfe and Jillian Stanphil. Their dedication, enthusiasm, and insights not only enriched our discussions but also contributed to refining the concepts explored in this book.

I want to thank my parents (Howard and Mary Beth), who inspired me. I want to thank Ralph Chips for being the greatest dog and companion. My deepest appreciation goes to my wife, Lisa Korby, for her unwavering support and patience throughout the demands of this project.

Introduction | The Sound of Resistance

In 2009, the Eurozone threatened an already reeling world economy. In the heart of the throng protesting at Syntagma Square in Athens was a sensory inundation of Greek fervor and conviction. The rhythmic chanting of two slogans in unison, each set to the traditional Greek rhythm of *dekapentasyllavos*, was like a pulsating drumbeat echoing off the buildings, a tangible reminder of shared Greek identity and centuries of cultural heritage. In this cacophony, the meaning behind the chants became an audible roar of demand. The resonating sounds carried an imperative force, echoing through the winding city streets, amplifying the collective will of the Greek people against their perceived oppression. The voices crescendoed and then faded, while the moments of silence held a palpable tension, almost like a deep breath before the next surge of verbal outcry. An undertone of grit and desperation imbued the chants with raw intensity, underscoring the seriousness of the protesters' demands. In the labyrinthine heart of old Athens, every concrete wall vibrated with the impassioned cries of the protesters, elevating the event to a visceral experience that resonated in the witnesses' core.

The protests arose in response to Greece's rising deficit. As one of the European Union member countries that had adopted the euro, Greece had stopped receiving foreign investment, causing their deficits to soar. Countries might ordinarily devalue their currency to remediate this problem, but the transnational nature of the euro put this option outside their control. As the unequal accumulation of debt threatened to tank the euro, the European Union acted swiftly with nongovernmental actors, such as the International Monetary Fund, to design a plan to balance Greece's debt-to-income ratio. Yet soon after, the 2009 Greece national elections brought the Panhellenic Socialist Movement (PASOK) to power on the promise of extending social benefits. The PASOK was almost immediately forced to implement a strict austerity program, widely blamed on the German government for refusing to lend Greece more money. The vice president, Theodoros Pangalos, warned that tanks would be required to secure banks if austerity measures were not passed. This reminded several Greeks of the military dictatorship known as "the Colonel's Junta," which ruled from 1967 to 1974. On May 2, 2010, Greece officially adopted an economic adjustment program, which enacted an austerity package that significantly curtailed social service programs.

The subsequent cuts and a 27 percent unemployment rate spawned public resistance, such as protests outside the Greek parliament in Syntagma Square on June 28 and 29, 2011. One of the primary protest chants called out the vice president of the PASOK: "Παλιοφασίστα Πάγκαλε μας απειλείς με βία μαζί με την απόλυση και την ανεργία" ("Dirty fascist Pangalos, you threaten us with violence along with dismissal and unemployment"). Another said, "Η Χούντα δεν τελείωσε το '73 εμείς θα την κηδέψουμε σε τούτη την πλατεία" ("The Junta did not end in '73. We are going to bury it in this square").[1] These slogans, which were also painted on walls, expressed the view that the government no longer represented the will of the people.

The Syntagma Square protest provides a representative anecdote for what I call a "sound tactic," which is the sound (adjective) use of sound (noun) in the act of demanding. The protesters at Syntagma Square were not making a request; by the time a group uses a sound tactic, all other communication channels have been exhausted, leaving the group no option but to insist on the legitimacy of its rights. Sound tactics attempt to constitute a group opposing a powerful institution obligated to enact their demands but that cannot be trusted to do so without public pressure. In this case, the protesters used sound to remind audiences of the relationship between the people and the government. The Greek people voted for leaders based on their promises and believed those leaders had a moral duty to deliver. The sentiment of this moral duty existed as a kind of ineffable feeling. This would be sound because it satisfies the necessary conditions—chief among them being that it rendered the nature of the demand audible; if an interlocutor cannot hear, you cannot create an obligation. But since there is no way the members of parliament could reasonably deny hearing them, it made an intersubjective relationship between them, which allowed for local normative roles and responsibilities so meta-deliberation could occur. The sounds marked a crucial distinction about what it means to be Greek, including questions of who is owed what and what it means to be democratic. These questions are visceral; they escape full capture in any textual representation.

We need additional context to understand how the Greek protest chants functioned as robust demands. In their analysis of this protest, Dimitris Serafis, E. Dimitris Kitis, and Argiris Archakis note that both slogans are "constituted by two iambic 15-meter parts (*dekapentasyllavos*)," which is "a general feature of many protest slogans, resonating with Greece's traditional demotic (popular) songs sung (and danced) in chorus at family, community and cultural events."[2] Nina Topintzi and Stefano Versace further explain that *dekapentasyllavos* spans "several centuries and poetic genres, including folk songs, medieval and early modern vernacular poetry, as well as much learned Byzantine writing in the ceremonial and exegetical traditions."[3] For those who grew up in Greece, this meter is familiar, as it has been carried across time through the oral tradition. The *dekapentasyllavos* interpolates an audience through a shared sense of time and place in Greek culture as a sound tactic. It conjures feelings of a Greek identity that rejects foreign rule. To be Greek involves commitments to the shared language, land, religion, and food, as well as some shared values, all woven through the *dekapentasyllavos*.

The sound speaks to the immediate presence of the specifically Greek people and the strength of their convictions; it was proof that they had managed to come together, seizing the window of time to enact their rights. The dense city center of Athens provided the ideal acoustics to amplify this feeling. The force of the protest reverberated off buildings and spread across the streets. People came out, chanted, and protested the cuts for two days. At times, friction erupted into moments of violence as police and citizens clashed in the streets. As an old city that emerged in the times of an oral society and became increasingly dense, the walls of the Plaka provided ideal spaces to write the lyrics so anyone could come to participate and join the assemblage of bodies. The hard concrete wall invited waveforms to vibrate and propagate across a downtown metroplex, and the labyrinthine structure enabled the reverberations to grow and amplify. The concrete obscured the source of any individual sound, creating an affect of *the Greek people* demanding to be heard. The sounds of the protesters— a unified, sensory collective—represented a presence that demanded accountability from the people in parliament. The event exerted its presence in news cycles for the broader international community, thus participating in a more expansive political spectacle.

The protest merged form and content because the ability of sound to gather audiences under a collective identity was integral to the protesters' argument. Their overall argument was straightforward:

1. Greek people are entitled to their social benefits.
2. If the state was cutting its social benefits, then it was fascist because it no longer represented their will.

But the function of the chants was less to generate reasoned dialogue about this stated proposition and more to constitute the Greek people as a collective presence. The government could not be trusted to make the right choice, so they must be forced to concede to the people's will. The Greek people, warranted from *dekapentasyllavos*, felt they must demonstrate how significantly the PASOK violated procedure. The PASOK promised to represent the people, and they broke that promise. The very people they voted for betrayed them, so any process for remediation would be called into question. This underwrote the substance of the protesters' claim that "right makes might"—the idea that the person making the demand occupies the moral high ground on an issue. Thus, an ideal moral tension emerged: any attempt by the PASOK to disrupt the protesters' voices with force only served to cede more of the moral high ground to the protesters.

Ultimately, the Greek parliament passed the austerity measures, and more instability followed. The textual slogans persisted on the walls as a reminder and future invocation. This performative sound tactic redesigned the communication environment and changed people's relationship with the Greek parliament. There were debates about what it meant to be Greek, who qualified for benefits, and the duty of the government. This mode of address created a set of relationships that distributed responsibilities and obligations between parliament and the people. Long after the Syntagma Square protest ended, the tactics that animated them persisted.

A *dekapentasyllavos* provides a classic example of a topos, a commonplace from which one draws arguments in rhetorical invention. The Greek chant provides an index of public feelings from which others might draw when advocating in public. Yet this topos is unique in how sound draws attention to temporal dimensions and things like rhythm, reverberation, and velocity. Unlike other topoi, the experience moves along a logic of intensity, in which the audience experiences how near the Greek people were based on the experience in time. For the Greek people, a mixture of all three dimensions gave *dekapentasyllavos* its unique character; the rhythm of the chant imbued it with meaning, the reverberation from the acropolis ensured the people felt more salient than before, and the quickness from which it emerged drove home the urgency of their plight. For spectators worldwide, the presence of the Greek people was felt in the rhymes of a *dekapentasyllavos* as it echoed off the dense urban acropolis, was transduced into newspaper headlines, and flickered across the public screen as a short segment on news networks.[4]

However, these tactics do not owe allegiance to any specific ideological stance but instead offer topoi to propel a variety of reasons. This principle is echoed in the notion that the misuse of valuable assets, including the power of speech, can lead to harm. Just as Aristotle suggests in his treatise on rhetoric, complemented by an emphasis on wisdom, the effective use of such assets requires ethical judgment. For instance, the *dekapentasyllavos* became a rallying cry for the far-right extremist group Golden Dawn to cast out immigrants. Here the power of speech, a fundamentally valuable asset, was employed not with wisdom and ethical consideration but as a tool for division. For Golden Dawn, this expression of what it means to be Greek became a way to sonically define us (the Greeks) against them (the immigrants). This example starkly illustrates how, when used correctly, assets like speech can bring immense benefits, yet when misused, they can cause significant damage. The ethical dimension of using such powerful tools underscores the necessity of integrating wisdom into our discourse, aiming to harness the potential of our assets for constructive rather than destructive ends.

This book is about the sounds made by those seeking change, how those people make a decision that is itself sound, and the possibilities that sounds offer us in our drive to hold those in power accountable. We live in an era marked by an increasing number of diverse social movements, all utilizing sound tactics to voice their demands. This intriguing use of sound ranges across the social and political spectrum, from the activities driven by President Trump's followers to the impassioned calls for justice and equality by Black Lives Matter activists. This spans the globe and goes beyond the confines of the nation-state and its citizens to implicate the flows of global capitalism and transnational networks. Understanding these sound tactics and their implications is not only fascinating but essential if we are to comprehend the underlying dynamics that shape our world today. The way we understand social movements as presences that manifest in everyday life provides an essential way to negotiate everyday politics. In this book, I delve into these phenomena, elucidating the profound ways sound is employed to convey and amplify demands and structure conversation, argument, and deliberation within these movements. This analysis offers invaluable insights into how movements use sound to engage with institutions, construct shared identities, and negotiate the public screen. But to understand how sound can be deployed tactically, we must first understand the rhetoric of sound.

Under What Conditions Can Sound Be Rhetorical?

The word "sound" in *Sound Tactics* serves a dual function. As a social practice, a sound tactic involves an agent using sound to pressure an addressee to accede. Additionally, the tactic must be intentional and morally grounded. In the complete sense, a sound tactic results from an agent under constraint using sound (adjective) judgment to implement sound (noun) to realize a goal. Sound tactics are not strictly instrumental—sometimes they work, sometimes they do not—but since the nature of the demand is moral, they prompt a moral debate that can lead to recurring social movements. A social movement here can beget policy change, cultural categories, revaluation of values, or other just social change. My gambit is that those sound tactics exert force to constrain the available moves that populate an argumentative ecology that enables and constrains a rich set of deliberative possibilities.

The first definition of sound is a noun that can be heard and felt. Such a definition places sound firmly in the realm of the phenomenological. There is no universal definition of sound but rather a culturally contingent understanding; one person might consider something noise, while another group might find it rich with meaning. This understanding of sound comes from a tradition of media theory that I discuss in the next section. Suffice it to say that this tradition recognizes that sound is a "durational" object that bundles together many sensations into a whole. Sounds can come from everywhere; we are immersed in them throughout our day.

There are several ways of defining "tactics," but something that unifies them is an emphasis on intention. Yet a more substantial discussion of a tactic comes from teasing out the difference between a strategy and a tactic. In his treatise on the practice of everyday life, Michel de Certeau distinguishes a strategy from a tactic by orienting them along the lines of unequal power relations between agents and institutions. While a strategy comes from a place of "will and power," the tactic "has at its disposal no base where it can capitalize on its advantages, prepare its expansions, and secure independence with respect to circumstances."[5] In other words, tactics invoke a power relationship where the agent does not occupy a place of power and must "constantly manipulate events to turn them into 'opportunities.'"[6] So, when the agent undertakes their goal, they undertake significant risk because they already operate at a power deficit. If your opponent has more power, you look for ways to harness that power to your advantage.

The practical judgment these agents use to turn events into opportunities raises a second definition of sound, an adjective: "showing or based on good judgment," which comes from the rhetorical tradition of exercising reason. It describes how an agent might audit their potential options when deciding how they want to advance an argument. While rhetoric and argument can be conflated, they are not the same. An argument can be considered an inferential relationship between a claim and data. Rhetoric, on the other hand, describes an inquiry into the available means of persuasive options. As a specific method, rhetoric audits the underlying contingent conditions to identify how agents might leverage familiar tropes to reach practical goals. Critical to this perspective is an agent with the capacity to make choices. While it is impossible to generate predictive claims, this method notes similarities that yield better choices. The rhetorical approach to argumentation produces topoi (or places), which helps us think about responses for generic situations.

Sounds

If sound tactics are how agents leverage sound against institutions, then "sound" as a noun provides the qualitative experience to underwrite a tactic. The concept of a "sound object" stakes out particular ground in definitional debates in sound studies. My definition of sound comes from a tradition of experimental music (*musique concrete*) that diverged from *hearing* sound simply as the indicator of something else; for example, "What's that?" "That's the sound *of a* door." Instead, this tradition seeks to experiment with bracketing the origins of a sound to consider the experience itself. For instance, we do not hear street noise in the chant of the opening anecdote but an attribution to the Greek people themselves. The specific site of the sound allows us to listen to *the Greek people* standing up and demanding change. Crucially, this provides the capacity to build indexical relationships between sign and signified.

From this tradition, sounds are not static entities. They index multiple dimensions (e.g., vibrations, electromagnetic waves, verbal inputs) to create a sensory experience holistically and link them to ideological structures. This process enlists public categories to help make sense of vibrations as narrative wholes. For instance, consider when a foley artist (the person who creates nonmusical sounds for movies) decides how to craft the sound for a scene. They must draw from publicly available resources, such as cultural assumptions and iconic sonic representations (synecdoche, perhaps). If someone wanted to place a podcast scene in a harbor—and get the audience to accept that it is a harbor—they might select a sample of "/foghorn/," a sound that culturally signals "we're in a harbor now." The association of foghorns and harbors is not the domain of the private individual but the product of general, contingent rhetorical categories. The capacity for hearing what feels like foghorns comes from public resources that associate foghorns, harbors, and expectations of the deep, resonant tones that associate the two. These ideas go beyond foghorns, moving up the ladder of abstraction to encompass the style of events, periods, and moods. Sound can provide a register to operate on feelings. Many sounds seem to help the public recognize an emergency (siren), cue a period of history (harpsichord), or modulate collective mood (the orchestral swell in a movie).

Tia DeNora's research extensively explores how sound can "get into action" of everyday life. For DeNora, sound provides an essential set of preexisting social resources that agents rely on to guide social interaction and define the contours of the agency.[7] She argues that sound functions as an ideological apparatus, effectively ordering the social. Through extensive interviews with participants about their music consumption habits, she concludes that as auditors move through space, "the audio-environment is thus part of what actors refer to in their reflexive monitoring of situations; it is one of the things that actors may consider to determine what is, should or could be going on."[8] Sound configures an embedded and embodied environment that agents rely on to make decisions on how to comport themselves, attune their energy, and dictate conduct. Unsurprisingly, it is strategically employed in places from the restaurant that plays the most incredible music to brand itself hip to an airplane that selects instrumentals to welcome passengers and soothe anxieties.

Take one of DeNora's interview subjects, Jennifer, a young woman who wanted to organize a party into a more mature event.[9] The party, we are told, is not like the other ones Jennifer experienced with loud music, cheap beer, and snacks; this one featured pretty music in different languages, mixed drinks, and desserts. Critical to setting the right tone for this party was her choice of contemporary "music in other languages," which exhibited social capital that was meaningful to her guests, "commensurate with their values of glamour, relaxed pace, sophistication, and romance."[10] Listening to music in other languages suggested a worldliness that set the tone for the event. For uncertain party guests, the materiality of the contemporary music also determined their conduct. For listeners, the notes conjured images of faraway lands they might one day visit and a sense of refined class characteristics that signify world travelers. If you are supposed to act like a worldly traveler, then the energy of the composition, coupled with sensations of worldliness, invites polite conversation and regulated conduct. An attendee dancing might seem a significant norm violation in such a setting, perhaps even drawing scorn. Music brings together materially produced vibrations with culturally acquired cachet. Form and content inseparably contextualize how to act.

Jennifer's musical ambience is simple enough, but the question of governing large-scale social spaces becomes much more difficult. Here, in the cacophonous environment of the public screen, any intentionally planned sonic act must compete with the noises of everyday life. Publics comprise distributed, vibrating assemblages vying for dominance across different times and spaces. These assemblages are linked to disparate horizontal, transitional networks that disseminate constantly. Moreso than ever, humans absorb sounds from an enormous arena of unknown sources. What Jennifer experiences is emblematic of how we engage media generally and what is called "the acousmatic situation" in our media environment. Combined with the proliferative condition of sound reproduction and recording, it highlights how contemporary technology constantly dislocates, relocates, and colocates sounds and bodies within temporary aural configurations. Even if listeners cannot identify a sound's source, it has an infinitely reproducible set of indexical experiences.

Sound Bodies

In today's age, the indeterminacy of sonic sources often prompts us to engage in imaginative supplementation; we attribute transcendental qualities or an active role to the origin of the sound. This disconnection between sound and its source generates a sense of tension and intrigue as listeners are left to visualize the unseen source. Though this concept may seem abstract, it's deeply intertwined with everyday experiences. Consider watching a movie with a voice-over. As we hear a voice, we instinctively visualize its corresponding body. Even if we lack knowledge of the speaker's physical appearance, our minds automatically populate the void with a physical form.

When faced with sounds whose sources are not visually apparent, such as the vague roar of a crowd, we instinctively fill the void with attributes born from our imagination. This type of unseen source—a presence to which we attribute sound—is what Brian Kane, in his book *Sight Unseen*, calls the "sonic body" (or a body that makes sound). The term "body" here evokes the presence we attribute to human agents. These agents are not limited to physical visibility and occupy a realm where the auditory can evoke the presence of the supernatural, from ghosts to deities. Their characteristics—shape, size, and presence—are subject to our imagination, often assuming an omnipresent or even panoptic nature, leaving us to wonder about their distance, magnitude, and the extent of their presence. The sound body is our imaginative response to auditory cues, painting vivid, often meaningful narratives when the source remains unseen or unknown.

Kane discusses an intriguing phenomenon occurring near Moodus, a quaint village in East Haddam, Connecticut, famous for its mysterious underground rumblings and tremors. The name "Moodus" originates from "Machemoodus," a term from the indigenous Wangunk people meaning "Place of Noises." The noises, initially believed to be caused by volcanic activity and subterranean vibrations, remain unverified and open to interpretation due to their unseen sources. Kane explores a spectrum of explanations, from spiritual and religious beliefs to natural scientific phenomena like seismic activity, gas dynamics, electricity, chemical reactions, magma movement, and geological shifts. Each theory reflects the cultural lens through which it is viewed, with Native Americans interpreting the sounds as the voices of gods, while European settlers pondered a mix of natural and supernatural explanations. The enigmatic nature of these sounds and their unclear origins encourage the imaginative construction of agents, whether they be spirits, gods, or natural forces.

I need to be clear: the experience of sound bodies is not the metaphysics of presence that Jacques Derrida warns about. But the creation of sound reproduction technologies can be used to structure unique relationships of absence and presence. Derrida explains that there isn't a singular, unmediated route to experience the "true reality" that preexisted language. He argues that the notion of having a direct, more authentic access to experience is false. Every method of experiencing life is an intricate organization of absence and presence, or spacing, of durational intervals. But these different organizations are always already culturally determined. In other words, in a unit of experience there are always complex cultural codes of signification that enable some things to appear salient and meaningful and others not. Although the modes may change, the influence of culture does not.

Instead of a metaphysics the experience of listening to acousmatic sound creates the feeling of sound intersects with what Joshua Gunn calls "presence affects."[11] He argues that presence affects emerge through the body's keeping track of cultural experience (the body keeps score) and how it draws from those embodied memories to interpret the present. From the perspective of psychoanalysis, Gunn writes, "Taking into account the Afterwards [sic] of understanding, it may be that what we mean by 'presence' is simply another word for affect, an experience of body-in-feeling before the fixity of representation. Presence."[12] When we feel a presence, that is the product of us making meaning out of an event that has passed. This relies on rhetorical categories that provide internal durational spacing. In other words, we know how we feel about something only after the event happens and we can attribute causality and cut out an agent, starting a chain of events.

Gunn's analysis of Electronic Voice Phenomena (EVP) serves as a compelling justification for the nuanced existence of presence affects where recordings purportedly capture voices of the deceased. EVP showcases how sound, especially recorded sound, can evoke a profound sense of presence from what is fundamentally an absence—the voices of the dead. When examining the rhetorical process, he found EVP relied on a complex procedure that involved priming, attribution, expert testimony, and audio to create sonic bodies. Yet there is affectivity that accompanies it, the designation of presence that endows it with significant rhetorical power. Through EVP, listeners report experiencing a range of emotional responses, from comfort and nostalgia to unease and fear, triggered by the apparent return of a voice from the past. These responses underscore the capacity of sound to store and mobilize past experiences in ways that are felt in the present. The very act of playing back EVP recordings manifests how sound can structure unique relationships of absence and presence, demonstrating that presence is not solely a matter of physical or temporal immediacy but deeply imbued with memory, emotion, and the ineffable.

As I will explain more in the second chapter, the acousmatic situation gives a generalizable presupposition that we never know the exact origin of a sound. When streams of broadcasts are grounded in signals like television, radio, podcast, and streaming, this provides a way to make sense of the infinitely reproduced world. We can never know the origin of the source because defining any one cause is an arbitrary cut. Yet as different causes come together, listeners are invited to speculate and imagine the origin—the body that causes the sounds (or the sound body)—that operates as a presence behind the public screen.

Although the sound body is unbounded, it conveys the immediacy, proximity, and urgency typically associated with a physical presence. The ascription of agency means these bodies can have intention, make demands, undertake responsibility, and confer burdens. Sound bodies can help us understand our digital environment, where the agency is distributed across various devices. These elusive entities possess seemingly divine powers, occupying all-seeing vantage points without being seen. Despite remaining unseen, sound bodies wield extraordinary power and exist beyond the public's gaze, exhibiting omnipresent, panoptic abilities. Some of the ways they may have impact include the immersive capacities and proximity of an experience. The larger-than-life entities can be on the periphery of everyday life or at other times intimately in the center.

Like the social movements I discuss in this book, sound bodies are unrestricted to individuals. As social movement studies aptly demonstrate, agents are not sole speakers but can include collectivities, assemblages, and other formations. This means that social movements are far more than just the product of a person but involve constitutive elements. Michael C. McGee demonstrates that social movement is *rhetorical all the way down*. Instead of focusing on a preexisting leader addressing a predefined audience using rhetoric as a tool to bring about an end, the entire process is understood as rhetorical. In a world where sound bodies create an unseen agent, unconstrained by physical limits, we see an interesting parallel with the abstract nature of social movements. Like sound bodies, social movements—the "agents" in this context—are more than their physical, visible components, such as protest marches or dynamic speakers. They exist beyond the individuals that make them up, constituting collective identities and causes that solely their visual aspects can't define. Therefore, sound bodies challenge our conventional understanding of agency, pushing us to consider how agency exceeds physical visibility and recognize the transcendent qualities of sound in a social movement's abstract collective identity. Using sound bodies to understand social movements gives an analytic language to describe how these agents gain a presence with the potential to exist anywhere and everywhere.

The sound body provides a way to register political agents outside the sight of the public screen or the public square. Consider the context of our opening Greek anecdote where agency, size, and feeling of the protest were attributed to cacophonous sound rather than just images flickering across the screen and graffiti on the wall. Each place provides a coordinate of everyday life that constellates the sensual salience of the event. In other words, *the tactic creates the conditions for how a sound body is felt.* This is a dynamic relationship that changes over time as each tactic might be deployed. There is an intimacy between the different demands and the presence that exerts their force through each tactic. Diverse media assemblages carry this presence across networks. For some, the Greek people are felt immediately as they move through Athens; for others, their presence reverberates through transnational media networks as part of the nightly news, muting its impact. In this book, I explore how these sounds and their associated feelings might add up to some broader set of tools for social movements and their implications for sound studies, rhetoric, and argumentation.

In the chapters ahead, the sound tactics I examine create imaginative conditions for the auditor to constitute the source of the sound; in other words, a physical sound chosen with appropriate contextual judgment can build the structure of feelings for a listener to identify an agent. The sound thus participates in constructing a collective speaker, allowing social movements to define the value and normative terrain of their demand. As I will demonstrate, whether it is the institution of the school, the family, or the government listening to the demand matters, as this impacts the moral terms of the discussion. The constraint of being a specific agent helps define the institutions' obligations, allowing the sound body to identify when they have exhausted all the normal means of seeking justice. Agents can use sound to shift the imagined body to a space beyond the perception of everyday life, enabling them to be everywhere and nowhere. It gives them extra power as they create a narrative tension with the substance of their claim that "right makes might."

Sound Reasoning

The practice of making an argument involves the social act of offering a premise and a conclusion. Several relationships between an audience and a speaker can constitute an argument encounter, from increasing someone's adherence to a set of beliefs to surmounting another's reasonable doubt. But what makes an argument sound rather than just valid? The term *validity* comes from logic, which involves abstracting symbols away from the social and making a mathematical determination of whether the conclusion is entailed in the premises.[13] While validity can be assessed through the form of an argument, soundness is a different kind of property. Soundness is a holistic assessment of whether an argument is good or good *for something*: soundness represents a pragmatic judgment about whether an argument holds together. Therefore, there is an inevitable social component to soundness. This social component can be considered in different ways.

One way we can judge an argument is through its function to regulate disagreements; this view is characteristic of the "dialectical" approach associated with the Amsterdam School of Argumentation.[14] Dialectical schools of thought assume that people enter into dialogue to exchange arguments and resolve their differences of opinion. This picture of social life shows that people can come together as neutral, deliberating subjects and persuading one another through objective, rational reasoning. If someone interrupts or exits this process, that person would be considered unreasonable. The underwriting assumption is that people naturally want to cooperate, and questions of power and privilege will not intervene in how arguments are heard. In this analysis, we can figure out what a North Star might be and use it to determine the best judgments, providing a framework for decision-making.

Yet this account, despite its attractions, is only abstractly social and doesn't apply to many contexts.[15] Argumentation is an emergent, self-regulating activity where people will debate what counts as a good argument, assert their definition of what should be in a proposal, and even challenge who counts as an expert.[16] We do, of course, have discourses, codified over diachronic time, that situate the synchronic exchanges. A fuller account would situate arguers in an institutional, social, and political context (this was, in part, the project of rhetoric in the late twentieth century). The holistic judgment of soundness then references the multiple commitments of the social worlds in which argument happens. The debate that happens occurs within a broader ecological set of discourses that adds a public and institutional dimension to the dialogic structures—it's not just that this person I'm talking to has a burden of rejoinder; it's also that those large institutions, in the right setting, may as well.

This is all to say that arguments do not happen ex nihilo, and arguers do not operate in a vacuum; their place within a social infrastructure recognizes implicitly that they operate within a chain of other commitments. This position recognizes that people live within intersubjective agreements that exert influence on how people act. These are generated from several commitments in formal places like the institutional structures that guide our social lives and informal areas like agreements during interactions. *Sound* as an adjective includes people making decisions by surveying the local normative terrain while attending to the shifting circumstances; it is a pragmatic, phronetic perspective that explores the banal practices that ordinary people use to self-regulate their disagreements. Indeed, in everyday conversation, simple speech acts such as accusing, proposing, and demanding all modify a chain of commitments that draw from local normative expectations. Making a sound argument is about developing a prudent practice that aligns the means of persuasion with the responsibilities of operating within a set of local commitments. When an agent acts, groups become constituted, obligations are met, and risks are distributed.

For arguers to display good judgment, their intent matters. After all, for it to be wise, it must be purposeful. In making an argument, a speaker is responsible for advancing a position they believe they can defend—something they can act on—and inviting the listener to trust them. As a social act, arguing generates a set of duties and responsibilities that create conditions for judgments, and judgment, perhaps most importantly, asks how to *situate* something in a constantly shifting social and institutional landscape. The critical first step is to determine how different claims can be rendered into other value priorities in a contrasting agonistic field to enable politics to happen in the first place. When the Greek citizens showed up to demand change, their intent was transparent. They conjured the public memory of the Junta of 1973 and constituted the Greek people *within that framework* to clearly define the affective stakes for the terrain of the deliberation. The narrative tension for the government was placing them between the people and the global financial system; memories of past use of government force provided additional context, further constraining the options for how parliament might respond.

Good judgment is an area of virtue in a world of constrained agency that allows agents to navigate toward an ostensibly virtuous goal in a social arena composed of shifting forces that link culture, power, markets, and governments. We live in a world of flickering devices, TikTok, vibes, and distractions. It is sometimes hard to believe that we all occupy the same time space. This may be because manifold time spaces proliferate, fragmenting, sphering, and propagating distinct worlds and experiences. This worldview assumes that communication does not start with dialogue—two people coming together in debate and deliberation—instead, an idea comes from the speaker (in some cases both the person and the device), out into the air, and lands on any vast number of listeners. In a world of mass-mediated dissemination, the speaker and listener can quickly become disassociated and unable to cocreate operational norms. Ultimately, a group's agency emerges under those moments of constraint when it can tactically make a demand.

I claim that sound and soundness are two sides of a rhetorical coin. Sound (the adjective) attends to how an agent attunes their commitments and obligations in each situation, and sound (the noun) is how that agent communicates them. We must gather the attention to make the demand and consider how making new reasons apparent might create opportunities for new loci of conversations. So, when we think about soundness, the larger question comes from how we judge the choices, given the constrained menu of options. Just like there are only so many ways sound, as a noun, can be made, there are only so many paths available to an actor, given the local constraints. Soundness involves a capacity for practical judgment, or "phronesis," but it is perhaps more accurate to say that soundness requires phronesis (like formal proof requires reason). Phronesis has a long cultural history stretching from the Sophists to the Aristotelians, through Rome and the Renaissance, and even to now.

Amid this backdrop of digital fragmentation, protesters adeptly navigate through the clutter using the very mechanisms that disperse attention to concentrate focus. The acousmatic nature of their tactics—where the source of a message or sound is unseen—plays into their hands, allowing them to craft and project powerful identities and messages without a centralized point of origin. This approach capitalizes on the digital era's essence, where voices can emerge from anywhere, anytime, resonating across the globe without a fixed location. In leveraging the acousmatic situation, protesters exploit the fragmented digital landscape to create omnipresent narratives. These narratives can surface on various platforms simultaneously, creating a sense of ubiquity and immediacy. The obscured origins of these messages make them more intriguing and compelling, prompting audiences to engage more deeply as they try to piece together the source and the full story.

Tactical Demands

Speaking in public provides an ordinary means of organizing how we think about everyday life; it illustrates how we undertake responsibilities, confer obligations, and make commitments.[17] In her essay on how speech acts structure the prospect for argumentation, Jean Goodwin demonstrates the potential of the practice of someone offering a plan to change the plans. In such a case, Goodwin explains, the speech promises to meet a "substantial burden of proof" required to alter the status quo; this normative obligation confers a cue upon the listener that they can reasonably accept claims made by the speaker and assume that "her proposal could withstand critical scrutiny."[18] The proposal establishes a communication environment that helps define the roles of the speaker and audience, the substance of the discussion, and the rules for the conversation. She contrasts this to gossiping sharply, when "a speaker expressly waives a commitment to veracity and even sincerity," which organizes an entirely different social interaction.[19] Conversation types impose certain norms that help generate expectations, burdens, and relations between speakers. Critical in gossip, proposing, and other similar conversation types, the speaker must be conspicuous with intent. The speech act designs the communicative environment only when the addressee knows the type of speech act in which they are participating.

Like a proposal, a demand is a speech act that prefigures a communicative environment. A demand involves an intention to influence an addressee to accede by arguing, in effect, that in this case "right makes might." Justness becomes a powerful mechanism of pressure. Requesting, in contrast, includes the opportunity for the institution to decline.[20] A demand underscores the feeling that the speaker does not trust the addressee to do the right thing. The transgressing of some norm licenses an audience to infer that the speaker would not undertake such a significant risk without first trying the proper channels.[21] This constrains the number of available social moves afforded to the addressees. Yet these social obligations can be easily evaded depending on the different contexts in which demands are made and how much force these obligations have. In the proper context, a demand can be leveraged to compel someone with more power to change.

The demanding process produces an agonism requiring groups to identify themselves in opposition. It involves hailing an institution and calling that institution, as a subject, into being. This process creates a relationship whereby the value divide between the agent and the institution animates the claims (of the demand), compelling the addressee to accede. The size of the embodied risk undertaken by the agent making the demand underwrites the force of the obligation it imposes on both actors. In other words, the greater the norm violation, the more credibility the audience can give the demand because they can be licensed to infer that the speaker would not take such a chance without good reason. The result is a high-stakes risk that trades in reputations and resentments. The highly charged feeling around such demands gives them moral force to propel new arguments elsewhere. Often the discourse itself can be about values. The organization of the demand acts on different value hierarchies of what is right, which then animate discussions about what to do. A demand's efficacy depends on the context in which it can be sustained, dismissed, or cause a backlash. But under the right conditions, a demand can be leveraged to give rights, increase wages, prevent death, or topple regimes.

The process of making a demand involves an agent rendering their intent audible. In other words, they literally have to tell us what they want. Only in making the intention transparent and impossible to ignore does it generate the sort of obligations that the agent undertakes while also conferring obligations onto another. While making the intention clear, the agent must satisfy two conditions for an act to be considered a demand: the first is procedural, and the second is substantive.[22]

First, a demand assumes that a procedural condition is met. The demand, as opposed to a request, comes from the speaker's decision to act outside of norms when making the intent to influence an institution audible. The procedural assumption is that the agent has tried every reasonable action to resolve the disagreement before stepping outside the bounds of decorum. The audible norm violation demonstrates that normal channels have failed, and the audience is licensed to infer that the institutional system cannot be trusted to fix the problem itself. Moreover, the agent making such a scene suggests that the institution cannot be trusted to do the right thing. Of course, the inverse of this indicates that if the demander has not made reasonable attempts to resolve the issue within the appropriate channels (the first condition), then they can face significant criticism, leading to the common refrain that "they should have just followed the rules and it would have been fixed." When an agent takes the risk to assert that the procedural condition has been met and traditional channels have failed, then the audible violations of decorum lay the foundation for their demand; these violations of decency come in many forms, some more overt than others, and the events critiqued in this book demonstrate a variety of such violations.

The second component that must be fulfilled is that a demand assumes a moral substance condition is met. This can be thought of as an argument that one is occupying the moral high ground, or to use the shorthand that I will apply throughout this book, that "right makes might." In their excellent analysis of the demand, Beth Innocenti and Nichole Kathol write that when groups protest institutions, the argument hinges on the claim that the institutions have failed to live up to their duty. To make this point clear, the agent bringing forward the demand must make their claim audible.

The acknowledgment of the demand thus creates an intersubjective situation that begins an agonistic political environment. When the agent is recognized, a series of intersubjective norms emerge. Significantly, Innocenti and Kathol write that "bringing to bear the norm of 'right makes might' constrains addressees from exercising institution or coercive power because doing so would put them at risk of criticism for using strong-arm tactics or abusing their position of authority and for failing to see the rightness of the speaker's position."[23] The exercising of the argument hinges on occupying the moral high ground. The most successful demanding strategies often involve the loudest displays that invoke outstanding norm violations and, thus, an undertaking of significant risk by the agents. The greater the institutional backlash, the stronger the demand is perceived by onlooking spectators. The substance of the demand licenses an audience to infer that the institution will change its behavior to no longer be in the wrong.

Of course, we must be clear eyed in recognizing that these obligations will only sometimes secure responses by compulsion. What counts, then, as a successful demand is the communication environment; the ultimate goal is to create the position for the communication conditions to change. Sometimes the discussion that results from demands causes the addressee to accede, leading to material change. Other times, the subsequent discourse compels the larger public to become involved, a second mechanism for creating change. There might be debates around the valuation of the demand itself. When new value hierarchies are uncovered, the ensuing discourse around them can lead to a transvaluation of values. Regardless of the outcome, the demand's efficacy concerns the different communication environments it underwrites. These discourses are hardly binary, but we must account for the situational nuance that emerges from the different tactics and the nuanced discussion that then appears in how they sustain discourse and deliberation.

Did the Greek people display good judgment when they demanded more from their government? Were the tactics sound? These questions concern the sort of conditions that the protests created for deliberation and debate. Since the original discussion that followed the protest raised issues from and around neoliberal capitalism, the state's role, elected officials' obligations, and the shifting geopolitical map, the constitutive fallout from the protests suggests a productive impact. The people had no other means to express their concerns. In an era of hyper-capitalism and the public screen, they needed to make a sound that spoke to and of themselves. The resulting deliberation contributed to the development of new concepts, the redistribution of sentiments, and the emergence of new entities. The sound nature of the controversy speaks to its salience and its ebb and flow over time.

So, if a demand demonstrates a violation of norms and evidence that right makes might, sounds are designed to amplify those feelings. Sound as a noun provides the substance for those very feelings, giving unique resources to contribute to that claim, tying intent to the reason for the protest. The ways those feelings reverberate have qualitative differences. A sound tactic attends to how the *immediate, intense,* and *immersive* resources for sound enable obligations to feel urgent, salient, and compelling. As I will discuss in the following chapter, each of these different features of what I will call a waveform helps uncover the unique warrant structures that aid social movements along these temporal registers. The experience of creating and listening to sound tactics produced by sound bodies adds to the claim's justification. Each chapter in this book explores how these tactics happen within the context of different institutions, each one setting the stage from which the agents must deploy their tactics and simultaneously defining the stakes of how sound might be considered, well, sound.

Book Preview

Like any other speech act, a sound tactic is seen as a stand-alone event and part of a web of interactions, each with its consequences and responses. Each act creates ripples that shape the ongoing discourse, providing a stage for continuous negotiation, understanding, and sometimes misunderstanding, all of which are integral to the human social fabric. The metaphor of the conversation as the primary problematic in making sense of the social comes from speech teachers. *Speech teachers* describes a specific group of people with a deep commitment to the teaching of public speaking that emerged at the turn of the twentieth century. Their core belief was that a conversation was the primary metaphor for discourse and could be applied widely. This idea has remained influential and provides a framework for understanding speech as an exchange of ideas and a dynamic interaction that structures our social and civic life. A demand is not simply made and received; it is performed, interpreted, and responded to within a complex conversational space. Creating a demand can subtly reshape this space, influencing the trajectory of the discourse and affecting the relationships between the participants.

The practice of speech instruction emerged as something wholly different from other subjects in the university—organized in everyday life and articulated somewhere between sound and the civic. The second chapter will tell the story of renegade speech teachers who drew heavily on Greco-Roman history, specifically Aristotle, to teach burgeoning urban populations how to navigate complex relationships (such as how individuals could coexist in shared time and space while pursuing their visions of a good life) and acquire new skills necessary for changing job markets. Critical here is a story of democracy that orients our understanding of rhetoric as a matter of practical instruction. These teachers saw their role in a new educational system that moved from making elites run society to giving everyday citizens skills to self-govern.[24]

Speech teachers embody democratic pragmatism, as demonstrated by James Albert Winans in his 1915 work *Public Speaking*. Winans championed fostering students' critical thinking and deep comprehension rather than encouraging simple information memorization. His goal was for students to actively understand and engage in the present moment with the audience, moving beyond passive rule absorption. While rhetoric in the field of speech might have started as interest in the experience of the presence between the audience and the speaker required to cultivate this capacity, the arrival of the text shifts the problem from fleeting feelings to abstract spatial relations. To help get a richer understanding of sound that allows me to apply it in the context of civic action and social currency, I advocate for a return to presence.

To fully explain the implications of sound bodies on the civic, in the next chapter I outline a transdisciplinary exchange borrowing from sound studies. Acousmatics is an essential concept in sound studies, as it highlights sound's crucial role in shaping our perception and understanding of the world. In the acousmatic situation, the focus is placed on the sound itself, divorced from its source but leaving a lingering itch to discover an origin; there is a metaphysical desire to endow something with agency. Acousmatics is a valuable tool for exploring the relationship between sound, technology, and culture and examining how sound conveys meaning and shapes our world experience. The acousmatic situation of a listener unable to ever know the source provides a helpful axiom for understanding the digital world where data and information are often abstracted and impossible to trace. I seek to use this understanding of sound to illuminate an understanding of speech in the contemporary civic sphere.

As I argue more in the next chapter, the Pythagorean curtain (or the acousmatics situation) becomes crucial in examining the mechanics of speech and sound. This concept emphasizes the spaces between source, cause, and effect that facilitate sound reproduction. Rather than residing in a single instrument or entity, the object of study becomes situated in these interstitial spaces within the public domain where cause and effect are rendered knowable. While a waveform obscures our ability to definitively know a source, the Pythagorean curtain accounts for how movements can extend their presence across vast temporal and spatial expanses. People might not visually comprehend these movements, but they can sense their causes and attribute origins, highlighting the influential role of unseen forces in our societal understanding.

At the same time, a waveform is a technique of abstraction to think about how each of these tactics might be conceptualized in time; as I will discuss more in the next chapter, a critical part of this abstraction is that it tempers sound that desires to be universalized, providing a contingent metaphor to understand events. The possibilities afforded by the waveform are explored thoroughly in chapter 2. These waveforms can always be missed, of course, in the cacophonous public screen and thus require a specific audience to be recognized. I divide topoi into three interrelated temporal registers: immediacy, intensity, and immersion. Immediacy deals with how quickly a sound starts and stops, offering places to modify urgency; intensity, meanwhile, comes as a sound dissipates and a choice to make new sound comes, pressuring the listener toward action; finally, immersion is about how sound vibrations fill a space, providing a sense of proximity. The language of the waveform then structures the rest of the book; each chapter spends time attending to one potential resource. In each chapter, the duration of the sonic experience provides a resource for feeling. Since this is about tactics, the groups wielding them come from a weaker position, using sound to leverage institutions. Those feelings help them constitute their force, be recognized, and, finally, compel engagement.

Chapter 3 starts with student advocacy after a school shooting on February 14, 2018, at Marjory Stoneman Douglas High School. These students needed to act quickly, and their concern is the sonorous resource of immediacy. They were worried that another school shooting was imminent and sought to keep the American public's attention while they had it. The students subsequently intersected with a vast infrastructure of nonprofits, celebrities, and resources that enabled them to quickly mobilize and produce the March for Our Lives event. The urgency of stopping gun violence looms large. It is perhaps best represented in X González's concluding speech at the March for Our Lives rally, which used the temporal proprieties of sound to create what I call a "cut-out," building up anticipation and then violating it with four minutes and twenty-two seconds of silence. The expectation violation was not just an attention-getter; it was designed to show the audience what it felt like to be in the school when the shooting occurred. The tactic represented what it felt like to be there in the moment. The extreme pain of remaining silent in a setting usually filled with noise underscores the sense that children cannot be forced to sit in this situation any longer.

This chapter adds to the conversation on sound tactics by demonstrating that the waveform extends beyond the moment in "the blink of an ear"; for example, a particular moment of González standing in the middle of the cut-out proliferates across platforms. The tension cuts across and brings the audience and the sound body together in a moment of vulnerability. The tactic created a relationship between the kids, who have been forced to sit in pain, and the adults entrusted to protect them but who have failed to do so. Right after González's speech, the image of them standing in the cut-out propagated throughout the public; the enthymeme of the silence enabled their argument to shape the continued discourse on guns—just as the rhetorical text has vast flexibility in contemporary rhetoric, the metaphor of the waveform also gives us an extended purchase to understand social movements because it comes in different shapes, sizes, and timescales. In this case, the immediacy of the movement is captured in the waveform of X González's speech, tying their demand to end gun violence with the immediate sounds (or lack thereof) of the moment. The urgency that builds, only to evaporate, perhaps gives us a way to think about how some of these tactics might operate.

Yet only some social movements are given access to the media resources that March for Our Lives received. Other groups must find innovative ways to generate momentum and pressure an institution to act. Intensity provides a way to generate force because every listener must choose to discern a signal from noise. Speakers can be tactical in their local environment to make an interlocutor confront them. Chapter 4 attends to another social movement, HU Resist, which started at Howard University shortly after the inauguration of Donald J. Trump.

This collective coalesced around the concern that Howard was serving the federal government at the expense of Black liberation. Like many nascent social movements, this group of students initially found it challenging to constitute itself as a relevant agent capable of making demands.

HU Resist elevated their campaign through the art of the heckle, drawing on a legacy of resourcefulness born from necessity. Faced with barriers to traditional forms of advocacy and planning, they adeptly navigated their constraints, seeking opportunities hidden within their immediate circumstances. Through improvisation, HU Resist crafted a series of innovative tactics, turning the university's environment into a stage for their protest. This strategic use of heckling—turning every interaction into a chance to press their demands—forced the administration into a dialogue they would have otherwise avoided. The narrative of this chapter traces how HU Resist harnessed this improvisation to fuel their cause, employing a variety of methods over eighteen months to amplify their message and shift the collective perception of what was possible, anchoring their intensity in the creativity and persistence of their heckling.

HU Resist succeeded because of the gumption that drove them to improvise and change their tactics over time. While they might have started with just a few people and fewer resources, their capacity to innovate across several waveforms enabled the group to grow, change, and adapt. HU Resist's ability to improvise and heckle the financial aid scandal helped them articulate their demand with the song "Bitch Better Have My Money," which ultimately compelled one of the most significant public concessions from the administration. The virality of their dance, coupled with the occupation of administration space, placed pressure on the administration to make a choice: adhere to their demands or risk looking more corrupt. The pressure translates to the university having to choose between forcibly removing the students or conceding to what the students demanded.

Chapter 5 focuses on how the intensity of students can change into the immersive power of the people. When the Québec government, responding to student protests, imposed the controversial Bill 78, which precluded public gatherings and stipulated government approval for all demonstrations, the people demanded their freedoms back. Every night, people emerged to bang their pots and pans; in doing so, they would tap into the social imaginary of the *charivari*—a transnational idea of the people—holding a liberal democratic government accountable. The extraordinary step of the masses coming out at eight o'clock every night for several months created the identity of a people committed to a liberal check on the institution of the government. If the government is meant to serve the people, then this repeated action suggests that the government has failed.

This chapter highlights the resource of immersion to show how demand might go from a small student protest to an all-encompassing "the people." Sound operates as a critical resource linking the audible intent to a feeling of salience that underwrites the force of the appeal. The people were *everywhere*, coming out nightly and saturating the streets and social media feeds. This demonstration often included musicking, a sound tactic inviting anyone in the community to grab what they wanted to use to participate in the music-making. It became a nightly party that brought people into the streets, including populations that ordinarily would not be part of a protest, such as children, older people, and people with disabilities. The practice of musicking was accompanied by social media posts that broadcast the nightly demonstrations outside the traditional coverage, giving anyone who tuned in an imaginary association through the sound. The loud and immersive sound hailed auditors, emplacing them in a new democratic space. The Casseroles (as they came to be known due to their use of pots and pans) used the physical realities of the streets to create an immersive sound, letting the banging bounce off walls and echo across town; at the same time, they tapped into the environment of the news media to create sound waves that would reverberate across town and immerse the entire citizenship in the struggle. The spatiality of the people's musicking gave presence to the feeling of democracy. Ultimately, their demands structured public deliberation about the proper limits of government control.

In the book's conclusion, I again consider sound as an adjective by exploring an *unsound* tactic. In response to COVID-19 restrictions, Canadian truckers organized the "Canadian Trucker Freedom Convoy" in January 2021, which involved hundreds of trucks driving to Ottawa to protest the vaccine mandate for cross-border truckers and other COVID-19 measures. But when the truckers switched the demand from revoking a narrow law to dissolving the entire Canadian government, this fluctuation raised questions about the tactic's soundness. As a matter of phronesis, this radical departure from the local normative grounds raised questions about who was behind the sounds, making it impossible for the people to settle on an author of the demands. Just as fear and concern crop up around things that go bump in the night, the shifting questions around the original cause sowed concern around their tactic. When the audience cannot definitively imagine the source of the presence, the uncertainty sows doubt and raises new issues of trust, fueling disagreement.

Now that we have previewed the book's central themes, we turn to chapter 2, where we delve deeper into sound's potential as a resource for moving the social. In doing so, we explore how sound might provide the very stuff of the political. The chapter takes a rhetorical approach to understanding sound and its potential opportunities, recognizing the contingent nature of an answer that always leaves room for the political without abstracting away from the lived realities of any participants. In this chapter, I am interested in discerning how listening can underwrite choices and obligations. I determine the ways it might be used to hold those in power accountable and explore how the principles that support sound can be wielded tactically by those with less ability to satisfy procedure and demonstrate the substance of their demand. Let us turn to the sound formations of waveforms.

1

Acousmatic Rhetoric, a Transdisciplinary Exchange

Sound Tactics brings various theories of sound together to advance an acousmatic rhetorical theory, taking us back to some of the underlying issues with the study of speech. When I say speech, I'm referring to a unique historical configuration tied to the founding of speech departments at the turn of the twentieth century that sought to operationalize rhetoric to the public speaking classroom. This is not a "turn" but a return to a configuration of rhetoric that emerged as it was being carved up into different technical areas of study. The discipline of speech, far from being an outdated relic, holds significant potential for theorizing the civic role of sound. While some may question drawing lines in rhetoric that focus on one history instead of another because it might prevent productive collaborations, the focus on these histories provides an enabling constraint.[1] The different historical conjunctures and the reasons for the decisions that were made provide a wealth of cultural resources that we can draw on in the contemporary moment.

Speech, as a discipline, carries a rich history that informs its inquiries and the knowledge it generates. Initially, communication models framed interaction as a direct exchange between speaker and listener, underestimating the complexities of audience engagement. Speech education recognizes the dynamic nature of public speaking, where speakers navigate the transient space between themselves and their audience, continually adapting to feedback. This adaptive process embodies a democratic dialogue, teaching speakers not only to articulate but also to read and respond to their audience's cues. Thus, speech education transcends imparting universal knowledge, focusing instead on equipping individuals with practical, situational skills essential for effective communication. This central concern animating the work of early speech instruction was how their discipline might ensure that someone taking a public speaking class was equipped to transfer their classroom skills beyond the university's walls and into the public.

These speech teachers retained a sense of rhetoric as a kind of soundness—an art that involved judgment—because they believed that speaking constituted a telos of community. These teachers wanted to work with students to cultivate the practices that underwrote the judgments required for democracy. Their early philosophical commitments retained a sense of the sonic and the civic that we urgently need, a kind of sonar that enables us to trace the ground of local democratic practice. As I will demonstrate, ironically enough, the text quickly usurped the speech as the object of study for rhetoricians in the newly developed field of speech, which occluded the vast potential contributions of early speech teachers. This book seeks to recover those potentials. In doing so, I advance a return to sound and a concept of civic obligation. Returning to a phronetic approach to rhetoric that takes sound seriously would enable us to move beyond disciplinary boundaries to contextualize sound tactics as a set of civic commitments.

When we focus on speech to understand presence affects, we can recognize its civic capacities and potential in a radically shifting media landscape, even when that presence is spliced, diced, and TikToked. A long history throughout the study of communication explains how speech involves the experience of presence affects as a good resource for advocacy. This provides us with an ideal heuristic to examine different situations and generate modest inferences about potential sound tactics for future civic use. This view has significant implications for our understanding of rhetoric because it is so much more than a techne (an art as it appeared in Plato's *Gorgias*); as the development of phronesis, a kind of praxis, rhetoric contextualizes the civic conduct for a member navigating the polis.

My theory of sound tactics results from a transdisciplinary inquiry at the intersection of rhetoric and sound studies. It addresses several interventions, noted here as they will develop throughout the book: This project contributes to the emerging interdisciplinary field of sound studies, which brings together the sciences, social sciences, arts, and humanities to investigate sound's impact on the world. I draw from acousmatics, a specific area of sound studies, to demonstrate how sound can be used as a resource for advocacy. At the same time, rhetoric brings a concept, problematics, and an understanding of the civic that sound studies lacks. It uses principles of invention that groups might adopt to bring their cause to the public. This book considers common principles that guide how sound can be used tactically. Perhaps, most importantly, it brings the other meaning of sound—that of good reasons—supplying a long history of using phronesis to think about judgment in rhetoric.

The interdisciplinary area of sound studies also faces a unique problem for which rhetorical methods might assist. When other disciplines come to sound studies, they can define sound and position it as a natural category. Robin James's recent book, *Sonic Episteme*, highlights a pernicious habit in sound studies to universalize *a* definition of sound as *the* definition of sound.[2] She argues that the result of this analysis "is that it naturalizes those existing imperfections and reinforces them rather than fixes them."[3] At the heart of James's critique is the universalization of technical reason, the tendency to focus on the what for so long that we forget to attend to the why. My contribution to sound studies requires us to turn to the relativizing moment between the speaker and the audience to evaluate rhetorical choices. Every definition of sound comes with choices. We need to return to the ground and attune to the specifics of the individual case. This move allows us to identify ways people can use sounds soundly.

An acousmatic rhetoric may shape values for holding those in power accountable to those who have less. We must be able to discern subject from object to study those moments of partisan, agonistic contestation when agents need to hold institutions accountable. As Kenneth Burke points out, this is rhetoric because it "deals with the possibilities of classification in its partisan aspects; it considers how individuals are at odds with one another or become identified with groups more or less at odds with one another."[4] Rhetoric is a political art that helps us go through what he calls "the flurries and flare-ups of the Human Barnyard, the Give and Take, the wavering line of pressure and counter pressure" as the social vacillates between cooperation and war. As speakers navigate this thorny terrain, they invent "common sensations, concepts, images, ideas, attitudes" to create identification.[5] Rhetoric allows us to delve into the transdisciplinary world of sound studies by giving language to the people, feelings, and ideas that play individual and crucial roles in moments of a contest between agents and institutions. Here rhetoric provides a valuable resource because it informs tactics to hold those in power accountable for their obligations. Rhetoric so conceived assumes a firm break between subjects to assess distributed roles and responsibilities.

Sound Tactics joins what Jonathan Sterne calls the "sonic imagination," a transdisciplinary conversation unified around a shared aspiration to study how sound impacts the world.[6] To contribute to this conversation, I propose the waveform as a theoretical concept to organize sound tactics into social movements. The metaphor of the waveform allows us to discern subject from object to explore those moments of partisan, agonistic contestation when agents must hold institutions accountable. The waveform and its attendant facets will enable us to assess how sound operates as a tactic in the case studies throughout the rest of the book. Immediacy, intensity, and immersion are the topoi that help us recognize those facets—topoi we examine that ultimately translate an agent's sound into feelings for listeners. After introducing the concept of the waveform, this chapter concludes with a discussion of the warrants that these topoi provide in an agent's attempt to leverage demands against an institution.

Sound Tactics provides an analysis of acousmatic rhetoric that links sound and argument to inform tactics in social movements. Such a practical account sutures an agent's intention, decision-making capacity, and desire to hold people in power accountable. This perspective subscribes to humanism, which focuses on the everyday experiences of sound as presence. The process comes from a musicological tradition of inviting practitioners to step outside formalism and invent sounds. Acousmatics is a contingent way of understanding sound as a particular kind of phenomenological object dictated through cultural traditions of audition that discern signal from noise. These embodied feelings draw from disparate rules and impact ways of knowing. When the inaccessibility of a source is made the condition for sound, acousmatics supplies literature with a language of intensity, immediacy, and immersion. I introduce the metaphor of a waveform as a way to think more broadly about the principles that organize tactics in order to understand our digital engagement in social movements. These chapters aim to construct a common framework that opens the potential for creating sonic phronesis.

What Is Sound?

Almost any sound studies book will tell you that to speak of "a sound" is a misnomer. The idea of sound can cover everything from a post-human process (vibrational ontology), which can help scientists explain stars, matter, and space, to providing phenomenologists with a cultural object to elaborate n. In his introduction to *The Sound Studies Reader*, Sterne observes that sound represents a vast interdisciplinary area of inquiry unifying everyone from the acoustic engineers who measure frequencies, to musicians composing melodies, to marketers using those compositions for advertisements, to the cultural critics responding to all of the above. Each of these disciplines defines sound differently, and those definitions have corresponding implications for how one proceeds to study sound as an object. Some perspectives on sound studies emphasize the materiality of their object and posit an objective world of oscillation that can lead to universal definitions, concepts, and theories. Frequencies might be measured, systematic propositions examined, predictions offered, and theories proffered. Suppose the sound is understood as only vibration. In that case, sound studies can go far beyond the realm of humans to encompass everything, for the entire universe might be understood as strings vibrating on different axes of time. On the contrary, if we are only interested in what people can *hear*, we will delimit an entirely different set of questions and problems.

The fact that sound does not have a single definition means there is no coherent object of research around which to structure the interdisciplinary field of sound studies. This lack of coherence has created tension between those who approach sound as a material object and those who consider it a cultural phenomenon. A material perspective recognizes that sound as pure vibration is a unifying force transcending traditional binaries. The cultural perspective, on the other hand, is primarily concerned with the ideological-affective impact of sound.[7] While a wide range of fields contribute to one or both views, one prominent tradition in sound studies comes from the musical avant-garde: acousmatics. This approach is located firmly in the sound-as-cultural-phenomenon camp and stresses understanding sound as a phenomenological study area.

Acousmatics

The story of acousmatics follows the composer Pierre Schaeffer, an experimental artist interested in how electronic music could alter how we *know* sound.[8] His project, which was called *musique concrete*, tried to get at sounds that were not traditionally associated with musical composition. Schaeffer wanted to produce a "symphony of noises" to recast and reorganize sound, distancing it from everyday life's ordinary, anecdotal experience. His premise was that everyday listening started with sound's relegation to being secondary to something else. He argued that when we engage in the everyday act of listening, we often seek to use the information from some signal to corroborate information tied to the visual cause. Some examples include listening for familiar cues when we hear a creaky door, a bus's whoosh, and a bell's ring. But he worried we could never experience these sounds as anything more. When we are engaged in such ordinary listening, we miss the rich world that sounds might create for us. What if, he pondered, we could liberate sounds from their causes and explore the internal textures and feelings of the sounds themselves? Schaeffer sought a new way to theorize sound acoustically, defined as "a noise that one hears without seeing what caused it."[9] He believed that this new definition allowed listeners to focus on the *qualities* of the "sound object" [*objet sonore*] itself instead of always being aware of the source of a sound.

Schaeffer found inspiration in the philosopher Pythagoras's teaching method of standing behind a curtain, making a sound, then forcing his students to agree on what they heard without any visual context to stabilize meaning. Schaeffer writes that "Pythagoras' disciples would have to give up naming, describing, and understanding what they were hearing in *common*; a particular listener would even have to give up understanding himself from one moment to the next."[10] He was fascinated by the ways a group of disciples must come together and create a common language for the description of a shared experience without recourse to the visual referent. The teacher's presence guided students to concentrate on creating the sound object, while the absence allowed their imaginations to flourish. The mode of inquiry "would be how to rediscover, through confronting subjectivities, something several experimenters might agree on."[11] The space between the subjective and objective offered a common cultural framework to discern signal from noise. In other words, as each person named the experience of the sound, the group might find a common language for the *experience of sound*.

Schaeffer's Pythagoras story is not supported by archival material, but it does provide an animating myth. The story accompanies many retellings of acousmatic theory because it provides a clever cipher to ground Schaeffer's acousmatic theory and draws attention to the interplay of presence and absence.[12] As a set of philosophical commitments, acoustemology finds strong resonance with phenomenology. As several other scholars have noted, the Pythagorean veil performed a resonance with a method of an epoche, a "bracketing," where listeners refrain from judgment about the external world to experience it anew, questioning received assumptions about a perceived object. Although the acousmatic experience might allow for speculation on inferential causes, barring direct access, it shifts the attention to the knowledge of the feeling created by a sound. While the listener may draw inward on experience, they simultaneously draw from shared cultural facts that could inform further speculation. In theory, this situation would allow students to question the prevailing science of the day.

In his attempts to mimic Pythagoras's approach, Schaeffer used a tape recorder to capture and loop sound, cleaving the signal from the source. Schaeffer ultimately theorized that the difference "between the experience of Pythagoras and our experience of radio and recordings" is "negligible" because we are finally trying to identify common categories for sensations without visual referents.[13] After playing the sound enough that it lost connection with its origin, Schaeffer would then listen and attempt to chart the different components and compartments of the sound itself. He outlined a variety of complex markings for types and kinds of sounds and parts of their internal form. The goal was to separate the sound object from its indexical signification and focus on the potential qualities of the sound. He hoped this could allow him to conjure new musical relationships for his symphony.

The audio preproduction enabled Schaeffer to bracket the sound and explore the world anew. His experiments posited a tripartite ontology suggesting that all sound is transmitted from a source, causes an object, and creates an effect. Put more technically, the three steps progress as such: (1) a source emits a vibration, (2) which causes the experience of a sound object, and the result is (3) an adequate description of qualities that can repeat to many different listeners. The acousmatic removes the initial source from consideration, allowing for focus only on the object and the effect. What happens if we no longer focus on the source and instead focus on some of the events as such and the potential unique effects that are repeatable? It was *an object bound in time but that flows like an event.* Yet due to the era's technology, it could be repeated, ad infinitum. He would hope that each object could act as units, put into relation as a new potential composition. The concept of acousmatics suggests a kind of audition that attributes a sound not to an instrument played, the magnetic tape, the notation, or the individual but to somewhere in between. All sound must be transmitted from somewhere, yet if we are unable to know the original source, then we are always in an acousmatic situation.[14]

While there are some initial issues with this conceptualization, the tripartite ontology of source, object, and effect offers a language for approaching sound through a generalizable condition that allows us to make sense of the media environment.[15] We can never know the origin of the source because defining a cause is always an arbitrary cut. Consider listening to an album on a device of your choosing. What counts as the music source? The source could be the headphone, the speaker, or the MP3; each could be the source of a sound. Instead of rhetorically constructing a cause, the shift to qualities of experience looks at what can be repeated across contexts. The Pythagorean veil thus offers a metaphor to describe the contemporary audio experience without a verifiable source. This metaphor suggests that when the source of a sound is removed, listeners must rely on cultural frameworks and shared experiences to interpret and make sense of the cause. The Pythagorean veil suddenly becomes a public screen where audiovisual objects circulate independently, ripped from their sources.

Michel Chion picked up and extended the work on the acousmatic situation in relation to audiovisual materials; he asserts that audio and visual elements are separate and then later combined to make up our unified audiovisual environment. If we can infinitely repeat certain sounds, then audio tracks are recorded separately from visuals and then they are brought together. That is to say that because you did not "see" the recording of the soundtrack, but then it is played at the same time, it is something different. The term *value added* was coined because of the effect brought about by combining two separate elements into a larger whole. Chion will refer to how sounds magnetize to certain objects on the screen. Although the source of the sound might not be immediately perceivable, audiovisual causal relations are created. The concept is beneficial for understanding how sound overlays video since, by unifying disparate images, sound imparts a sense of temporality to a scene, giving it a distinct beginning, middle, and end; the ability to perceive a scene as a singular entity demonstrates the power of sound to integrate separate frames into a cohesive whole. The visual anchors the scene on and off the screen to help situate the listener in a particular space—just like there may be a stage or a screen, and a domain that exists beyond it, outside of the realm of sight.

The imaginary place of the listener is a point of audition (POA), the auditory perspective from which an audience experiences a scene, dictating not only the specific sounds heard but also their intensity, direction, and emotional resonance. A point of audition involves two operations at the same times, both emplacing a listener: "from where do I hear, from what point in the space represented."[16] Distinct from the point of view (POV), which frames visual experience, POA enriches narrative depth, suggesting spatial context, character emotions, or unseen elements through auditory cues. For instance, hearing a character's environment—be it rustling leaves or distant chatter—crafts an immersive, subjective soundscape that complements or contrasts visual storytelling. This auditory layering can amplify tension, underscore thematic elements, or deepen character connections, weaving a richer, more textured narrative experience that parallels, yet diverges from, the visual narrative structure. Other literature on the senses calls this emplacement, but POA provides the framework for how the body senses the immediate, immersive, and intense features that underwrite an acousmatic rhetoric.

Over the course of the book I will discuss that a point of audition is not tied to a public screen but exists in several concentric circles, from a literal spot in the city where you hear protesters coming down the street, to a point of audition of someone watching a live television address of a speech, to someone watching the national coverage of a protest on their campus as they feel national pressure. The POA acts as the lens through which we "hear" a scene, while the sound body is the imagined presence we attribute to unseen sources of sound. Together, they form a dynamic interplay where POA frames our auditory perspective, and the sound body fills this framework with depth, character, and emotional resonance.

A Return to the Sound Body

This book's transdisciplinary engagement will complicate rhetoric as a field of inquiry. A vast presence, like the roar of a crowd or the hum of city life, reflects how the sound body offers a new language to describe the contemporary sound experience. In the imaginary outside the public screen are presences or agents creating feelings. To that, I turn to Brian Kane's research. He found that in an era of acousmatic sound, we often search for potential causes, which results in our *imagining* causes. As Kane notes, "One central, replicated feature of acousmatic listening appears to be that the underdetermination of the sonic source encourages imaginative supplementation. The sonic body projected onto acousmatic sound is considered transcendent. Acousmatic listening is often deployed to grant auditory access to transcendental spheres, different in kind from the purely sonic effect."[17]

In other words, when there is an effect with an uncertain origin, we speculate on the cause. There are a number of different kinds of causes. A category can be agential. We can list several mythical examples of giving agency to things that go bump in the night. This invites the rhetorical construction of the cause in an imaginative space. The choice of the "body" as a metaphor in the "sonic body" is purposeful because it refers to a kind of presence affect. Here we are not limited to worldly presence, as the sonic has housed the likes of ghosts and gods. In fact, the "sound body" concept mirrors Thomas Aquinas's first cause argument by postulating an unseen originating presence behind perceived phenomena. Just as Aquinas contends that the universe's existence necessitates a divine first cause, our instinct to attribute agency to acousmatic sounds reflects a tendency to ascribe metaphysical power to unseen entities. This parallel suggests that we readily imbue both cosmic origins and everyday sonic experiences with transcendent, almost divine qualities, granting these imperceptible "beings" significant influence over our perceived reality.

But as we move increasingly into the secular realm, we might think of these bodies as human agents. When sounds emerge, loud ones (such as something happening in the streets each night or something that expands to include the realm of digital devices) invite a communal search for the potential cause. The sound body helps audiences create mental images of characters, objects, or spaces based on the sounds they hear. The disconnection between the sound and its source creates tension, intrigue, or mystery as the audience is left to imagine what the unseen source might look like. There is a need to create an imaginary supplementation about the potential conditions around the cause of sounds; here the imagination can be filled with any number of cultural assumptions.

This situation of unseen sources being ascribed imagined, but culturally rooted characteristics can apply to both individual and collective agents. As I will discuss in the ensuing chapters, we might think of agents as sound bodies. Such an association troubles the relationship of sound to the visible; whether a single person, a group of people, or an imaginary entity, the combined visual and auditory representation creates an impression of their presence (presence affect). This raises questions about the sound body's permeability, size, reach, and dissonance. What might appear outside the screen might also cut across the entire city, like masses that move across space or presences that shift across landscapes. The sound body does not know the limits of time or space. Sound bodies change in size and scale, an effect that has become exaggerated as we progress through the age of mass-mediated devices. Sound bodies can appear everywhere: on the radio, on the television, through ambient devices, and even through wearables. Although these bodies do not need to subscribe to our traditional understanding of the visual body, they may. They can also be the all-powerful, all-knowing, all-seeing body. It is important to note that they exist within overlapping frameworks that have institutions and power.[18]

The idea that people can come from all places to meet on some different plane of existence is what prefigured many early conversations that underwrite the understanding of "digital space." As Frances Dyson argues, "Audio has naturalized what could be called the disembodying effects of new media technologies, [paving] the way for further mediations of the embodied subject." Thus, she argues, "It is no coincidence, then, that the diverse technologies we associate with new media reconstitute the experience characteristic of the aural."[19] The skepticism that emerged around audio devices as early as the phonograph anticipated many of the early debates about the projection of presence we face today with Deep Fakes and artificial intelligence. It is not difficult to draw parallels between debates about the origin of an unknown source and contemporary debates about the credibility of sources.

As the proliferation of digital media normalizes agents' potential to emerge and transcend the bounds of time, space, and regionality, we need a language for those social entities that transcend the game board. How might we account for the presence of organizations that feel larger than life? What about the emergence of artificial intelligence to which people are increasingly attributing presence affects? These vary in shape, size, and proximity and often exist in an omnipresent position that can seem almost panoptic. In these cases, it becomes impossible to determine how far away a presence is, how large it might be, and how present it may become in our lives. Whether or not we can see the presence, it can function as a relevant character in social situations, standing in as an all-knowing narrator or an all-powerful monster. This perspective offers a language for agents who do not have a visible body for us to see but whose power we can feel in our everyday lives: social movements, corporations, government regimes, and artificial intelligence. These entities can be salient and distributed, giving us the low-grade feeling that they might be lurking around us. In other cases, they grow to the size of gods and monsters, reaching across the country to touch us. We may even feel them coming after us.

While the experience of presence can transcend platforms and media, we must recognize that sounds distribute burdens, risks, and responsibilities differently for different bodies.[20] *Sound Tactics* asks how we might use the localized norms and assumptions governing how sound is tactical. What does it mean for a sound body to undertake standards and responsibilities? How can unseen forces come together in a way that challenges the status quo? How might we use and exert normative force and demand change? Hold those in power accountable? Shift the discourse? What does sound inquiry offer? The rest of this book will explore theories and case studies that make good on the promise of understanding the power of sound in argumentation, focusing on tactics that make a difference. A sound tactic focuses on the unique capacities of sound while teaching the norms of judgment required for speech. Such work operates within the dynamic unfolding of time, bringing one together with another in an immediate civic temporality.

The remainder of this chapter will combine two traditions to illustrate my methodological intervention of the waveform. On the one hand, I am interested in how a way of doing something becomes elaborated into a series of disciplinary structures. On the other, I question how an object of inquiry can be known, evaluated, and studied. The formation of a discipline and the formation of an object are intrinsically linked, as one frames the understanding and development of the other. Happenstance stories provide the metaphors that help determine our ways of knowing. The accompanying context that we use to ground them is important to the values that underwrite the study together. What pulls sound and soundness together? To answer this question, we must reclaim speech about rhetoric and argument.

Speech, Rhetoric, Argument

When colleges first came to the United States, they were tied with a narrow range of possible services. Later, with industrialization, the growth of higher education in the United States accompanied more practical goals. As people flocked to the cities, they needed to learn to speak and write, leading to the rise of new departments to accommodate those needs. "Speech," which became professionalized through the organization now known as the National Communication Association, isolated talking as a unique set of skills, and the history of the discipline gave speech a civic sense through the rhetorical capacity for judgment. I will argue that speech started as a home for rhetoric as a techne in a booming industrialized economy but carried with it instruction in phronesis for civic engagement. I will focus on how the study of public speaking constituted an object of research and a set of metaphors that helped scholars build criticism as a professional project. The public became implicated in a democratic "conversation" about underwriting a research agenda that helped with the speech teacher's duty of developing phronesis that contributed to an interdisciplinary conversation. How people reached judgments in a democratic discussion provided a framework that evolved into reasoning that animated a scene of rhetorical criticism.

Scholars and activists take for granted that words and language are the same whether spoken or written. Sometimes that is true, but it is also a habit of thought that can close our minds to the unique contributions of speech. By speech, of course, I mean so much more than the spoken word. The differences between reading aloud and giving a speech are put most plainly by James A. Winans, author of an early public speaking textbook who invests a speech with the capacity to invoke feeling in a particular moment with a particular audience: "Not all speech-making is oratory, but there can be little doubt that the chief purpose of public speaking is persuasion. It is in persuasion that the spoken word is superior to the written.... When men are to be aroused to act, to vote, to change a habit, to adopt a course of conduct, to kindle with enthusiasm, then the speaker is needed."[21]

While the written text enabled and constrained specific modes of communication, the speech was always concerned with a particular moment's contingent circumstances. The discipline of communication draws from a history of teaching public speaking that was attuned to presence, contingency, and statecraft. This history provides a unique perspective to offer in the uptick of sound and rhetoric: speech as a field has always been concerned with the cultural conditions that underwrote an audience's reception when they heard a particular speech.

The discipline of public speaking positioned a classroom as the ideal place to teach speech. The classroom was a laboratory where teachers and students navigated a public arena with stakes, different levels of commitment, distinct values, and attention differences. This is very different from the "ideal speaking situation"; it is a profoundly pragmatic space filled with people from other places with their own goals. Winans was early to recognize that the meaning of "public" can change across different contexts, arguing, "We must fit into and serve the communities in which we are placed, rather than offer work better adapted to special schools of expression."[22] He realized that as more than just a specific set of content, public speaking taught a democratic capacity to reason in public. The hope was that the class would allow students to balance the forms taught with the ability to adjust those rules as necessary in future situations: "I have wished students using this book to become intelligent on the subject, not merely to learn rules."[23] Winans constructs a distinction between "intelligence" and passive "learning" to suggest that the latter aligns more with the elocutionist practice of learning a specific form instead of the more classical practice of making situated decisions, as the former implies. He wished to drive home the idea that speech compelled students to decide when to use the skills they had learned in class; speech not only required but cultivated the capacity for good judgment.

Winans's imagined public speaking situation is the uniquely sonic and civic space of a conversation. The distinction between private and public is not a matter of audience or size but speech performance. He locates this quality of "public" speaking among other things students do in everyday life. The conversation provides a model of belonging that recognizes how daily interactions make up the civic sphere. Although some have critiqued conversation as a model of civic engagement, Winans's understanding of a public speech as a conversation is entirely different from the popular understanding of that term.[24] While we may engage in some conversations through "give-and-take," as is associated with turn taking, Winans notes that conversations come in many different shapes, including some in "which one party does all or nearly all of the talking."[25] More than anything, Winans's treatment of public speaking as conversation points to an understanding of speaking as a recursive situation between speaker and audience. He encourages teachers to impart habits that will ensure students can exercise situated judgments in different conversations.[26] Winans writes that the ultimate goal is "thinking on his feet; he creates, or re-creates, the thought at the moment of delivery."[27] The speaker is always recursively responding to feedback from the audience, deciding what to do, and moving on. The fluid dynamic of thinking about public speech as a conversation creates the opportunity to adapt in the moment, whether positive, negative, or somewhere in between. When considering what makes a situated judgment, we can consider how it contributes to and designs broader conversations. Phronesis always involves balancing between the individual and the community; sound reason involves the temporal dimension.

The allure of the conversational metaphor becomes well worn as it is replicated in subsequent public speaking textbooks.[28] We should distinguish the conversation from the normative confines of the dialogue. Sometimes people assume that a conversation is too polite of a model for thinking of the civic. They imagine a place with too many rules, which does not allow for friction and agonism. But this is not the function of Winans's version of conversation; the model of the conversation is for the speaker. The public speech as conversation must focus on the day's moral issues to effect long-term change. Speakers must be intentional and attentive to the unfolding situation. Otherwise, they risk becoming inattentive or soliloquizing. Ideally, they can set their tone, read the audience, and respond in a way that fits the situation. The speaker must learn to observe the "signs of thoughts and moods of his hearers"[29] and act accordingly. The goal is that a speaker can tell if "the other party to this conversation is interested or bored, approves or disapproves, understands or is puzzled, and he amplifies a point or touches it lightly."[30] The goal is to be in a relationship with another; otherwise, they risk not being part of the conversation.

Winans makes a good point. Yet someone might imagine how the idealized context of a public speech changed over time, and this change made a corresponding impact on the scholarly imaginary. While the experience of the public speaking instructor might have pervaded the sense of the early researcher in the speech field, the text, literally and most often metaphorically, pervades the imagination of later critics. As I will explain in the next few sections of this chapter, the rise of the text crystalized in the vision of textual analysis as a professional practice for scholars of rhetoric. This mode of understanding offers much insight, but it is a perspective that leaves something important behind. It aligned with an academy in the throes of the linguistic turn and a structuralist economy. The unit of analysis would change from the speech as conversation to the speech text. The text became the primary way for experience to become knowable. This gave rhetorical critics transdisciplinary power because we could speak to other humanities scholars who also focused on the text. The emergence of the oratorical text was a trace that even the early rhetorical scholars talked about, so it was not wholly new, and one might see it as the product of institutional necessity (since people published in journals, text-based forums). But something important was lost in the field's move away from public speaking as a conversation in which a speaker exchanged sounds with an audience.

The Break from English

As higher education became more appealing and accessible to a broader range of students, new courses and disciplines emerged to keep pace with the developing technologies of the era, positioning college as a gateway to opportunity. As society recognized the importance of training people in reading and writing, practicing English became a crucial skill for the general populace. Teachers adopted Scottish logician Alexander Bain's 1866 textbook, *English Composition and Rhetoric*, during this period. The book emphasizes that writing is grounded in producing specific products, ends, genres, or modes. For many, this text and the underlying assumption that rhetoric adhered to specific genres set the stage for establishing a new field of study. Ideas around writing started with conversations about the modes of rhetoric, and the modes set their agenda for how rhetoric as composition would be studied.

At the same time, starting in the 1880s, a group of English teachers agitated for what would become the study of speech. Founding the National Association of Academic Teachers of Public Speaking (NAATPS), these teachers argued for an approach to rhetoric grounded in the ephemeral moment. The early scholars of this nascent field argued that rhetorical practice should be in the shared recursive interaction between speaker and audience. This perspective underwrote a new problematic where public speaking was seen as part of a broader movement of taking politics out of formal institutions and into the domain of everyday life. The classroom was another forum where students could practice their art and test their ability to persuade others in a shared moment.

On November 28, 1912, a sort of "declaration of independence" was ratified by a group of speech teachers working in English departments; it made a case for separating English from speech. At the core, the practice and teaching of public speaking were inherently different from those of writing, so an existence separate from English departments would give students specialized instruction focused on speech rather than the written word. Contextually, this group of scholars sought to define themselves as distinct from English but not the same as elocutionists.[31] These early scholars used "speech" to encompass everything from public speaking to an emerging area of speech science.

The historical conjuncture in which speech teachers emerged was unique. If someone wanted to get an education in speaking, there were two choices: the elocutionists offered to teach "public speaking" in an overtly expressive manner, or someone could enroll in a public speaking class (usually found in newly formed English departments). Elocutionists focused on performance mechanics such as projection, articulation, and inflection. For them, the audience was irrelevant; elocution was about following the rules for a speech. Partly in response to elocutionists, speech teachers emerged with a distinctively "civic conception of rhetoric" centered around "the source of community and politics"; this approach united "scholarship with teaching using the animating myth: that public address, social movements, and political communication" were the focus of their art.[32] This group of scholars took their cues from a Greco-Roman conception of rhetoric to fashion an approach to what it meant to speak in public. This means that they sought to always situate the act of speaking in relation to a specific community instead of a universal audience. Phronesis provides a way for each speaker to talk to different kinds of audiences.

This meliorative practice of public speaking sought to make people better; the speech teacher cultivated civic judgment around the capacity to expound, convince, and persuade. Good speech was always situated in an unfolding conversation. For instance, Winans writes in his public speaking textbook, "I wish you to see that public speaking is a perfectly normal act, which calls for no strange, artificial methods, but only for an extension and development of that most familiar act, conversation. If you grasp this idea, you will be saved from much wasted effort."[33] For the student to know the difference between public and private, speakers need to recognize that conversations describe a kind of civic organization between speaker and listener. Throughout the book, "conversation" becomes the touchstone for how Winans envisioned speech operation as distinct from elocution. While elocution asks people to learn universal rules for performance, public speaking would teach people how to engage in a kind of democratic conversation that demands contingent changes. He argues that the distinction between private and public is not a matter of audience size but the quality of the encounter.

The new NAATPS organization needed a means to professionalize itself, which begot a journal to publish research, the *Quarterly Journal of Public Speaking* (now the *Quarterly Journal of Speech*), in 1915. The journal gave speech a home for scholarly communication, which was much needed; as Charles Woolbert signaled, "In speech we find the substance of a discipline that can and ought to be of the utmost value."[34] One of the chief concerns was how this new thing should be researched, evaluated, corrected, and taught. James Winans's contribution calling for "The Need for Research" sought justification that he could use to rebut folk approaches to public speaking, make better teachers, and legitimatize the field. In the early pages of the journal, there were several debates about the goals of teaching, its priority vis-à-vis research, and the classroom's connections to society.[35] Speech was understood as the currency of social interaction and practical skill required across a variety of contexts.

In the second issue of the *Quarterly Journal of Public Speaking*, Woolbert's essay, "The Organization of Departments of Speech Science in Universities," carves out a unique, temporal site for speech: "English is concerned with the past more than with the present, while speech science must occupy itself more with the present."[36] Woolbert, indeed a bit tongue in cheek, elaborates on the contrast with public address:

> Picture an individual enjoying the finest fruits of a course of study in English, and what do you see? A man sitting at ease, preferably alone, surrounded by books, enveloped in a soul-satisfying silence, taking in the ideas and feelings of the ages to himself. Then draw the likeness of a man filling the highest purpose of a course in speech studies, and what have we? A man in action, evaluated upon a public platform, set before a gathering of others, bidding for the eye and ear of everyone present and giving forth vital ideas and feelings to the people before him. Here you have at a glance the difference in the genius of the subjects taught as English and subjects taught as speech science.[37]

What constitutes the differences between the two fields are sensory economies, relations of time, and imaginations that are the subject of inquiry. While writing involves techniques such as reading, looking, and engaging the imaginary, public speaking calls for a dynamic immediacy of a shared duration.

As the discipline expanded, speech was conceptualized as a collection of ordinary human activities done in everyday conversations. Insofar as democracy was moving from formal institutions to everyday life, both Winans and Woolbert recognized the value in the practical art of teaching people how to speak. Ultimately, the two men belonged to the two major factions in the early days of speech, the Cornell school and the Midwest/Illinois school, the latter becoming associated with the social science tradition of speech. Yet when speech first existed in a constellation, Woolbert would not identify as a traditional positivist. Keith argues that Woolbert identified more as a pragmatist and Deweyan, employing a method focused on "distrusting authority, inspecting evidence and outcome, and situating knowledge in a context of use."[38]

Winans is associated with the rise of the Cornell school and humanistic inquiry. It was literally in Ithaca, New York, working with Winans, that young Assistant Professor of Public Speaking Herbert Wichelns found the necessity for writing "The Literary Criticism of Oratory," which would later appear in a book commemorating the career of Winans.[39] The research serves as a space to help legitimatize the nascent field of communication and its object of inquiry. In this essay, Wichelns justifies an understanding of rhetoric and the need for speech departments by explaining that rhetoric's "chief aim is to know how critics have spoken of orators."[40] A vital move in justifying a discipline was delimiting an object of inquiry. He argues that literature is concerned with discovering a transcendent truth beyond time, while oratory emerges in response to specific conditions.

Wichelns associated rhetoric with "statecraft"—tying oratory to sovereignty, citizenship, and contingency.[41] Rhetoric, he writes, "is bound up with the things of the moment," which can exist in an "occasion, its terms, its background."[42] The rhetor must attend to the details of *a* specific situation and its *concomitant* political ramifications and be ready to address them. Wichelns encouraged critics to be present at the speech event because as speeches change from sound to text, critics are "free to regard any speech merely as an essay, as literary effort deposited at the shrine of the muses in hope of being blessed with immortality."[43] For Wichelns, there is value in considering the spoken word *as* spoken, as sound experienced at the moment. He warns that with historic public address, there is an impossible difficulty in "reconstructing the conditions under which the speech was delivered." Nonetheless, he identifies those moments when sound is experienced as critical to rhetorical insight.[44] If rhetoric is understood as the study and practice of communication about that which is contingent, it follows that the assessment of rhetoric is not just about the persuasive effect (which is impossible to define anyway) but has a deeper, more philosophical foundation anchored in a *sensation of presence*. Perhaps most crucially, we can trace the importance of phronesis here, which ties to an older approach of rhetoric as practical wisdom.

As many have noted, "speech" is an early titular term for the communication discipline, but it has come to mean many different things. While there might have been disagreement over how to approach it, everyone in the field that broke off from English agreed on an everyday object of concern: speech. Joshua Gunn and Jenny Rice report that in 1918, the name "Speech Department" was suggested by those who would create these new units, and by 1930 most had adopted the title. But Gunn and Rice found across the early archive of publications that speech did not have a consistent meaning, including everything from the metaphor of conversation to material voice, to the whole gambit of human expression. The term speech offered, they write, "a meeting place of the human body and language, of *both* affect and the word, of *both* feeling and meaning. And the affective component of speech was once considered an important domain of study for budding social scientists as well as scholars of oratory and rhetoric."[45] From the founding of the discipline up until the middle of the twentieth century, "speech" as a label was ubiquitous, appearing in journals, departments, course titles, and majors.[46] As Gerry Philipsen observes, "For fifty-one years, from 1918–1969, 'speech' was arguably the crucial substance term."[47] Yet with time, "speech" declined as an organizing term and was usurped by "communication."[48] In this period and within the community of those who studied rhetoric, there was a growing trend to supplant and occlude speech as an object of inquiry.

In William Eadie's archival investigation into communication disciplines' histories, he notices people slipping away from the term early in the 1950s. As people returned from World War II, there was a boom in the study of communication. However, there was some frustration with speech. For instance, Eadie notes the establishment of the National Society for the Study of Communication (NSSC), initially formed by social scientists dissatisfied with the discipline's focus on something as ephemeral as rhetoric. This society would eventually become the International Communication Association. But in the 1950s, "Speech scholars, led by Elwood Murray ... and W. Charles Redding ... attempted to bring the theory development process together by forming the avowedly interdisciplinary NSSC and creating *The Journal of Communication* as its scholarly publication."[49] This early offshoot of the discipline signaled dismay in the study of speech and represented early attempts to stabilize the object.

In their work, Murray and Redding predict a future in which communication scholars have moved away from speech and toward the more stable objects. Consider Redding's 1957 speech analysis, which highlights how rhetoric should be concerned with "a close, sentence-by-sentence scrutiny of oral or written discourse for the purpose of determining what kinds of 'meanings' the words may represent."[50] From a stable object like a speech text, Redding hypothesizes that a critic can obviously use the precision tools of content analysis to ferret out the ways that the speaker has handled their "available means of persuasion."[51] In other words, a turn to a stable object like a speech text might offer the critic something concrete to study. By advocating for the analysis of speech texts, Redding previewed a future in which communication scholars would prioritize the stability and durability of an object.

Through several publications, Joshua Gunn has accounted for some of the historical conditions that influenced speech's decline, such as a disciplinary desire to acquire more epistemic credibility, distance itself from Nazis/Fascists/Communists, and be more enticing to students. But his claim is that, ironically, in the process of adjusting to its audience, speech went from attempting to operationalize something anchored in presence to being disregarded because it was too difficult to discipline. As I will discuss more in the next section, one of the primary events that led to disciplined speech was the emergence of another object of inquiry: close textual criticism. The emergence of the text displaced speech as an object of inquiry.

Close Textual Analysis

Although the field of speech might have started with political oratory as its center, it would become increasingly wed to the text. Like several other disciplines located in the humanities, rhetoric would become ensnared in the linguistic turn. We might identify many points as the text's inauguration at the center of the field. One event that sanctioned the text as a legitimate object for the study of rhetoric was the first in a series of Biennial Public Address Conferences titled "Putting Text in Context," held in 1988 at the University of Wisconsin–Madison.[52] Although rhetoric was initially separated from English based on the ineffability of speech, the Public Address Conference announced the arrival of the "oratorical text" as the "*sine qua non* of making a difference" across the humanities.[53]

The critical unit of analysis would be the text. One of the most well-known proponents of this approach to scholarship, Michael Leff, explains that in a "text," there is "a whole that assigns meaning to a region of shared public experience and solicits an audience to embrace the meaning it constructs."[54] For Leff, the metaphor of the text permeates his call for a method of close reading and close textual analysis. When form and content are no longer alienated from one another, "the two blend together within the unfolding development of a discourse, a development that simultaneously holds the discourse together and holds it out as a way of influencing the world in which it appears. Form, then, plays a decisive role in rhetorical discourse, but only as it promotes the function of the discourse, as it acts to produce an effect on auditors and to do some work in the social world."[55] Rhetorical acts are verbs responsive to specific situations and deserve to be studied as such, not disregarded to get to some deeper content or abstracted to understand some larger recurrent ideology. Rhetoricians can listen to what they can *do in the world*. But rather than considering speech as sounds produced in civic spaces, these scholars focus on the form of an oratorial text made up of words preserved in writing.

The conference centered the text, inviting different critics to focus on "a single speech text, and appreciation of the critical effort obviously demands a reading of the speeches themselves."[56] Like an arena for a sporting event, the text provided a place for a reader to follow along as each critic elucidated the interworking and strategy of an orator and evaluated their choices to a specific exigency by reading a manuscript of that orator's speech. Leff and one of his coauthors, Fred Kauffeld, continue, "The responses all suggest alternative interpretations of the same text or texts, and the reader perhaps can sense how subsequent discussion might follow from a consideration of these differing perspectives."[57] In the agon of contested readings of a shared text, scholars found a site for endless academic conversation. The conference codified the practice of reading speeches as an object of study and embraced arguing about how orators responded to the situations they faced. Rhetoricians could challenge taken-for-granted assumptions about the history of an object, uncover terministic screens, and apply different hermeneutics to illuminate critical historical moments. Rhetorical criticism provided a set of methods to investigate the relationship between an oratorical text (meaning a written speech manuscript) and its context.

The conference's assumption (and the assumption of close textual analysis in general) is that rhetorical ideas become meaningful when tested against case studies. Rhetorical judgment is not about abstracting to a universal theory but about recognizing practical wisdom in how orators respond to exigency. Rhetorical theory does not abstract hierarchically but moves laterally, from case to case; we can make inferences and understand how some concepts can move between cases by applying what we learn from one case to the next. To theorize within cases is to find what potential modes of invention are available and selected in a particular case; to theorize across cases is to recognize the situations that might repeat and the lessons that emerge, which can be useful in similar situations. Rhetorical criticism might provide rough outlines that can be applied in other circumstances, but it will not give a set of rules or offer predictive analytics.

While close textual analysis represents a significant step forward for rhetorical criticism, the insistence on examining the written text applied constraints on the nascent field. As a set of metaphorical entailments, the discussion of the text makes a few meta-theoretical assumptions that eschew the potential rhetorical resources available to the rhetor. A textual approach defines the form of rhetoric as something that can be linguistically explicable, mapped as relations between words set out linearly in space. A focus on text assumes that rhetoric's effects can be derived from reading off a paper. But someone reading a text (whether it be a speech text or an essay about a speech text) conceptualizes flow as a sequential movement of give-and-take between discrete actors. Such an approach assumes that an intentionally produced document (such as a preserved speech manuscript) creates an inseparable gulf of time and distance between the rhetor and the audience. Finally, a textual approach locates the force of rhetoric as discrete, externalized, illocutionary effects. While this approach certainly has merit, it also potentially misses other topoi of rhetorical events and might miss other ways to move the social.

The concept of judgment in rhetoric extends beyond merely discerning the meaning of a text; it is about evaluating the choices made by the rhetor, understanding the context in which the rhetoric was produced, and assessing the impact of the rhetorical act. This nuanced judgment is crucial when examining rhetoric in a broader sense, outside the realm of the written text. As we delve into other facets of rhetorical events—spoken discourse, digital communication, or visual rhetoric—we carry the critical judgment honed through textual analysis. The text has taught us the importance of close examination, understanding form and content as intertwined, and viewing rhetorical acts as responsive to specific situations. As we navigate through the broader landscape of rhetoric, this refined sense of judgment enables us to excavate deeper meanings, uncover latent ideologies, and identify the myriad ways rhetorical acts can shape and influence the world. But we also need to move beyond what the textual analyst has given us to study such objects as the speech event, the image event, and the sound tactic.

This is not the first time a social movement scholar has pointed out that "the *metaphor* of the 'text' may hinder considering fully the possibilities of movement discourses."[58] The text represents just one medium; other media and modes of communication contain other potentials for social movements. By focusing on sound, I join other scholars who explore rhetorical resources outside the page by shifting the norms around what a rhetorical critic examines, creating space for recognizing that some tactics might exist outside linear arguments on a page and the medium of exchange that is selected might materially affect bodies. If practical wisdom concerns learning how to adapt to constraints, what affordances would another mode of control provide?

Waveform

So far, this chapter has argued that rhetoric is a practical art that equips citizens with the means to advocate in public. The goal of a rhetorical critic is not to generate a predictive theory but to thicken concepts that generate an understanding of how one might respond to contingent constraints. Criticism aims to develop analogic inferences that look across particulars while simultaneously realizing we might not be able to explain every single aspect of a case. As I have demonstrated, these precepts and ideas come from closely examining case studies where agents use sound in the civic realm. But oddly, the scholars so tied to speech, so eager to differentiate themselves from students of the written text, ended up tying themselves to textual forms. What happens if we keep the focus on the kind of judgment valued by the rhetorical tradition but change the object?

The turn to sound studies seeks to bring us back to a discussion of speech in the public forum. From rhetoric, we focus on rhetorical judgment and the normative assumptions that accompany it. But each example of social movement studied in this book also uses a theory of acousmatic sound to think about possibilities of social action. As we move beyond the text as the primary metaphor for speech, acousmatic rhetoric offers a way to think about sound as the object of rhetorical criticism. But how might we *know* acousmatics and describe the principles that emerge from advocates using sound tactics in public? I substitute the text metaphor with a waveform metaphor as a way to think about how sound offers resources for invention. This becomes the object of analysis.

Defined, a waveform is a graphical representation of sound that traces topoi in time. Most often, waveforms come from the audio recording world, where they are used to visualize sound to understand some part of its behavior. These never appear in the wild but involve many cultural practices. I use a waveform as a metaphor to organize the different public feelings that sound tactics may draw from to generate social movement. While the waveform and its image do not get us any closer to reality, the conceptual language of the waveform and accompanying discourses around audio do foreground relations in time, which is an increasingly important medium for civic engagement.

The most traditional waveform is the expression of a complex system; from a microphone and an algorithm, an object of knowledge is created and becomes the subject of evaluation and adjustment. In the audio recording world, a waveform is a visual representation of sound that measures vibration along three coordinates: amplitude, frequency, and time. If a vibration displaces molecules in the time space, amplitude measures how far the molecules go, and frequency measures how often this action repeats. The waves can be rounded, squared, or even triangular, depending on the context. For the technically trained listener, a waveform crystallizes a moment that can be evaluated and assessed. While the sound is ordinarily a subjective experience located *in* the immediacy of time, the waveform renders it objective and stable *outside* time. The fixed image affords duration for deliberations, technical edits, or many other kinds of critical judgment. The waveform can foreground a language of time for us to think about how argument types, or topoi, can be used in situations. Each chapter, thus, represents a kind of waveform, which is an acousmatic reduction grounded in a hermeneutic epoche.[59]

These acousmatic topoi are formed from overlapping features of immediacy, immersion, and intensity. Immediacy involves the relationship between the time of a vibration's start and end. In any perception of sound, there can be many different sounds starting and stopping, giving the potential for many other points of identification. Immersion encompasses vibration's capacity to reverberate in space and impart a temporal signature that helps locate someone in an area; think of the difference between an echo in a canyon and the roar of a crowd when you're in a stadium. Finally, intensity describes the pressure put on a listener to act. Intensity provides the feelings that underwrite the force to compel another to act. Each of these features and the corresponding impact of this experience offer rhetorical intervention potential for social movements.

Immediacy refers to a class of claims surrounding the passage of time. Immediacy shapes the assumption of when things should be. As vibrations come into existence, the attack and release provide opportunities to set, satisfy, and violate expectations that can contribute to the feeling of what should be done, when it should be done, and in what kind of manner. Audiences anticipate the time between the end of a sound (the release) and the start of another (the attack). How we expect these intervals and whether they satisfy or violate expectations are all coded with signification layers, providing a material foundation to shape events. Tia DeNora, in *Music in Everyday Life*, gives an ordinary example of how people use music to convey time as a resource for going to the gym: pumping them up before they go work out. We wake up to our favorite playlist as it signals the time of the morning for a workout to commence. The sound gives the listener a beat to sync with and indicates that it is *time* to work out.[60] By extension, when a group hears a sound tactic, that sound can create a sense of urgency—it is time for advocacy, to join them, to act. Sound can *pump people up* to work or set the mood for action.

The next chapter explores the potential of the cut-out, which foregrounds immediacy. This tactic comes from and moves around a sense of timing and urgency. What can be more urgent for a generation of students growing up under the threat of school shootings? For X González, this urgency is contextualized in the contingent circumstance of a march to end gun violence in a country brimming with guns. For them, this moment performs the unexplained terror of waiting for a mass shooting to end. As a resource for invention, the feeling of urgency underwrites their different techniques to move people to action as they hold them for over four minutes in agonizing silence, unsure of what is happening. Their call is even more prescient, given the context of the American gun debate and that the next shooting can happen at any moment. The shared experience of waiting for the next moment imposes a collective sense of timing: right now.

Intensity refers to a feeling of choice. As a signal is discerned from noise, there is a need to choose the next step; the various vibrations surrounding us always necessitate the creation of the next sound. Propagation comes from a constantly difficult-to-source world, but we must make continuous decisions. In a world populated by constraints that always, in some sense, occlude the origin of a sound, we must make judgments as waveforms dissipate, even though we always lack some information. Intensity accounts for the qualitative experience that accompanies any choice. Sometimes we refer to an old, habituated way of discerning signal from noise, and we need to notice it. Other times, sound skirts its material constraints as it forces consideration, hijacking attention. Intensity speaks to the surplus feeling that exceeds any moment and helps provide for the next by directing the sense of awareness and considering the timing and specific material constraints of the situation.

Chapter 4 explores HU Resist's effective use of heckling in a year-and-a-half-long campaign, highlighting how their targeted and clever disruptions drew in more supporters over time. By frequently challenging the administration, HU Resist amplified the pressure on Howard University to accept their demands. Notably, in response to a corruption scandal, their heckle using a viral dance to "Bitch Better Have My Money" intensified an occupation of the administration building. This increasing intensity forced the university to either respond positively to demands or face growing discontent from both the campus and the wider public. The chapter illustrates the power of heckling as not just noise but a strategic tool that can shift narratives and compel institutional change, demonstrating its impact through a series of escalating public confrontations.

Immersion refers to how sounds situate listeners in a place or territory. As a vibration propagates through space, a large portion of the sound energy follows indirect paths as it reflects off the ground and the environment of the milieu: walls, ceilings, and façades. The environment exerts agency as it shapes sound; textured surfaces, like upholstery and carpet, absorb reverberation, dampening and contouring the wave. Each echo locates space as flat, hard surfaces reverberate and extend or lengthen the wave. These give a sense of salience and proximity. As a listener attempts to discern meaning from sound, sensual knots come together to form where you are in a place—we make judgments about where these little sounds come from all the time to help inform where we are in a room, a home, or an environment. These become, of course, more elaborate as we add a more symbolic attachment. Where we are, how we feel attached, and the proximity to others are grounded in a complex system of echolocation that involves mediating another cultural material binary.

The potential of the immersion waveform happens in Canada in chapter 5 (when people took to the streets and banged pots and pans, becoming known as the Casseroles); the emerging democratic carnival gave a sense of the salience and proximity of the growing democratic movement. As people poured into the streets every night, the sounds of their pots and pans playing in the street would reach the far neighborhoods. Their social media would also populate the feeds and flood the zone of the news coverage. Their sound body emerges as a global agent on the public screen. The immersive experience of the Casseroles coming out and demanding change every night gave a sense of how widely shared the sentiment was and roughly the distribution of that sentiment. Moreover, it gave the lawmakers a sense of how near and persistent the people were. In an increasingly digitized world, the immersive qualities of the Casseroles were amplified and helped speak to the salience of the moment.

As a lever to compel the action of a listener to movement, these three interrelated parts of the waveform describe how sound provides a resource for persuasion: through immediacy (the quickness or slowing of duration), intensity (the changing force), and immersion (the ubiquity of a movement). These different facets provide a structure of feeling that underwrites a sound reason. They help shape how acousmatic objects might invite reason's absence and presence. These three dimensions provide metaphoric entailments that draw into relief relations of time and force. Of course, waveforms are like texts in that they require cultural techniques of interpretation that help discern public categories of meaning. And, like a text, a waveform is operationalized as a set of metaphoric entailments, providing a master term to arrange the unfolding of signification. This is another form that shows some facets while concealing others. If the goal is to attend to the conditions of invention that organize sound tactics, the waveform gives enabling constraints that inform phronesis.

Because waveforms are flat expressions of the movement of sound, an acousmatic approach recognizes that they must be interpreted and tied to different cultural practices. Such an approach cannot suggest and universalize a specific view of sound as a neutral configuration of signal and noise at its center. Instead, the waveform is culturally situated across different case studies. I will draw analogically across additional case studies in this book to make my arguments. I am interested in practical agents intentionally trying to realize a goal. In each example, various iterations of sound and noise repeat the agent's purpose of compelling someone to act. That is to say, a consistent meta-theoretical assumption that holds for all this work is an intentional listener that can discern signal from noise.

The potential for the infinite repetition and amplification of these waveforms can be as personal as a unified sound on the street, the videos on the screen, and the stories making headlines on the news. It may exist in the countless shares, likes, reposts, and retweets. The replicative nature of digital media mirrors the continual propagation of sound waves, further obscuring the origin and extending the influence of a sound tactic. These waveforms, characterized by properties like amplitude, frequency, attack, and decay, reflect various public narratives and collective sentiments, as seen in the rapid response of the March for Our Lives campaign, the unpredictable peaks of the HU Resist movement, and the sustained crescendo of the Casseroles' protests.

Waveforms Reflecting the Sonic Body

Sounds vary in shape, size, and proximity. Often, they exist in an omnipresent position, almost panoptic, but how far away they are and how large they might be present meta-calculations of a demand. Each of these different social movements began with the emergence of a distinct sonic body making a demand. Working in concert with each of these groups was the supposition of an imaginary plane where there would be an imagined sonic body exercising agency that could be felt. Sometimes the sound body could be seen, sometimes not. The immediacy, intensity, and immersion coordinates attend to the different sites that might amplify force over other units and periods that cut across platforms and spaces. The waveform metaphor aptly encapsulates how media narratives, like sound waves, can emanate from multiple, often indeterminate, sources and reverberate across vast digital landscapes. When related to the concept of the "sound body," the waveform shows how these narratives unfold, escalate, and recede. Making judgments about the sound body is a potent analytical tool that uncovers digital media's subtle interplay of sound, time, and collective emotion.

In this era of globalization, concepts of space and presence have transcended the confines of traditional time, place, and nation-state (the usual coordinates of statecraft). Entities like multinational corporations and transnational actors, including social movements, are becoming increasingly influential and difficult to pin down. How does power operate to both control and disrupt space? There is an increasing need to reconceptualize social movements not as confined to specific geographic boundaries but as transnational organizations. Given that we are constantly immersed in the "public screen" of digital and social media, sound bodies provide a language to discuss how agents operate within this ambient environment—where we exist and interact—where presence is distributed and perceived. If there is a public screen, then we need a language for extended bits that impact our surroundings. The language of an acousmatic gets at all the things that are happening around us as we stand in a point of audition. A public screen exists in a place where some acoustics and actions may be outside the purview of the screen but shape what is happening.

Rhetoric's focus on practical cases fits neatly beside evaluations of how sound shapes the potential for discourse. A rhetorical techne and practice, through the judicious use of sound across different contexts, can be a practical tool for achieving objectives. An approach that draws on the metaphor of the waveform encourages us to rethink presence and agency—which we get through the sound body—in different ways conducive to our ecological environment. The introduction of the sound body enables us to grapple with how presence can be salient and distributed, a low-grade feeling of lurking, or all around us, or it might be apparent and salient. This approach enables analysis of social movements to go beyond the platform of politics and think more granularly about the sources of power that might underwrite and drive the propagation of movements as they shift, change, and move. Rhetoric can help organize topoi, finding the principles that might help manage how sound can be deployed.

To see how acousmatic rhetoric can help describe the resources that sound offers agents in their attempt to make demands against institutions, we turn first to the March for Our Lives and the Parkland Kids. In a clear example of leveraging a sound tactic in a moment of particular importance, the Parkland Kids harnessed the power of immediacy to advocate for change in a way that unexpectedly transformed the course of youth advocacy and the gun debate. The public got to experience their tragedy live on Snapchat, which gave rise to the Parkland Kids' vulnerable sound body. As they came out to advocate for gun rights, the Parkland Kids became a ubiquitous movement sprawled across the news, mobilizing the memory of their tragedy to demand reform on gun violence. But when X González came out at the March for Our Lives, their strategic use of immediacy, or how sound shapes time and virality, brought the audience back and exerted pressure to move the social.

2

The Cut-Out and the Parkland Kid

For the student survivors of the February 14, 2018, Marjory Stoneman Douglas (MSD) shooting, the fact that they were the latest statistic was far from a surprise; they had grown up in an era of normalized gun violence. In the United States, MSD added its name to a long list of "school shootings." Although happening prior, I use this term to refer to a specific kind of media, framing those dates back to the Columbine High School shooting in Littleton, Colorado, in April 1999, when two students killed twelve classmates and one teacher before taking their own lives. The corresponding media spectacle captured national attention as the country attempted to make meaning out of the event. These students stood on the cusp of the emerging Generation Z. Almost every student who attended Parkland was born after the landmark shooting in Columbine and, therefore, after the corresponding federal funding for and implementation of active school shooter drills, safety protocols, and metal detectors.

The March for Our Lives event that Parkland students held in the aftermath of the MSD shooting happened against a backdrop of the constant threat of school shootings that had ushered in an era where living under the shadow of potential violence was the norm. This reality had forced schools into a perpetual state of heightened security, with frequent searches and seizures becoming commonplace. Yet despite these measures, the issue of gun violence only continued to escalate among the youth. At the time of the Parkland shooting, more than thirty-nine thousand people had died by gun violence. Not all gun violence gets national coverage, but even the discussions of spectacular violence fade quickly. In 2018, *The Atlantic* reported that the average length of a mass shooting headline typically dwindled after just six days, overshadowing the ongoing violence that plagues everyday life.[1] If spectacular gun violence was not covered, the ordinary use of guns, which is a salient part of American life, would not get any attention. What once was unimaginably shocking was met with resignation and calls for thoughts and prayers. The Parkland students recognized that they needed to shake up the contours of the debate by demonstrating that the adults had lost the moral high ground to lead the conversation.

Sound supplied an essential means of invention because it worked through immediacy, the way a sound can cue the experience of time. MSD student X González deployed a sound tactic titled a "cut-out," which built up expectations, violated them, and finally released them. While much of the national conversation centered only on the "silent" part of the cut-out, this is just a fragment of the speech that must be understood in the context of the entire performance. As a sound tactic, the cut-out describes a specific temporal form—a buildup of expectation, a violation, and a release—that conveys a meaning: the dread of experiencing a school shooting and the relief that comes from action. As the audience takes this journey through time, an emotional bond is forged with a student's experience in a school shooting. In the trajectory of this cut-out, satisfaction only comes when tension is broken, which happens when González returns to the discussion about a need for action, prompting the audience to be inclined to a similar action-oriented debate around guns.

González's decision to drag the audience through the dread of time unfolding in a discomfiting break from normality before releasing the tension in a speech that called for action provided an iconic experience that reverberated. Like all sound tactics, the cut-out exists *in time*, and its capacity to propagate in public resides in latent capacities to *transduce* or change in substance. The feeling that we needed to do something now was the warrant underwriting urgency. When González changed from the speaker who created a visceral moment that transfixed the country into a symbol of youth activism and the virtue of youth taking over the conversation, they inspired generations of youth activists over the long durée.

The sound tactics employed laid bare the assertion that parents have failed to live up to their obligation to care for their families because they subject children to the fear of the constant potential for harm. The sound tactic of the Parkland Kids operated to invert the traditional norms of the gun debate by suggesting that the current stakeholders were not the right people to be having the conversation in the first place. While parents should be the speaker, the demands entailed ceding authority to the kids, who were operating as nonpartisan stakeholders due to their unique experience growing up in this securitized state. The hope is this new expertise will at least move the needle forward toward gains that can make up some incremental change toward eliminating the ongoing violence.

The map of this chapter will unfurl as follows: First, I wish to introduce the work that demonstrates how sound constitutes an experience of time. Once we have established how sound operates to form the perception of time rhetorically, the chapter will introduce the Parkland shooting and situate the constitution of the Parkland Kid. Next, I will turn to the March for Our Lives, where X González utilized the tactic of the cut-out. Here I will spend some extra time unpacking how the cut-out draws on acousmatics to manipulate perceptions of time and create an effect on the listener. The cut-out is a generic waveform, one that exists in many kinds of music, but it is how González uses the cut-out in their speech under this circumstance that solidifies it as a crucial sound tactic. In González's case, the address intersected with the affordances of the camera, which realized an emotional moment expressed as a photo.

While the sound tactic generated attention through the cut-out, the image of González remaining silent became an iconic image of youth mobilized for social change. It was not just the speech but the way the event mobilized the media and the memory of the shooting that propagated the Parkland Kid through the public. The image provided a context that underwrote subsequent coverage, and not just of Parkland; it became an index for generational politics. I will conclude with how the space of generational politics creates room for new debates for the stake of the planet. The Parkland Kids became part of another sound body and part of a larger movement of youth democratic politics.

Sound's Immediacy

To make sense of the cut-out, we must contextualize how the experience of listening to a sound locates an auditor in a dynamic flux of time. Listeners discern meaningful sound from noise, holding onto it, sensing it, and expanding the circumference of their attention to accommodate its shape, feel, and intensity. In his landmark work on the phenomenology of sound, Don Ihde writes that "sound dances timefully within experience. Sound embodies the sense of time."[2] For the ordinary listener, sound emergence and recession within the passage of everyday life compose the immediate present. The experience of listening does not occur in discrete, atomized moments—where each "sound" occupies an unsteady flow, like a skipping record—but instead appears as a unity within a continuous flow. Each instant is perceived within a larger temporal span of a living present, a duration, as it recedes into a recent past. Different sequences are gathered and associated—people use and deploy sound to make it a part of everyday life. These associations are indexed with varying life experiences to become entangled parts of the social scene.

In one of his many additions to the acousmatic project, Michel Chion gives us language for how the experience of sound in time helps provide feeling to a particular duration through a temporal focal point—an unfolding period experienced as a unified gestalt with distinct material shapes. Earlier I spoke about this being a point of audition (POA). While we might visualize and analyze these shapes through the metaphor of a waveform, Chion suggests an interior mental space that "feels like the present," the few moments, "the duration," "or the blink," which cannot be too strictly defined—depending on the sound, it can pass quickly, or it can drag.[3] Chion suggests that the listener's capacity to anticipate a sound's completion modulates this subjective sense of time. If a listener feels like they know the conclusion, they might be inclined to move on to other potential sounds.

Sounds link different frames together into a coherent sense of linear progression. When the same sound connects structures, they causally follow one another. For example, a montage of faces during an audience reaction has no implicit sense of time. But when set to a dialogue soundtrack, it creates a sense of linear progression. When a video already contains movement with a clear trajectory, like someone walking, sound acts as a vector that infuses the image with an ephemeral quality. For example, when paired with the idea of dripping water, Chion writes, "the sound of a droplet imposes a real and irreversible time on what we see, in that it presents a trajectory in time (small impact, then delicate resonance) by the logics of gravity and return to inertia."[4] In other words, sound gives each frame an irreversible sense of starting and ending. It provides the spectator with an orientation toward events, instructing them to anticipate. Sound sets or violates the expectations for a scene. Anticipation is not merely reactive; it is an active force that constitutes people's affective existence.

Chion gives an example of a single, isolated piano note to describe the general shape of a sound in time. He selected a single piano note because if one follows it to an extreme limit until it fades entirely to extinction, it far exceeds the average duration window for a piano note and would feel like it drags. A listener, Chion suggests, rarely listens this long because they often anticipate that the intensity of the note will dissipate toward extinction. But invert the same note, listening to it from its softest remaining sound to the moment when the key was struck so that the listener does not know when the sound may end, then the experience of time drags with it. Chion continues, "The same sound inverted, which takes the form of slow building of intensity and disappears as soon as that intensity reaches its maximum, will be listened to much more actively and continuously, and so it will seem longer."[5] Underwriting the latent tendency for the listener to follow a building intensity, and thus for sound to draw out longer, Chion posits listeners attend to amplification, or building sound, because it "might grow infinitely, covering up all other sounds, invading us, submerging us, and disarming us—all by preventing us not only from hearing but also from making ourselves heard."[6] When auditors do not know what will happen but anticipate the following note, the interval drags on until satisfaction. As our anticipation is piqued and satisfied, it contributes to a feeling of time's passage.

Chion's point is that listening to the inverted piano note extends its duration because of the listener's anticipation; this has more to do with the temporal shape of the note's duration than any arbitrary sign or signified relationship to the piano key. Chion's inverted message is unique because it encourages an auditor to focus attention and contort the experience for fear it may not end. Because sound can encourage listeners to anticipate when it might end, it *narrows* attention, creating a shape in which time seems significantly slowed down and elongated. Chion's hypothetical listener could be held there for a while, languishing in pain, gripped by a note that might not eventually break. Of course, when the listener recognizes the end, they may *expand* attention, speeding up time and opening the mind to other things. The inverted piano note can help contour the temporal shape of a sound by manipulating anticipation. The figure of a sound's duration creates a variety of different forms. Sound's capacity to induce listeners to anticipate, narrow, expand, and modulate attention supplies a powerful resource. If the shape of time can be meaningful, it gives rhetoricians a powerful resource for invention. Indeed, if a form can be a kind of content that makes an argument through the experience of that form, then a form that evokes duration or immediacy can be a site to create meaning.

The waveform provides a metaphor to examine how durational immediacy can be shaped to move the auditor. These shapes are not blank forms without substance but rather communicate messages themselves. This was certainly the case for X González. The survivor of the horrific shooting needed a way to express how terrifying it was to hide while not knowing what was happening to their friends during a school shooting. Simply saying they were scared was not enough to convey their experience. So, they turned to a sound tactic, the cut-out, to set up and ultimately violate their audience's expectations. This provided the feeling of the Parkland Kid, a site for them to identify with and join the debate. They used sound to contour a duration that resembled their experience through the cut-out, and the result was iconic.

Marjory Stoneman Douglas Shooting

On the afternoon of February 14, 2018, an armed student with an AR-15 walked into Marjory Stoneman Douglas High School in Parkland, Florida, and pulled the fire alarm. As students, staff, and faculty poured into the hall, the student opened fire, murdering fourteen students and three staff and wounding many others.[7] While the shooter roamed the halls, trapped students turned to social media platforms, like Snapchat, to capture and disseminate their experience to friends and family.

Usually, in the aftermath of a school shooting, a familiar pattern of narrative and imagery emerges: aerial shots of the school, first responders on the scene, emotional survivors, mourners at vigils, and images of the shooter. These representations constitute the public's understanding of these tragedies. However, this portrayal is sanitized, focusing on the emotional impact rather than the violence within the school. This repetitive imagery shapes the debate surrounding school shootings, often framing it as a question of the best means to protect children. The discussion typically positions gun rights activists against gun control advocates, each with differing views on how to ensure school safety. What immediately differentiated MSD from other school shootings was the introduction of Snapchat and its capacity to share raw, first-person perspectives. This disrupts this narrative, allowing new stakeholders, like students, to influence the debate.

Snapchat, a popular social media platform among teens, enables users to record and post ephemeral audiovisual stories, or "snaps." Its realness and immediacy contrast with the curated content of professional organizations, providing observers with a sense of immediate presence. The platform's Snap Maps feature further extends its interactivity, transforming private snaps into potentially public events by tracking their frequency, location, and dispersion. Snap Maps uses an algorithm to create a real-time "heat map," highlighting emerging stories based on activity density. This combination of mobility, camera, audio, and a vast dissemination network has revolutionized the public perception of events like school shootings. Snapchat replaces the traditional aerial shots with first-person perspectives from inside the unfolding tragedy. This shift parallels how frontline camera equipment during the Vietnam War changed public perception. The platform demands interpretation through these authentic and immediate fragments and opens opportunities for new voices to shape the narrative. As legacy newscasters once did, viral content creators can now influence public understanding.

The snaps gave the public an intimate view of the shooting dispersed through first-person perspectives of shaky camera angles, screams, sniffles, bullets reverberating, cries, lifeless bodies, blood, panicked whispers, shattering glass, footsteps, and heavy breathing. The public's sensorium pierced the school's walls during the shooting for the first time, experiencing the students' perspectives in real time. For those who did not tune into the massacre live, major television networks picked up the snaps and posts and brought them into the living rooms of the public, blurring out some of the images but retaining the scary sounds. The myriad pictures provided an intimate perspective of a school shooting that previous media coverage had not.

Snapchat extended the range of the public's eyes and ears, live *inside* MSD as the shooting unfolded. Short bursts of videos showed first-person perspectives of cowering students, bullet-ridden computers, pools of blood, lifeless bodies, and more. Speakers relayed screams, gasps, sobs, cries, moans, and gunshots. Snapchat opened space to extend the public's sensorium into a new realm, the school shooting, but it lacked the capacity for the public to make *sense* of what was witnessed. Student survivors of the Parkland shooting seized on the opening and responded with speeches, helping to create the figure of the Parkland Kid and, with it, a way to approach the gun debate. This group of kids advanced a new demand in public; fed up with the world the adults left them, they claimed that adults had failed to protect them and demanded change. The Parkland Kid, as a sound body, emerged.[8]

The emergence of the student was relevant because in the previous conversation, they were largely absent. But in this new context, their experience as a survivor and credibility growing up in this era became salient. As a set of advocates, the students could tactically wield their experience to demand change. In the process of a tragedy, their presence was captured, narrated through the mass-mediated shooting experience, as it was picked up and rebroadcast worldwide. The body behind the screens could be linked to those who were vulnerable and had experienced the tragic result of an adult society that did not live up to its obligations. The residual expertise of the sound body provided a powerful rhetorical resource. This sound tactic works through immediacy—the temporal waveform brings people together through the feeling that this problem must be addressed urgently. The students could express their feelings that the situation had become so unbearable that it needed to change.

The news coverage brought the intimate experience of a school shooting, detached it from its origin, and repeated it throughout the public. The fragments became a salient part of the public screen, and the presence of the vulnerable kid became a sensed figure. Ultimately, the presence of the kids and their vulnerable bodies came together in the kid's perspective when they spoke out and started advocating for themselves. On Saturday, February 17, González rode down to a gun control rally, writing their speech, "We Call BS," on the way. In Fort Lauderdale, Florida, González was greeted by a few hundred members of the local community, as well as politicians and other Parkland families, giving what the *New Yorker* would call "the defining moment of a gun control rally."[9] González used "generational terms like student, kid, teacher, and adult. The term student, for instance, appears 11 times in the short address and is often accompanied by references to specific classes and concomitant instruments like textbooks, tests, and pencils."[10] They offered the generational divide as a talking point on the gun debate, which did not easily fall into the traditional battle lines of a time before.

The speech took the stance of a generation forced to grow up in an era of school shootings. For them, they have only ever known a world in which gun violence defined their existence. The speech claimed older generations might have grappled with gun violence, but this would be the first generation to be defined by it. They are faced with the possibility of someone coming to the school and shooting them. An actual shooter did not need to go to the school to shape these students' coming of age because school shootings had already organized their adolescence. These students grew up around metal detectors, clear backpacks, armed officers, viral videos of shooters, classroom debates, threats, rumors of lists, and numerous other shootings, adding to the fear that they could be next. This speech claimed the older generation was beholden to big money or incompetence, while this generation just wanted to ensure they could eliminate the scourge of gun violence. González's use of generational conflict drew into relief the divide between kids and parents.

This early speech used the family metaphor to constitute the social world, dividing children's and parents' primary duties and responsibilities. Since a child is not a fully formed member of society, it is incumbent on the parents to care for them. In this formation, parents undertake the caretaker role with a responsibility to ensure children are not harmed. Underwriting this normative standard is the assumption that the parents have the resources and mental faculty to make these decisions. If parents were to intentionally put a child in harm's way, they would be violating these expectations and thus no longer able to serve as guardians of the child. These expectations go beyond the intent to suggest negligence when inaction results in an inability to meet essential obligations. When the family becomes a trope to understand the social world, the debate pivots on whether the adults have satisfied their care obligations. The fact that adults have failed to live up to their responsibility to protect children is a prevalent theme in the address. As Lisa Miller and Andres Kudacki point out, "In [their] black tank top, with raggedy friendship bracelets stacked on [their] wrist, [X González] looked, as the comments said, so *relatable*—[they] could have been any teenager you know."[11] As they gave their speech, they offered a stand-in for any kid giving an address to the public.

It is in the context of the family that González's demand is taken up. They demand to surrender the gun debate to the kids. In this representative anecdote, González calls for a shift in the agency when they exclaim, "And maybe the adults have gotten used to saying, 'It is what it is,' but if we students have learned anything, it's that if you don't study, you will fail. And in this case, if you actively do nothing, people continually end up dead, so it's time to start doing something."[12]

In this passage, González forcefully demands that adults surrender gun policy to the kids because the adults have failed to live up to their responsibilities. The claim that adults have gotten used to saying, "It is what it is," after a shooting is set out as evidence of that abrogation of duty. According to González, parents fall into a practice of "actively [doing] nothing," an oxymoron that creates a tension that implicates the adults' incompetence in creating a situation where "people continually end up dead." The lack of an agent in that sentence enacts González's point—it does not require any work for the status quo of mass shootings to continue. If the adults have failed to meet their obligations, they must hand over the care of the family to someone else. González points out that kids have particular expertise. Attending school, they have learned that if you don't study, you fail. González points out elsewhere in this speech that after the shooting, "We have to be studying our notes to make sure that our arguments based on politics and political history are watertight." They were the ones who knew how to compose well-researched public arguments to show us how to move forward. González's speech went viral and propelled them into the national spotlight.[13] The kids became symbols of the argument that the adults have failed to live up to the expected standards of care.

Sensing the political momentum, González joined with the other visible survivors of the Parkland shooting, such as David Hogg, Kalyn Corin, Cameron Kasky, and Delaney Tarr, to constitute the Parkland Kids, who planned what would eventually become the "March for Our Lives" in Washington, DC.[14] Miller and Kudacki paint the scene: as González stood on the stoop talking to Demi Lovato on their cell, Tarr was inside figuring out the appropriate talking points, such as being bipartisan because this is "a nonpartisan issue."[15] Hogg stayed the night and woke up to do an early morning spot with González on *New Day with Chris Cuomo*. The students could not keep up with the media attention, so they recruited help from "a couple of Douglas alumni who were home from college offering support and [from] a mom friend with a background in PR."[16] Soon, the kids got professional representation from 42West, a celebrity PR agency. González and the Parkland Kids became a household name after being invited onto various nationally televised shows, from news interviews to Dr. Phil to Ellen DeGeneres.[17] The group soon incorporated the March for Our Lives Action Fund as a 501(c)(4) and devised a board of directors. Even though there was a board of directors, the Parkland Kids insisted they maintain a voice in the nonprofit.

The March for Our Lives

The March for Our Lives event was scheduled for March 24, 2018, roughly six weeks after the initial shooting. The Parkland Kids planned a march for six weeks down the line because they wanted to keep Parkland and guns in the national conversation longer than the traditional media cycle. By putting a significant action on the calendar farther away, the movement ensured they had another media event in the future, empowering them to take charge of the narrative's timeline. Deena Katz, an organizer behind the Women's March, helped coordinate and submit the permits for March for Our Lives.[18]

The Parkland Kids tapped vast gun control networks to sponsor marches and gatherings nationwide. The students worked with institutionalized social movements, such as Moms Demand Action, MoveOn, the Women's March LA,

Representative Gabrielle Gifford's foundation, and Everytown for Gun Safety, to design, fundraise, and plan their march.[19] They raised 3.3 million dollars for their march on Washington.[20] *Buzzfeed News* reported that some organizations provided logistics, like Representative Gifford's foundation, which worked with Everytown and Moms Demand Action to coordinate concurrent protests. MoveOn encouraged "its millions of members to follow and promote the March for Our Lives movement on social media and attend the rally."[21] Everytown helped secure large donations, such as a one-million-dollar donation from Eli Broad. Even groups indirectly involved, like Planned Parenthood, aided with portable toilets for the march.

On the March for Our Lives event day, people turned out en masse to support the movement. Every continent, save Antarctica, and every state had a *concurrent* protest. One hundred eighty thousand people marched on Washington, DC.[22] The well-attended event was dotted with people waving clipboards, wearing neon yellow shirts emblazoned with the words "Register to Vote!" and yelling, "It takes less than three minutes."[23] It had a party-like atmosphere, with celebrity performances from Ariana Grande, Miley Cyrus, and Lin-Manuel Miranda. In addition to many of the Parkland Kids themselves, the event featured speakers such as Edna Chavez, a high school senior in Los Angeles who lost her brother to gun violence, and Yolanda Renee King, the nine-year-old granddaughter of Martin Luther King Jr. González was the last speaker scheduled to appear. The speeches were aired live online, on network television, and on some cable news channels. González's finale was scheduled to appear right before performing artist Jennifer Hudson.

When it was finally their turn, González walked up to the stage wearing ripped jeans, tight-cropped hair, a choker necklace, and a militant green bomber jacket—dotted with patches of the Cuban flag, among others, and lines from their earlier speech, "We Call BS," and other statements—over their March for Our Lives shirt. As the last speaker of the March for Our Lives, González served an important symbolic role, a punctuation mark for the event. They needed to capitalize on the momentum generated from the event, bring the community together, and underscore the urgency to act now. Their demand hinged on the argument that no more time is wasted. Adults have failed, and too many people have died, and it's time for the adults to hand over the reins to the kids. To do that, González used a cut-out, a temporal break that underscored the immediacy and urgency of their demand.

The Cut-Out

The demand followed the logic of González's earlier speech that the adults needed to hand control over to the kids; the cut-out underscored the immediacy with which this needed to happen. Indeed, the thrust of the reason why the standard means of letting the parents solve the problem would not work is based on the timing. There is tremendous uncertainty surrounding when the next shooting would occur, and González used sound to impose on the audience the feelings attached to this reality. They used their voice as an instrument to modulate intensity and time to place the audience in the shooting. While some might call González's move "silence," such a term misses the important vocal work that González did to create a temporal shape that incited embodied feelings. They relied on the sound tactic of the "cut-out," which is a temporal shape that involves a sequence of (1) setting a sonorous expectation, (2) an extreme violation of that expectation, leaving the audience in anticipation, and (3) a release. The cut-out enabled González to render an iconic experience that gave the audience a reason to fight for gun reform. Each member of the audience, regardless of where they were located—at the march or watching on TV—lingered in the anguish of the more than four-minute-long cut-out. The introduction of González's voice in releasing the cut-out amplified the urgency in the call to action, as it paired a swift feeling of relief with a need to act against gun violence.

While there is a generic form of cut-out, there are several ways to set and violate expectations through it. In this address, González accomplished the cut-out by first selecting the expectation through a sonorous trope of augmentation, as when a musician slowly lengthens the duration of a melody. The sonority of the first part of the speech conveys a sense of a typical day unfolding. They then switched to the diminution, another sonorous trope. This move incrementally shortened time values and intensified the pitch before González suddenly stopped—leaving the audience in the agony of silence. The pause was not a moment of reflection, but it instead iconically imposed on the audience González's personal experience of the school shooting. The eventual release of the cut-out is the release of shared pain, infusing the audience with surplus energy, which González capitalized on for their call to action. This gave the audience an embodied reason to go out and fight for gun regulation. Together, these three parts—augmentation/diminution, drop, and release—created a temporal shape, the cut-out. The cut-out lasted the exact length of time as the shooting itself;

the temporal form was the content being conveyed: an experience of what the shooting was like and how it inspired activism.

If the sonic body of the kid lingered in the periphery of the public screen, the cut-out served to propel the Parkland Kid's vulnerability into the forefront of the public. Although you might only be seeing González, they represented a part of the whole of the Parkland Kids. The immediate presence of the experience was cut out and repeated across different programs as the speech went viral. González came to stand in for the generic body of the kid, and the enthymematic picture of González imported the silence and reminded the audience of the entire sonic body.

Building on Immediacy

González walked out onto the stage and performed the following:

> In a little over six minutes, seventeen of our friends were taken from us, fifteen were injured, and everyone, absolutely everyone in the Douglas community, was forever altered. Six minutes and twenty seconds with an AR-15, and my friend Carmen would never complain to me about piano practice; Aaron Feis would never call Kyra "Miss Sunshine"; Alex Schachter would never walk into school with his brother Ryan; Scott Beigel would never joke around with Cameron at camp; Helena Ramsey would never hang out after school with Max; Gina Montalto would never wait for her friend Liam at lunch; Joaquin Oliver would never play basketball with Sam or Dylan; Alaina Petty would never; Cara Loughran would never; Chris Hixon would never; Luke Hoyer would never; Martin Duque Anguiano would never; Peter Wang would never; Alyssa Alhadeff would never; Jaime Guttenberg would never; Meadow Pollack would never.[24]

Then they stood in silence. The crowd watched, also silent.

A chant of "never again" started and then faded out. González still stood.

Finally, the beeping of an electric timer rang out. "Since the time that I came out here, it has been six minutes and twenty seconds," they said. "The shooter has ceased shooting and will soon abandon his rifle, blend in with the students as they escape, and walk free for an hour before arrest." Then they concluded, "Fight for your lives before it's someone else's job."

In the first part of the speech, González employs augmentation, a technique that builds on successive intervals bit by bit to increase the experience of duration. This is often found in classical music. Once a potential length is reached, it contracts and starts over again. The result builds a rhythm, stretching the time experience for the listener. Instead of "ear blinks," we might think of keynotes. The repetition provides an organizing logic that structures other sensations. Augmentation gives the audience a slower perception of time. As it slowly builds the extension of time, the audience knows what to expect, allowing them to anticipate successive growth correctly. González defined each interval by a simple melody of ascension in pitch, extension, and descension at the end, elongating the listener's experience of duration interval by interval.

Consider, for example, when González builds out a sense of duration at the start: "Everyone, everyone, in the Douglas community was forever altered. Everyone who was there understood. Everyone touched by the cold grip of gun violence understands." The anaphoric "everyone" marks each interval, providing an inflection point where González ascends their pitch before releasing the intensity in their voice to create a descending rhythm. When González starts this refrain, they ascend with an "everyone," then descend and extend with the first syllable in "abs" and release with "solutely." They repeat the process, starting with the following "everyone," ascend with "in the Douglas Community was forever," and descend on "altered." Now the length of the refrain is a little bit longer of an interval. They begin the following sentence with the ascension starting again with "everyone," extend over "who was there," and then descend with "understands." Finally, the set concludes as González ascends, "Everyone who has," plateaus over "been touched by the cold," and finally descends with "grip of gun violence understands." The repetition creates and satisfies the audience's expectations, augmenting the tempo and extending the experience of duration. Because the audience knows what to expect, it makes sense for an average period. Each interval sets the stage for the next, providing the conditions for the next break's length, intensity, and duration. After four repetitions of augmentations around the word "everyone," González continues to build the same gap but changes the critical phrase from "everyone" to "no one," this time with "no one" augmenting and elongating time for another four repetitions. González repeats the same rhythmic structure of ascension and descension, intensity and release, and with each repetition the interval grows incrementally longer.

The cycle of expectation and satisfaction, extension and contraction, ascension and descension, all signal the typical pattern of life. González places the audience in the quotidian rhythms, building an understanding that any ordinary day could be February 14 at MSD. Like a day unfolding, intervals build on one another; each moment teems with intensities that peak and release and build on one another. Moments slide into memory, replete with all the stirrings that set the conditions for the next day. Yet something is haunting about González's voice. The dissonance in the rhyme scheme between "no one" and "everyone" casts an eerie shadow, as if something is almost imperceptibly off—perhaps the record skips, but maybe you heard it wrong the first time—a kind of sonorous foreshadowing. As González transitions to the next part of the speech, augmentation condenses into a memory of stability, a sonorous point of comparison for the coming change in tempo and tone that will occur in the next section. Refrains provide points of comparison, and this quotidian pattern gives the audience an iconic issue to compare to the coming chaos. If the first part of the speech were measured and consistent, then the second part would be fast and intense with the removal of intervals, ultimately culminating in a cut-out.

In the second part of the speech, González uses the sonic trope of diminution, which progressively shortens intervals by removing words, phrases, or sounds to speed up time and switch up the temporality. For the listener, this accelerates time, increasing velocity and shortening the duration of intervals. The phrase "would never" becomes the inflection point where González intensifies their pitch. While they conditioned the audience to expect an eventual release in the first movement, they only intensified their rise, fomenting anticipation for a release that might never come and painfully elongating time. As González intensifies the audience's emotion, they introduce the name of each slain student and remind the audience that they "would never" act again. That's sixteen repetitions of the "would never" refrain. Each intensification reminds the audience of death and further grips us by naming eight classmates with whom the dead children would never again interact. Each named death iconically brings more pain to the collective feeling of the audience, more dread without the promised release.

The second refrain places the audience in the moment of the shooting. González proclaims, "Six minutes and 20 seconds with an AR-15, and my friend

Carmen would never complain to me about piano practice." Here they start the process of diminution, giving the audience the first "would never" and establishing the most extended interval—including references to themself ("my friend" and "to me"). Next, each phrase has the name of the fallen, "would never," a verb, and an indirect object. Each repetition of "would never" intensifies González's vocal pitch, violating the audience's expectation of a potential release and building up tension for the audience. González speeds up, quickening time: "Aaron Feis would never call Kyra 'Miss Sunshine.'" The time of the speech accelerates, bringing the chaos of the shooting, along with the student deaths, directly to the audience. The increased speed also increases pain, as González ratchets up the dread with each intensification and deferment of release. Each "would never" results in another intensification of the collective pain of the audience—the hits come faster and faster. These seven instances of "would never" have a subject sentence, an intensification, a verb, and an object. González accelerates again. The final eight are a bleak reminder of the real toll of gun violence, with just the name and "would never" and leaving the lost action unstated: "Alaina Petty would never; Cara Loughran would never; Chris Hixon would never; Luke Hoyer would never; Martin Duque Anguiano would never; Peter Wang would never; Alyssa Alhadeff would never; Jamie Guttenberg would never; Jamie Pollack would never."

The repetition of "would never" strings together into an iconic pattern of the heartbeat of someone on life support, speeding up and then, without much warning, stopping. Each "would never" intensifies the pitch, and the promise of an end to the built tension is further delayed. What follows is not just silence for quiet reflection but elongated dread and agony as the audience is hooked, anticipating what González might do next.

González then stood silently for four minutes and twenty-six seconds. At rapt attention, the audience searched their face for a sign, studied their body language for what to do, and waited to see what they would do next. González stared off into the horizon, unmoving, holding their ground. Sometimes their eyes were open; sometimes they would shut them. Tears would stream down their cheeks, but they did not lift their arms to wipe them away. They stood, stiff back, closed lips, clenched jaw, erect neck. Their breath was audible, like lapping waves—in and out. All the while, González let the audience hang there. The audience, unified in anticipation, waited for González to say something, anything. The tense moments became palpable as the audience at March for Our Lives tried to figure out the proper reaction to González's stoic silence. The audience's four minutes and twenty-six seconds might have felt like hours. The quantitative measure of time does not capture the qualitative experience of duration.

Just like the students in the building were unsure what was happening in the adjacent building while a code red was called and a shooter roamed the halls, the audience was transported into the same disorientating, visceral pain. This was not a sensation that could ever be conveyed through language; it could only be experienced. The collective feelings created by the sonic elements opened a rhetorical space that everyone listening shared. A few minutes out into eternity, those watching on the various mediated platforms were caught off guard, too. Over the period, the live copresent audience engaged in a variety of reactions, including clapping, chanting, "Never again," and declaring, "We love you, Emma" (X González's name at the time). Yet each attempt at reaching the speaker was punctuated by silence when González offered no acknowledgment. The awkward encounters between González and their audience underscored the discord of the crowd. Bodies gathered together, uncomfortable, uncertain how to act, but overwhelmed with the need to do something with this surplus feeling. Media coverage caught images of disquiet and discord in an unsettled audience.

The final section of the speech frees the audience from the cut-out. A beep from the timer indicates that González can speak again. As they come out of the cut-out, they begin the last refrain: "Since the time that I came out here, it has been six minutes and 20 seconds; the shooter has ceased shooting and will soon abandon his rifle, blend in with the students as they escape, and walk free for an hour before arrest." González's voice also returns to the familiar rhythm of ascension, extension, and descension. Like the surviving students escaping from the school, a sudden relief passes over the crowd. González capitalizes on the ineffable experience of the cut-out's release, catalyzing the audience into action by ending the speech with a demand: "Fight for your lives before it's someone else's job." They start with an ascension, increasing pitch as they say "fight for your lives" and descend with "before it's someone else's job." The audience has suffered together across vast distances, regardless of how well they knew the names of the slain or González. The final section released the tension of the cut-out. Because the resolution of pain came with a call to action, this implicitly suggests that acting is how to resolve pain. Doing something helps alleviate some pain, which supplies a material reason to work.

Shortly after they left the stage, González's speech went viral, reverberating through mainstream platforms. Like the snaps before, the speech became detached from the origin; the experience of the silence came to stand in for the pain and vulnerability of their sound body. All the major cable networks had carried it live. In the twenty-four hours after the speech, it racked up over a half million clicks on YouTube and appeared on every major news broadcast, and stories landed on the front page of every major news publication.[25] The cut-out became the focal point of the coverage, the place that unified the audience and the coverage into a coherent whole, where the pain and the dread and feeling of community coalesced into a moment in time. The speech was celebrated for its power, a recurring theme; major news periodicals talked about "The Powerful Silence,"[26] "The Most Powerful Moment from the March for Our Lives Protest,"[27] and "A Powerful Protest."[28] Others warned that the speech "will crush you"[29] or might even "stick with you forever."[30] On Twitter, users declared the speech the "Loudest silence in the History of US Social Protest,"[31] "an incredible, chilling moment,"[32] and "one of the most remarkable political moments I've seen."[33] The collective moment of feeling, a moment in time, is remembered from the speech.

In much of the coverage after the speech, many people misquoted the amount of time of the silence, reporting different amounts of time, and later issued corrections. For example, the *Huffington Post* reported that González "honored shooting victims with six minutes of silence."[34] *Cosmopolitan* magazine wondered "what was going through [their] head during the painfully somber six minutes of silence [they] maintained during [their] speech."[35] *The Hill* tweeted, "Emma González holds six minutes of silence for slain classmates during March for Our Lives speech."[36] Similarly, *The Atlantic* observed that "González kept the silence—continuous, insistent—until six minutes and 20 seconds were up."[37] This might seem unremarkable, but when you look into the corrections it seems to be evidence of the power of the cut-out. For example, Jerry Weismann, a contributor who noted the wrong time, writes, "I wrote that her pause lasted six minutes and twenty seconds. I was wrong.... In empathizing with [González's] emotional expression, I went into time warp."[38]

Perhaps some reporters mistook the silence for the whole speech rather than just part of the speech. Regardless, the cut-out became the most memorable moment, sucking up and warping time. After their speech, González posted on Twitter, "Real Quick: my speech today was abt 6 mins & 30 secs, including both my speech and my silence. The fact that people think the silence was 6 minutes ... imagine how long it would have felt if it was 6 minutes, or how it would feel if you had to hide during that silence."[39] Perhaps this standard error was because the entire speech was six minutes and twenty seconds, and people misheard González state that the span measured the time since "I came out here," or perhaps it was because the silence stretched the audience's perception of time for those four minutes and twenty-six seconds. All in all, losing track of time sparked a sense of urgency to act *now*.

Picturing the Silence of González's Speech at March for Our Lives

Many images came from the March for Our Lives event. There were pictures of the National Mall brimming with bodies, collages of protest signs, stills of the speakers mid-speech, and candid shots of celebrities performing. Yet in the days that followed the March for Our Lives event, it was the image of González standing alone on the stage in silence that dominated the coverage of the events. In particular, the moment they stood in silence symbolized the event—the last moment lingered in the public memory to galvanize future action. There was no specific image of them standing there, but numerous photographs captured split-second differences. Just as a microphone recording of the speech captures each slight shift in tone or texture, there was a steady stream of pictures, each capturing a different part of the cut-out as González held the audience's attention hostage. Jim Watson at the *Agency Free Press* caught González with their eyes open, a tear remaining at the corner of their vision, just short of falling.[40] For Alex Brandon of the *Associated Press*, González's eyes were closed, a tear crawled down their face, but their hands were not in view.[41] González's likeness was suddenly everywhere, a ubiquitous part of our mediated environment; it appeared in newspapers, memes, TV shows, and several other platforms.

Photography is not a passive process that simply "records" life; rather, it is an active agent in the co-constitution of life. Sarah Kember and Joanna Zylinska write, "Life goes beyond and contests representation: it is a creation of images in the most radical sense. Photographic practice as we know it is just one instantiation of this creative process." They explain that photography is "of intermittent duration, of incised movement and captured time."[42] The process of "taking a picture" involves a perspective in a place, material technology brimming with affordances, light, disparate movements, shapes, cultural categories, and many more considerations. Snapping a photograph involves a dynamic relationship between a surface reflecting and refracting light and a lens apprehending it. Movements between the photographer and the object yield different expressions of this dynamic. The passage of time changes the light. Helping guide the modulation of this dynamic are broader cultural dispositions that might dictate what counts as a good picture. Capitalist interests provide lures that help show how people select a shot from a multiplicity of images. For a photographer navigating space, considerations such as impediments, cultural constrictions, or any other external factors constrain or enable perspective. What if a large object obstructs a view or a potential legal restriction prevents movement to a spot that might allow for a better idea? Instead of being the product of a person simply using an active technology imposed on the inert matter, a photo is an expression of a complex event.

Several photographers (independent contractors) vied to take the *best* picture of González's cut-out to sell to an image distributor (a pretty good lure). Random cameras provided numerous vantage points with many different perspectives, each offering its relational dynamic that yields an expression: how González's face and body relate to the podium, logos, and stage. One of these particular nodes is what allowed for the constellations to align for lines, coloring, platform, and missing logo. However, there is also the timing of the camera, as an aperture apprehends movements in time refracted by light, such as the rise and fall of González's chest, the tensile moment before they release their silence demanding our attention. Yet these moments caught in light are also measured against more extended, cultural contexts—how March for Our Lives relates to previous school shootings. The image has compositional elements that have a relationship of *resemblance* to the event. The picture is as silent as the moment in time right before the release. While there is significant scholarly attention to visual culture and how it impacts public reasoning, this conversation can be extended to explore the repetition of similar images that get picked up and endlessly repeated in different ways. A stock image uses repetition to invoke a context for discussing the public good. These images are not specific arguments but impose a structure of feeling, which in turn helps define the appropriate topic for discussion. One of these became a valance for youth activism that suggested ceding leadership to the kids because the adults no longer have the moral authority.

After the March for Our Lives event, an entire economy of photos was bought up and then circulated online. Consider Getty Images, one of the largest image distribution agencies, which sells images to various companies and spreads "widely in print publications from the pages of magazines and corporate pamphlets to the covers of greeting cards and novels. Stock images also proliferate digital media, from commercial websites to television advertisements, reaching vast audiences in every corner of visual life."[43] The wide availability of their images for easy licensing means they have greater reach than others, which gives them a unique power to shape expectations and norms.[44] These photographs traffic in aesthetic stereotypes for profit—images are often indexed under different headers where they think an image might be ideally used. With Getty, the market provides a mechanism of dissemination that spreads the message to stop gun violence. The surplus of capital offers a tool for social movement; we can see how "seamlessly capital appropriates the politics of identity and marginal representation into commodity form."[45] González's image was organized under such tabs as gun control, March for Our Lives, violence protest, speeches, Gulf states, one-person photo, and youth movement.

Getty's image of the cut-out is in landscape format, centering González from left to right. González stands alone, sandwiched behind a giant podium and a wall featuring a March for Our Lives logo behind them. González is in front of the movement, leading it toward the camera. They are also the face of the movement, as they stand erect, facing an invisible audience with no makeup, no hair, and nothing besides the podium. The lines of the microphones point toward their face. Finally, the picture says what cannot be said, conveying the emotional intensity of silence. It is the potential that the silence might break, of a release that might come when González says *something* and releases the cut-out. The photo provides a compact, iconic image of the demand, complete with an enthymeme standing in for the silence.

Like many other movements, the March for Our Lives event exited the news cycle. The feeling of immediate urgency that underwrote the claim to the moral high ground waned. Several other stories took its place. In the immediate aftermath heading into the 2018 midterms, two of the many new shooting stories included an anti-Semitic truck driver who killed eleven in a synagogue on October 27, 2018, in Pittsburgh, Pennsylvania, and a shooting on November 7, 2018, in Thousand Oaks, California, where a former Marine went into a crowded bar and opened fire, killing twelve.[46] Yet Getty's iconic image of González continued to exert force on how people might feel about the trajectory of efforts against gun control, centering the Parkland Kid in the public debate. *The Atlantic* proclaimed it was "The Year the Gun Conversation Changed," and the *Huffington Post* wrote, "2018 Was the Year We Turned the Tide on Ending Gun Violence."[47] Local news periodicals also picked up the iconic image. The *Spokesman-Review* claimed, "Parkland Attack Fueled Big Shift in America's Gun Politics."[48] The *Chicago Tribune* reported, "One Year After Parkland, Crown Point Student

Says the Need for Change Continues: 'It Doesn't Mean That You Stop.'"[49] While all these articles feature the same iconic Getty image, they all go further, propagating an image of gun violence and the family metaphor. The idea that guns implicate adults' capacity to live up to guardianship norms has now been enshrined in the debate.

Youth Studies and the Future

All these years later, the legacy of the Parkland Kids is how they drew into relief the failure of adults. The iconic image of González, licensed under the category "youth movement," unwrites a broader legacy of a shifting culture resource. In 2019, Greta Thunberg emerged as a prominent figure in climate activism, drawing significant inspiration from the student activists of the Parkland mass shooting. Thunberg's rhetoric sharply delineates the responsibilities of adults versus the younger generation, accusing adults of failing in their duty to safeguard the future for the youth.[50] In a March 2019 interview with *Rolling Stone*, Thunberg openly credited the Parkland students' strikes and activism as a catalyst for her own. She admired their courage and the clarity with which they challenged established powers, such as the National Rifle Association, despite historical precedents of such efforts falling short. Inspired by the Parkland students' determination to effect change irrespective of external support, Thunberg resolved to adopt a similar stance in her climate activism.[51]

Yet not everyone is afforded the space of a kid's innocence. Robin Bernstein writes that the position of "kid" is often afforded to structures of Whiteness. This raises questions about the potential of sound tactics. For Black groups, how sound can be used tactically presents a set of questions different from those for the Parkland Kids because they have another set of constraints, including an entire history of racism. I would be remiss not to point out that for the South Carolina student, the silence was not sufficient to stop her from being viewed as a threat when a school officer violently pulled her from her seat and threw her to the ground.[52]

As we transition from the Parkland Kids to HU Resist, we see how different groups have leveraged sound tactics to amplify their voices and demands for change. Both movements emerged in response to institutional failures that threatened the safety and well-being of young people. The Parkland students utilized the immediacy of sound to convey the visceral experience of a school shooting and galvanize support for gun control, while HU Resist employed strategic heckling and protest songs to challenge financial mismanagement and systemic issues at Howard University. In both cases, the activists skillfully navigated the public sphere using social media and traditional news outlets to extend the reach of their sonic bodies beyond their immediate physical locations.

However, key differences emerge in the tactics employed and the broader societal contexts of these movements. The Parkland Kids found themselves thrust into the national spotlight almost immediately, benefiting from widespread media coverage that often framed them as innocents demanding protection. In contrast, HU Resist, composed primarily of Black students, had to work more deliberately to gain national attention, navigating a complex history of student activism at historically Black colleges and universities (HBCUs) and contending with racial stereotypes that often frame Black protest as disruptive or threatening. While the Parkland Kids' use of silence as a powerful sound tactic resonated widely, HU Resist's deployment of call-and-response chants and protest songs drew from a rich tradition of Black oral culture and civil rights activism. These distinctions highlight how race, class, and historical context shape the reception and impact of youth-led movements, even as both groups sought to challenge entrenched power structures and demand accountability from institutions that had failed them.

3

Heckling and HU Resist

A concerned collective of Howard University students, HU Resist, formed during the early days of the Trump presidency. The group reasoned that if Howard University took federal money, the institution would be beholden to the Trump administration. When they realized that a member of the Trump administration, Betsy DeVos, was on the Board of Regents, they took action. Soon they realized the problem went much deeper than DeVos and Trump. For HU Resist, Howard became a binding site to repair a fractured Black class consciousness. For example, they saw how fellow students separated themselves from other people's struggles in *their* community—how classmates would ignore the people of color experiencing homelessness on the parameter of campus. In response to the fracking of solidarity, the protesters needed to unmask the machinations of the university and demonstrate how it propagated an agenda of capitalist white supremacy. They needed to intervene publicly in the official discourse and draw attention to the ways it reifies hegemonic power.

HU Resist provides a case study of the potential of the heckle. Paul McIlvenny explains, "An audience member hearable changes his or her participation status from a member of a collective audience to an individual in direct interaction with the speaker."[1] "Member hearable changes" identify the point when an audience member's audibility becomes perceivable and their agency is recognized. When making a demand, the norms around the audience become one of the places that can provide moral resources for the claim that right makes might. What differentiates a heckle from other kinds of audience participation is the way that it operates as a potential turn, moving the audience from spectator to the new speaker. As McIlvenny continues, "A heckle can urgently undermine an argument or an assertion by providing an alternative hearing: by disagreeing, by questioning or adding information that negates the premise or reveals a presupposition, by undermining the sequential import, or by ridiculing the speaker or the seriousness of a statement."[2] For those without power, it provides an avenue for a public hearing, and/or it can compel public figures to defend their positions with greater accountability and transparency. The original speaker faces a critical decision: engage with the heckler, concede the floor, or ignore the interruption. Each choice significantly influences the subsequent direction and nature of the discourse. The timing of this engagement is crucial, as it profoundly affects the perception and efficacy of the heckling as a tactical intervention. However, taking over the conversation comes with its inherent risks, as the attempt to hijack the agenda could backfire, reflecting the delicate balance hecklers must navigate in influencing public discourse.

Sonic intensity reflects the compelling force sound exerts on listeners to incite action. Sound, a competitive element in our auditory environment, can influence our decisions, acting as a resource of intensity. This refers to sound's capacity to pressure an audience into deciding their following action as a waveform ends, balancing on the edge of potentially overwhelming noise. Sound's temporal nature means we frequently face the choice to either succumb to our sonic environment or assert control, possibly through counter-sound. Thus, sonic intensity is an active dynamic shaping our interactions with the soundscape. Here agents are asked to make a pressing choice. How pressing, you ask? Some options are very acute: "We must act now!" Other times we have a vague sense that we should do something. The expression of the qualitative gradient is the terrain of intensity. Speakers and listeners make sense of the event through the mobilization of shared cultural categories. There are so many different audiovisual sources that we need public categories to add them together into meaning. We might know a presence's intensity as it propels into the public and demands to be addressed.[3]

The inception of HU Resist burgeoned into a formidable movement that projected its message across the national spectrum, leveraging public platforms to exert widespread influence. This escalation from local dissent to national prominence underlines the power of strategic heckling, demonstrating its potential to significantly pressure the targeted "speaker" or institution. Initially galvanized by their opposition to James Comey's speaking engagement, HU Resist expanded their agenda to confront the administration more broadly, especially in response to the unsatisfactory handling of student aid issues. This evolution illustrates the multifaceted utility of heckling as a tool for challenge and change, emphasizing the critical importance of timing in such tactics. Despite the inherent risk of backlash, HU Resist adeptly navigated the complexities of public dissent, showcasing the capacity of well-timed heckles to resonate across varied audiences.

Many months later, HU Resist would capitalize on its recruiting effort to occupy the administrative building and significantly grow its presence. When Howard was caught in the middle of a financial scandal, the protesters responded by occupying the building and heckling them with Rihanna's "Bitch Better Have My Money." The size of their sound body enabled them to pressure the administration into acting and making concessions. The sound body of HU Resist, as a collection of audiovisual elements and understood as a felt presence mediated through the public screen, became a subject in the public imagination. The conversation around Howard's practices started locally around the school and rose to the national level.

In exploring HU Resist's ascendancy, this chapter delves into their adept utilization of the evolving situation to advocate for reform. By amplifying their voice through sound and intensity, they engaged with the administration via conventional channels while grounding their actions in the rich heritage of Black Power and civil rights movements. Their strategic protest against Betsy DeVos, alongside their innovative use of Twitter and Periscope to document interactions with school officials, exemplified their savvy in maximizing visibility and mobilizing support. A pivotal moment in their campaign was the occupation of a building during a high-profile event, merging ceremony with protest to bolster their ranks and affirm their identity. The climax of their activism coincided with a financial aid scandal, wherein HU Resist's timing and choice of heckle to Howard's administration (Rihanna's song) encapsulated the students' grievances and demanded attention. This act of defiance, underscored by the viral spread of their protest, compelled the administration into a corner, transforming HU Resist from a campus-based entity into a nationally recognized force that necessitated administrative action.

HU Resist's journey from localized protest to national presence underscores the necessity of adaptability and improvisation in resistance movements. Drawing inspiration from a history of creative resilience among marginalized groups, they utilized available resources—technological, cultural, and historical—to craft a compelling narrative of dissent. By ingeniously deploying the materials at their disposal, HU Resist not only advanced their cause but also inscribed their actions within a long lineage of activist ingenuity, signaling the enduring power of tactical intensity and sound judgment in the quest for justice. Their tactics propagated in the public screen, but a sound body on the lower frequencies occupied counter-publics, supplying resources for future movements.

Intensity

Intensity encompasses how the materiality of a waveform can shape choice. An extreme example of this phenomenon is how a loud, sudden blast can trigger someone to jump. In this case, vibration bypasses cognition—hijacking attention. From the increased heart rate, comprehension as meaning is assigned to the culprit that caused the bustle, and safety is assessed. Yet this experience illustrates how vibration taps into a process that weighs the potential significance of an event and discerns meaning. This can happen across various spectra, from a proximate disturbance that vibrates a body to something more diffuse that lingers in the air and gives a heavy or uneasy feeling. These are differences not of kind but of degree; intensity commands attention and distributes choice. This can affect cultural fault lines, as in the case of the debates around fireworks and the affective traces of war around the Fourth of July. Intensity does not refer to volume; it relates to the pressure to animate a decision. It is not how loud the sound is but the process of assigning a potential threat.

In *Listening to War: Sound, Music, Trauma, and Survival in Wartime Iraq*, J. Martin Daughtry explores sound's strategic role in warfare through an ethnographic lens, focusing on its impact on soldiers and civilians during the Iraq War. Through a number of his interviews, Daughtry highlights how sound not only serves as a tactical tool on the battlefield but also underwrites the process of judgment. This study illuminates how intensity, from the sharp crack of gunfire to the ominous rumble of improvised explosive devices, informs and shapes the actions of military personnel. While soldiers may not be able to see an enemy, they can feel and infer their looming presence based on these vibrations.

Daughtry introduces the idea of "concentric circles" to describe the layers of sound engagement ranging from soldiers identifying weapon types by their sound to commanders feeling political pressure shaped by the media's portrayal of war sounds to act. On the battlefield, sound's "mass" is evident in its ability to do both. The physical experience of sound, described as visceral vibrations or the embodied impact of weapon calibers, underscores its importance in conveying critical intelligence. Changes in volume, frequency, and duration can reveal crucial shifts on the battlefield, providing vital information for combat decisions. Textures provide soldiers with valuable information as they move through the battlefield. At the same time, sound is also employed in psychological operations, such as using loud music or taunts to unsettle and intimidate opponents;

for example, coalition forces have been known to play recordings of heavy machinery, such as tanks and helicopters, at high volumes, creating the illusion of an imminent attack without the actual presence of these vehicles.

While the battlefield is one concentric circle, another is how sound radiates from the battlefield and is picked up across the public screen to shape the civic. The presence of the sound body—leaked videos from the battlefield into our homes—becomes an object of knowledge that also informs choices. When discourse about war enters into conversation, audiovisual fragments become new presences demanding action. Daughtry reminds the reader that the impact of these acousmatic objects "often persists long after the actual sound waves have died away."[4] The signal enters new assemblages that help replicate a story and drum up the intensity for something to happen, as in the case that we should go to war. Consider, for example, when there was a "strategic leak" of some disembodied audiovisual content of a drone strike released to help persuade the home front to be in favor of the war: "Their audiovisual products were intended to convince a global audience of the righteousness of their cause. Traveling through the globalized networks of twenty-four-hour news and the internet, these mediated narratives significantly increased the intensity and reach of the sonic campaigns of the Iraq war. They stretched the battle for the hearts and minds beyond the front lines."[5] Sound is separated from the signal, acquires meaning, and ascribes intensity to a visceral weight. Images from the front lines become packaged and consumed to shape public sentiment on the war.

The move into the news cycle demonstrated how presence became redistributed as the feelings of the Iraqi people came into the national news. Analytic intensity considers how presence may feel pressing and prescient, such as in a tight battle, or it may impart a lower-grade feeling of lurking and pervasiveness when it is salient and distributed. For example, widely viewed footage on WikiLeaks taken from a US military helicopter showed the crew firing on a group of men (including journalists) walking on a Baghdad street. The video, accompanied by audio of the helicopter crew's communication during the attack, sparked widespread outrage and renewed debate about the role of the US military in Iraq. The aesthetic and the look represented a discourse that mobilized a set of discussions about the roles and responsibilities of the United States in the war, particularly journalists.

What happened in the Iraq War applies to understanding how a college group on campus might pressure an institution to change its policies. In each of these examples, sound comes into meaning to demand some kind of choice; the need to mean this or that exerts a kind of pressure that can be operationalized for benefit. While "strategy" refers to tools of power used to control spaces or systems, "tactics" are choices (often spontaneous) for acts of resistance taken by agents with less capacity, like taking shortcuts or using products in unintended ways. For the students of HU Resist, intensity provided a means to pressure an institution to act through a tradition of improvisations. HU Resist thought about the different contingent possibilities they might select as opportunities to solidify and incrementally realize their identities. We can see how HU Resist used sound to hijack attention, advance their cultural categories to support their cause, and pressure a choice. At first they were able to generate awareness through minor violations of decorum, which in turn generated a modest amount of pressure to shape the discussion. But as the sound body increased, HU Resist could wield its influence to intensify its demands.

HU Resist

The collective of students known as HU Resist began to form at Howard University around the same time Donald Trump was elected president of the United States. Some of the earliest founders recount that they started the organization because they felt the institution was not contributing to Black Liberation and a legacy of activism. Alexis McKenney, for example, expressed frustration at the widely held sentiment that simply coming to Howard was enough to be "part of this legacy, and that existing here at this institution is resistance enough."[6] Other members took this critique a step farther and positioned Howard as having an explicit strategy to fragment any awareness of a collective Black struggle toward liberation. As another of HU Resist's founders, Jason Ajiake, explained, "Howard is supposed to create this new Black petite bourgeoisie class [of] lawyers, doctors, politicians. This is what Howard was chartered by Congress to do. To create that intermediary between the black masses and the white power structures."[7] A significant example of this division between the Black middle and working classes, which McKenney and Ajiake pointed to, was the tense relationship the institution fostered between the students and the surrounding community. When the university did not treat the local community as agents deserving of respect but as objects to be ignored, it did so with definitions like "Black Excellence" that positioned the students at Howard in contrast to the local community and perpetuated inequality. McKenney further argued that Howard promoted a "foundation of Black capitalism and Black excellence which makes a separation between who Howard students are and who the greater DC community is. It all connects into how we contribute to how we're socialized into thinking and playing into the federal government whether that's in our best interest as Black people as a whole or not."[8] HU Resist was formed to close the gaps between the students of Howard and the broader Black community; it sought to cocreate with them.

The perceived conflict between the federal government and Black Liberation reached a new impetus when Howard University's president, Wayne A. I. Frederick, joined the leaders of other historically Black universities in the Oval Office for a listening session with Donald Trump. HU Resist reasoned that if Howard University took federal money, the institution would be beholden to the Trump administration. The group took to Twitter to start launching critiques. Although these critiques generated some attention on campus, they crystallized when Betsy DeVos was invited to the school and students had a concrete event to organize around. They wanted to be explicit that the university needed to do all it could to separate itself from the Trump administration and everything it represented. The very first Twitter post for HU Resist listed demands from the new organization, which included, among other things, that "Howard officially declare itself a sanctuary campus," "reject federal funding and ban President Donald Trump from all university-affiliated buildings," " refuse to abandon its values in exchange for financial security," and commit to building the "Kwame Ture Community Center."[9] After establishing its online existence, HU Resist grew its presence on campus. For instance, they held a recruitment town hall where they captured photos and videos to demonstrate this growth on social media. Their campaign got them a meeting with President Frederick.

The students demonstrated an inclination toward improvisation by looking at what material, technological, and cultural resources were available to generate more intensity for their movement. If intensity comes from the assessment of a choice, then HU Resist hoped to generate that intensity by using the streaming platform Periscope to broadcast all forty-four minutes of the meeting with President Frederick.[10] Creating this public record projected their presence further onto the public screen, something they likely hoped would cement administration accountability. The stream showed members of HU Resist in a conference room while Frederick fielded questions from the group. The students appeared disinterested, some on their phones, others lying in their chairs. At the same time, Frederick was engaged, animated, and gesticulating as he explained his position regarding their interests to the students.[11] On the surface, this relaxed attitude suggests that the students assumed that the power of their claims and reasons would generate enough intensity to get Frederick to adhere to their position. For them, these conversations were less about reaching reconciliation with the opposing party than getting a concession or explanation in front of a vast, virtual audience. Yet what HU Resist did document was meeting the first step in making a demand: going through the normal means and meeting with the administration.

HU Resist used the technological affordance of social media to amplify the potential audience of the meeting, which could increase the intensity of the encounter. Their use of Periscope foreshadowed the rising trend of activists live streaming or recording their interactions with competing perspectives. The size of their potential audience, and thus the intensity of their message, was theoretically limitless. As often happens with social media, the actual performance of the live stream fell short of its potential reach. Several reasons could be attributed to this shortcoming, one being that an extended live stream needs to lend itself to the quick attention of the public screen. McKenney later explained, "After a few meetings with our administration and seeing where that was going, which was nowhere, I think we kind of re-shifted, and this year we're hoping to get a more community focus."[12] Even though the meeting was not helpful, it did demonstrate that the group tried, in good faith, to work with the administration. The group spent the summer regrouping, recruiting, and working with the community to devise a very different sound tactic in response to a new opportunity: the arrival of James Comey.

The group claimed that they protested Comey precisely because he had a history of impeding Black liberation despite being a liberal folk hero venerated for standing up to Trump. Because he was a national figure that commanded a national audience, this protest truly got their cause across the public screen. Although HU Resist started a localized event, they grew from their initially narrow set of circumstances to stand in nationally for the threat to freedom of expression. This new spotlight raises the question of timing because heckling (one of the tactics employed by HU Resist) can be perceived negatively; when backlash is swift, it triggers a heckler's veto, a trope that situates the students as rowdy and unable to confront a "mature" discussion about differences of perspective. Such a concern could undermine their attempt to engage a broader audience by eliciting images of unpopular discourse as the existence of an illiberal presence on college campuses. Instead, this activity traveled in the digital barber shop as the classic civil rights trope.[13] Here these students operated on lower frequencies and decided to mobilize civil rights memory in framing their concern and selecting and structuring their call-and-response to help define their identity. Much more than ego rhetoric, HU Resist helped define their presence as a presence.

Comey's Convocation

On August 23, 2017, Frederick announced that former FBI director James Comey would become the Gwendolyn S. and Colbert I. King Endowed Chair in Public Policy. Comey would deliver several community lectures as the endowed chair during the 2017–18 school year. The Howard University press release said the lecture series was "designed to foster fruitful discussion and spur meaningful interaction."[14] The first speeches were scheduled for the 2017 convocation, where he would welcome incoming first-year and transfer students. The institution invited Comey to deliver the address for Howard University's 150th convocation in 2018. Howard University's president anticipated that this might be a provocative pick. Frederick said, "I am pleased to welcome Mr. Comey to Howard. His expertise and understanding of the challenges we continue to face today will go a long way in sparking rich discussion and advancing meaningful debates across campus."[15] In this telling statement, Frederick shared his belief that Comey's presence would demonstrate a commitment to getting at the truth through the back-and-forth of argumentation. The speech would also be Comey's first public appearance since his high-profile firing from the FBI and the revelation that the president of the United States, Donald Trump, asked him to obstruct justice.

HU Resist took to Twitter to argue against the former leader of the FBI being appointed to welcome new students to Howard University. They raised significant issues related to Comey's commitment to the "Ferguson effect," which trades in pernicious, white supremacist logic by assuming that Black communities—which are more policed than white communities irrespective of citizen camera use—are naturally more prone to violence. They pointed out that this demonstrated Howard's history of working with the federal government to undermine Black liberation. Years earlier, Howard University worked with the FBI to turn over sensitive information about Kwame Ture (known as Stokely Carmichael when he started at Howard in 1960).[16] HU Resist provided an image of civil rights icon Kwame Ture in a Howard sweater. In 1961, Ture participated in several civil rights activities, including the Freedom Rides to desegregate the interstate bus system, a sit-in demonstration of Attorney General Robert Kennedy Jr.'s office, and helping register voters in Mississippi. In an early move to present the condition of memory of the event, a selection of images of Ture to highlight the FBI and Howard's misdeed brought us back to the era of civil rights, setting the context for justice and harm within the imaginary.

On September 22, 2017, approximately five hundred students, staff, and faculty went to Crampton Auditorium for convocation. HU Resist entered near the emergency exit in the tier directly below the projector booth. Its members sang collectively, synchronizing their voices through a choral effect. The choice of song, "We Shall Not Be Moved," is derived from a spiritual from the plantation era and became popular during the Civil Rights Movement.[17] HU Resist then shifted from a chorus to a collective "call-and-response" for which they were their audience:

Caller: I say I love being Black
Group: I say I love being Black
Caller: I say I love being Black
Group: I say I love being Black
Caller: I love the color of my skin
Group: I love the color of my skin
Caller: 'Cause it's the skin that I'm in
Group: 'Cause it's the skin that I'm in
Caller: I said I love being Black
Group: I said I love being Black
Caller: I love the texture of my hair
Group: I love the texture of my hair
Caller: And I rock it everywhere
Group: And I rock it everywhere
Caller: I said I love being Black
Group: I said I love being Black
Caller: I love the fullness of my lips
Group: I love the fullness of my lips
Caller: And the way I comb my hair
Group: And the way I comb my hair[18]

These are significant statements. This first sequence focuses on visual features commonly associated with Blackness—pigmentation, hair, and lips. The

"I" spoken by many people in unison foregrounds each as similarities that bond that group. As the group goes through each refrain, feelings intensify as each person speaks and is spoken to, hears others and is heard, affirms and is affirmed. The texture of their voices coming together and affirming each statement amasses weight. The sound grows and presses against the bodies of others in the room, vibrating and becoming louder. Some might think these students were calling together a sonic body occupying the space the way previous generations of civil rights activists took up room on buses, at counters, and in other public places. The ritual then moved to communal pronouns opposing a common enemy and concluded with affirmations of the group being among God's chosen people.

In terms of a heckle, by transitioning from a member of the audience into a chorus, HU Resist audibly shifted from being part of the audience to engaging directly with Comey, thereby altering the participation framework to a speaker-heckler-audience configuration. This shift not only brought the group into direct interaction with Comey but also redefined the dynamics of the event, as HU Resist's chants created a new focal point. Their actions exemplify how heckling can momentarily or significantly change the course of a discourse, inviting extended exchanges and potentially shifting the speaker's role as the primary source of information or authority.

But more so than any specific words, the importance of the practice itself and its power to affirm and give dignity to "the lived experience of Black people" was conveyed.[19] "Call-and-response" emerged from the Black oral tradition and has been carried into the contemporary moment through the gospel, stories, music, and ordinary banter.[20] There are various iterations of call-and-response, but they share the characteristic of connecting speaker and listener. The goal is to affirm each other's existence and establish a unified sense of an affirmative, collective identity. Anyone can join a call-and-response as they listen and take their turn calling and responding—symbolically and effectively unifying with the collective.[21] Newly forged communal bonds create opportunities for the community that did not exist before and, with these comes new rhetorical potential. For HU Resist, exchanging positive messages and affirming each other with a community made for explicit identification across differences, which viscerally drew new members to join the active dynamic.

Improvisation kicked in as the leaders took over the call-and-response by listening to the group and inserting their chants. After defining themselves as a singularity, they began defining the other. Suddenly one person yelled, "Get out here, Comey, you're not our homie." The group pivoted and started to repeat, "Comey, you're not our homie." The move from "I" to "our" marks the moment when the group explicitly defined itself as a community based in opposition to Comey. The opposite of Blackness and all its beauty was rhetorically Comey. Finally, they began chanting, "(K)no(w) justice, (k)no(w) peace." The lyrics could mean that without knowing divine justice through full emancipation, it is impossible to know peace. Of course, the lyrics also play on a bit of sonorous polysemy and could mean that there may be discord without justice.

A reporter for Howard University's student paper, *The Hilltop*, recalled the change in Crampton Auditorium as HU Resist started chanting: "The energy abruptly switched as the crowd loudly reacted with a mixture of cheers, groans and awkward laughter as the protest began."[22] The energy of the call-and-response spilled into the audience as some people got out of their seats and joined in by clapping, jeering, or generally calling out Comey. At the same time, others became irritated as whispers gave way to people in the audience yelling, "Let him speak." The amplification of the energy was visceral. At one point, the orchestra and choir attempted to mask the protesters with the ironic selection of Beethoven's "Hallelujah Chorus."[23] The accumulating sonic force of the call-and-response was essential to announcing and affirming their collective presence—even as competing sonic forces attempted to mask them.

All the while, Comey stood quietly on the stage with his hands folded. A couple of minutes later, his response was to dismiss the chanting as forceful but unproductive noise and reconfigure the situation into a debate between two sides on a quest for truth. He stated, "I hope you'll stay to listen to what I have to say, and I just listened to you for five minutes." He then appealed to the norms of a conversation to encourage the protesters to listen to what he had to say: "I love the enthusiasm of the young folks; I just wish they would understand what a conversation is. A conversation is where you speak, and I listen, and then I say, and you listen. And then we go back and forth and back and forth. And at the end of the conversation, we're both smarter."[24]

By acknowledging the group's "enthusiasm," Comey emphasized the mass and the positive valence of HU Resist's sound. The explicit reference to conversational norms was intended to carve out a space for Comey to speak. HU Resist's performance would be understood as their *turn*, and Comey would get his *turn*. Comey's rhetorical appeals manifested with the high sonic definition that mobilized norms of reasonableness to reshape the antagonistic relationship between him and the protesters. Even if they disagreed, the two sides could agree on the fair terms of engagement to reasonably resolve their disagreement. Such a mode of sonic exchange would allow each person to present their perspective. By saying that he listened, he indicated that he had satisfied the norms of a conversation's contractual relations. Since he fulfilled the duties imposed on him, it was unfair for HU Resist to deny him the opportunity to speak. This, in turn, conferred a moral obligation on HU Resist to listen to him. The group could face social rebuke if they didn't listen after exercising their right to say. Even if they disagreed, Comey argued that the two sides could agree on fair terms to resolve their conflict reasonably. HU Resist listened to Comey speak for a moment about the importance of listening to both sides, but then they seized the opportunity to retort: "White supremacy is not a debate!"

The Hilltop reported that when Comey's scripted remarks concluded, he received "a standing ovation, while the protesters simultaneously exited to the front of Crampton to continue their demonstration."[25] The split audience debated everything from Comey's invitation to HU Resist's tactics. Howard student Brianna Williams agreed with the protesters and appreciated their tactics. In contrast, others, such as Mikayli Solomon, said they might agree with their message but felt the call-and-response was "embarrassing."[26] In turn, criminology major Noelle Shaw was impressed that Comey even listened for a while, but other students, like Alexis Barge, took offense that Comey claimed to understand their struggle.[27] In short, the audience was divided. For some, what they heard was a meaningful exchange; for others, it was disruptive noise.

For HU Resist, the convocation performance might have polarized the crowd, but it earned them many recruits. While the organization was negligible during the first semester, the decision to attend *this* event ensured they had a captive audience of all first-year students. For those attending the event, the practice of discerning signal from noise was an intense experience. The high-profile nature of the event propelled HU Resist into the broader public.

The sound body of HU Resist grew as imagery from the event was projected across the public screen. The signal separated from the source and was reattached for one mainstream audience to become a proxy to talk about the feeling of campus culture writ large. The event propagated across the evening news of major broadcast networks like NBC, Fox, CBS, and Reuters. Newspapers such as the *New York Times*, *Politico*, and *The Atlantic* provided digital coverage with embedded video. With this coverage, the sound jumped from inside Crampton onto the national stage. While the in-person audience was divided in its interpretation of the events, the national audience largely viewed the act as a usurping of procedure rather than a sound tactic. The nuance of a call-and-response and the demands concerning the relationship between Howard and the federal government hadn't been heard. HU Resist had been recast as radicals who couldn't listen to the opposition. Thus, their protest was reconstituted as a heckler's veto.

The Heckler's Veto

The term "heckler's veto" emerged from the 1951 Supreme Court decision of *Feiner v. New York*, when Irving Feiner—a radical at the time—advocated for Black citizens to take up arms against the government to gain civil rights. His words angered many, whipped a crowd into a frenzy, and readied many to attack him. The police asked Feiner to stop, and when he refused, they arrested him. The police reasoned that if he continued speaking, then violence would surely follow. The pursuant legal case worked its way up to the Supreme Court, which held that denying a speaker's right to speech based on a crowd's potential for violence was appropriate. Justice Hugo Black was horrified in writing the dissent because "today's holding means that as a practical matter, minority speakers can be silenced in any city."[28] In other words, a crowd that does not like a speaker's content might stop it simply by becoming rowdy. Harry Kalven Jr., a famous legal scholar of the time, coined the term heckler's veto to describe this new power the audience might exercise over speakers' rights. He explains that "if the police can silence the speaker, the law in effect acknowledges a veto power in hecklers who can, by being hostile enough, get the law to silence any speaker of whom they do not approve."[29] The precedent from *Feiner v. New York* established that if the audience proves to be rowdy enough, it could exercise agency to infringe on others' rights.

Although no case has overruled *Feiner*, it holds little legal weight. As Timothy E. D. Horley explains, "A number of post-*Feiner* cases make it appear as though Justice Black's dissent has carried the day."[30] The court distinguished the precedent, which means they held the case to be so specific as to make the holding essentially meaningless. However, the narrative that a hostile audience may trump the rights of a speaker continued to be told in public debates over free speech rights. In particular, this narrative emerged as evidence of a "free speech crisis" on college campuses. From this perspective, the heckler's veto appears whenever students try to prevent a speaker from voicing an unpopular opinion. This narrative emerged and became refined over the turbulent time of the 1960s when there were numerous protests on college campuses. The theory goes that students are doing it again: creating disruptions and forcing their will on the speakers.

Consider a 2017 piece from the Foundation for Individual Rights in Education as a representative anecdote for the narrative. As in the *Feiner* case, a heckler's veto occurs when a rowdy crowd prevents speech. But while the *Feiner* case involved a group being worked up through address, in this case, students intentionally disrupted a speaker to censor an unpopular view. The heckler's veto is rooted in the misguided belief that an argument can be defeated by forcefully shutting up its proponents. On the college campuses of a free society, a viewpoint gains acceptance in the "marketplace of ideas" by the persuasive power of the arguments in support of it, not the *physical might* of its advocates. Rather than using force to silence a speaker, the response to speech with which one disagrees is more speech, not violence or censorship.[31]

The heckler is identified with "drowning out, shouting down, and assaulting" those with perspectives they do not want to hear.[32] This veto allegedly threatens democracy and free speech because the only response to those tactics is force—removing the potential disruption or preemptive action. If force is used, then the heckler exists outside of reason. Critical to the frame is the assumption that the heckler is not interested in listening to the other side but only seeks control to stop the planned event. The concern is that there will never be space for alternative perspectives because students will never allow dissent or different voices on college campuses.

The Heckler's Veto and HU Resist

The heckler's veto emerged as a descriptive term in the coverage of the event at Howard University. At the most basic level, it suggests that HU Resist did not follow the procedure because they did not let Comey exercise his right to speak. This is within the conventional norms of social sanction and derides HU Resist's credibility to advance a public reason (or even consider what they did put forth as a reason in the first place). Timothy Meads provides a representative anecdote in his blog post for *Town Hall*. HU Resist came in and chanted:

> "No justice, no peace," "F**K James Comey," and "We Shall Not Be Moved." Mob-style justice intent on thwarting adverse political ideologies from entering campus is nothing new. However, 2017 has seen an alarming spike in students believing that blocking their political opponents from speaking via protest, threats, and other measures is justifiable. This trend amongst college students is almost entirely driven by left-leaning students and outside groups such as the far-left, radical terror group known as Antifa. Recent polling suggests that college students are very comfortable with what is known as the "heckler's veto," or allowing the audience to shout so loudly that the speaker cannot get their message out.[33]

Here the protest is understood only by its volume and the desire to prevent another side from speaking. HU Resist is contextualized within a broader movement to exclude contrary views from being heard on campus. The importance of the protesters' voices becomes understood as a specific mechanism of the veto—they can prevent Comey from talking through the magnitude of their chant. The discussion becomes about the noise they produced rather than the signal they were sending.

As the media picked up the HU Resist event, the students were similarly represented as a frenzied mob, and more emphasis was placed on their sound tactics as a use of force. The reduction of the crowd to clenched fists, anger, yelling, and threats of force suggested that something dangerous might actualize. The racial implications of the call-and-response demonstrated the sonic color line's inevitable constraints that prevent advocacy. For instance, Adam Goldman from the *New York Times* wrote, "James B. Comey, the former F.B.I. director, was met with raised fists and chants of 'no justice, no peace.'"[34] Here the association is explicit: the students were angry, their fists were raised, and they threatened to violate the norms of peace. Merdie Nzanga of *NBC News* also foregrounded potential violence when she described HU Resist as an "angry group of students who were shouting 'we shall not be moved,' 'I love being Black,' and 'no justice, no peace.'"[35]

Again, the disruption is emphasized along with the promise that they are going nowhere once conditions change. Both reports allude to the use of force.

In reporting for CNN, Laura Jarrett and Katishi Maake observed that "[as Comey] began his speech welcoming new students at Howard University, protesters could be heard yelling from the back of the room, raising their fists and shouting."[36] Jarrett and Maake contrast Comey's welcoming and rare public appearance with the yelling and the raised fists to underscore the protesters' incivility and potential for violence. If HU Resist is willing to deviate from the norms of sonic decorum, then they will deride all etiquette. The intensity of their sounds becomes translated into their potential for violence, and they become coded as a threat.

Thus, the coverage reduced HU Resist to another example of a group trying to "shout down" an unpopular speaker. The *National Review* used the event to sound the alarm, writing, "The shout-down crisis is very much alive today; witness last Friday's high-profile disruption of former FBI Director James Comey at Howard University."[37] Jonathan Turley admonished Howard University for not issuing discipline or punishment. The Comey incident "was the latest example of protesters shutting down free speech on campus, and the university appeared unwilling or unable to enforce basic civility rules by removing and suspending the students."[38] *Inside Higher Ed* also situated this story within broader concerns about free speech: "The protest came as universities and their choices for speakers and lecturers have come under scrutiny, raising questions about who is deserving of those spots."[39]

The montage of perspectives demonstrates that the convocation address was yet another iteration of the heckler's veto, and HU Resist was indeed "inundated with criticism from white liberals on social media."[40] The threat to speech is seen as a threat to reason itself because when the space for reason is closed, all that is left is violence. There was a deep concern about an illiberal presence lurking on campus, which manifested here on this college campus. However, these associations between noise, violence, and race are old and must be located within a more profound history of the sonic color line.[41] When one side gets to define the contours of what reason sounds like, then those norms of decorum can be used to exclude organizations that it disagrees with. Whiteness pervades one side of the binary, representing ordered and good sound. In this binary, Blackness becomes its opposite. This broad, culturally contingent label can be applied to all things that render some bodies correct and others requiring regulation and discipline.[42] These regulations are used to carve up space, distribute bodies into the appropriate places and times, and contribute to a racialized politics of segregation.

HU Resist, the Black Barbershop, and Civil Rights Tactics

What cultural context might help explain the divide between those who viewed HU Resist's actions as powerful and those who characterized them as violent? The distinction between a heckle serving as a veto (or not) is really *how sound it is*. Understandably, this might not feel like a universalized stance, and the soundness depends on a number of factors such as the audience and the timing. Sometimes that sound travels in the lower registers outside the dominant range of audition. In her work on Black digital orality, Catherine Knight Steele provides the metaphor of the Black barbershop, which provides an early example of Black entrepreneurship, giving them the independence to move into the working- and middle-class services to care for their hair and engage the socializing practice of talk. Steele writes, "As a space hidden from the dominant gaze, the Black barbershop became a historical site of cultural importance for the black community."[43] These spaces became central to the building of a community, as barbers often became neighborhood leaders. Perhaps most importantly, she argues, the Black barbershop constitutes a counter-public, replete with its own sound body.[44]

Alongside physical locations that allowed communities to thrive away from an oppressive gaze, we also see how audio technologies facilitated aesthetic practices that enacted Black self-making and community on modernity's terms. The digital barbershop did what the physical one achieved; severing sound from source opened space for reinventing traditions and advancing new perspectives. When transmission origins are uncertain, dominant regimes lose the power to limit circulation based on clearly defined categories like the race or class of a speaker. Instead, ambiguity allows for generative repetition and framing, which enables alternative subjectivities and communities to flourish. Overall, the split between signal and source enabled by phonography provided conditions of possibility for modern Black cultural production to use technology to recalibrate some of its central topoi, enacting new forms of Black subjectivity and community.[45] There is a tradition of a sound body helping to facilitate Black community power, a history of echoes and the production of spaces outside the white gaze that provides freedom.[46]

For audience members who identified with this perspective and understood a similar cultural context, HU Resist's decision to heckle Comey was sound. HU Resist, and their supporters, defined themselves within the civil rights tradition. On their Twitter account, the group posted a live stream that said, "TW: This is How Campus Police Dealt with Students Outside the Administration Building," and linked to a chaotic video that featured a crowd of students of color, some police, and an audible struggle. The shifting point-of-view shots gave the viewer a visceral perspective of being in the group. HU Resist also tweeted that "challenging the status quo is never widely accepted at the moment," with graphics displaying the lack of public support for the Freedom Riders in 1961 and the March on Washington in 1963. Tweets like this positioned the group's occupation of the building as analogous to what happened during the Civil Rights Movement. Indeed, it informs the moral substance of their claim that their protest was not about shutting down Comey's speech; rather, it was in support of Black liberation.

These modern narratives extend from civil rights into current fights for justice, dignity, and equality amid systemic racism. Integrating HU Resist into the civil rights saga showcases it as a continuing chapter in the African American pursuit of rights, highlighting the enduring battle for racial justice and the evolution of resistance methods, united by a consistent quest for freedom and equality. HU Resist's engagement with digital media for organization and activism represents the adaptation of resistance into modern contexts. The trope of humanizing a hero is common in the Black barbershop. Steele writes that the "insertion of self and personal experience brings validity to the conversation rather than weakness to one's argument. Recentering one's experience, or the experience of the subculture within the dominant society, replicates the practice of folktales and songs common in the Black oral tradition."[47] The comparison of the experience enables them to position themselves on the right side of history.

After the convocation, HU Resist's sound presence expanded into homes across the country, and many contributed to the newly formed PayPal to support the group's growing national presence. Here another acousmatic body grew far beyond the confines of Howard University, both in time and space. HU Resist took the opportunity to bolster their standing as a group working in the tradition of civil rights. They accrued material resources to "provide hot meals for the houseless community around campus."[48] They held an event discussing civic activity with former Student Non-Violent Coordinating Committee members. Afterward, they worked "with local community organizations to combat gentrification in the area." They surveyed the "surrounding community about their needs" so that they could "continue to bridge the gap in a non-intrusive way."[49] The reach and distribution of their audiovisual presence expanded on social media, including in a promotional video showing them chanting together and planning their next meetings. As the organization grew, it sent surveys to listen to what the students demanded of the institution.

While they went to the convocation with one set of demands, they wanted to be sure that, in future instances, their claim to represent the students would be supported by evidence of their willingness to listen. At this point, HU Resist, as a sound body, had grown to a formidable size. This organization started small but became much broader, garnering stakeholders across the university, expanding its presence to a national level, and even earning some celebrity followers from the Comey event. In January, HU Resist started a blog on the online platform *Medium* to further advance itself as a "voice to challenge the flaws of the institution."[50] As a presence in the Black barbershop, the group recognized their role to offer a critique, and they used social media to express solidarity with other organizations, critique police brutality, and announce more workshops. Just as they improvised with a pivot between the lackluster performance of their audience with Frederick and Comey's speech, the group again sought out resources to employ sound in a way that might make a bigger mark. They took the time to collect and plan before their next significant move to commemorate the anniversary of the 1968 and 1989 occupations of the administration building at the end of March.

Financial Embezzlement at Howard

Two days before the anniversary of the 1968 and 1989 administration building (or A building) occupation, March 28, an anonymous whistleblower broke a story about financial embezzlement at Howard. An "open letter" surfaced on *Medium*'s blogging platform reporting the embezzlement. The embezzlement scandal centered around the misuse of financial aid funds by university employees registered for classes at Howard. These employees were alleged to have received financial aid grants and tuition remission benefits that exceeded the cost of attendance, allowing them to pocket the excess funds. In some cases, employees were said to have received double the amount of financial aid they were eligible for. This resulted in significant financial loss for the university and a lack of financial aid resources for other students in need. The letter alleged that "it was widely known that President Frederick instructed financial aid administrators to deny discretionary aid to students who were headaches for

Frederick and his administration. Specifically, student protesters, especially those affiliated with #HUResist, were denied financial assistance for their 'disruptive activities.'"[51] Frederick announced in a statement that an internal investigation revealed financial misconduct within the university's financial aid department. Although Frederick's statement did not delve into the specifics of these allegations, it did mention that six employees were terminated in September 2016 due to "gross misconduct and neglect of duties."

For HU Resist, this was an inadequate response, and they heckled him. We can only speculate about how much prior knowledge HU Resist had regarding the leak, but they were prepared with research in the form of surveys to amplify and direct the story. Releasing their survey's results along with information on the scandal created the condition for listening. For example, in the lead-up to the protest, they would share stories about the financial corruption scandal right after posting survey results showing that the student body harbored a widespread distrust of Howard University's handling of finances. The implication was obvious: students' suspicion of the institution was justified, and they were entitled to harness their power as students to correct the injustice.

HU Resist adeptly used the financial aid scandal to broaden their perceived focus from issues only about race to include the experience of being a student; as they explained via a March 28 Tweet: "It's not about HBCUs vs HBCUs [historically Black colleges and universities], it's not about PWIS [predominantly white institutions] vs HBCUs, it's about student power. Students all over the country lack power over their institutions and it's time we start demanding it. #StudentPowerHU."[52] They constituted the grounding for a new sound tactic about the relationship between students and institutes of higher learning. This created a set of relationships, duties, and obligations to which both parties could hold themselves accountable.

On March 29, 2018, HU Resist started the day with a party at the flagpole to rally the masses and begin their entry into the administration building. While hashtags constituted them as #students, they stayed consistent with the civil rights discourse. The selection of the date held a significant meaning; this represented the fiftieth anniversary of the occupation of the administration building during the Civil Rights era. The goal of the protest was to get the university to recognize the students' power and listen to the enumerated demands posted on Twitter. In a March 25 tweet they wrote, "In the words of Frederick Douglass, 'power concedes nothing without a demand.' These are our demands." The students demanded adequate housing, an end to tuition hikes, transparent salaries, an end to rape culture, faculty accountability, oversight for campus police, an end to food insecurity in and around campus (community center), Fredrick's resignation, and a voice on the board of trustees. More than three hundred students showed up and occupied the building. HU Resist filmed, tweeted, and sent press releases to local news affiliates. HU Resist also brought numerous supplies to ensure they could occupy the building for an extended period. The group entered with pillows, sleeping bags, food, and water.

Pragmatically, the students occupying the building provided the start of the demand, and this time it was loud and clear. When the students made their demands, they drew attention to the norm that the university has failed to live up to its obligation to adequately care for the needs of the students. When the administration could not stop internal members of its organization from stealing from the students, they lost the moral authority to care for the students. The university can no longer be trusted to appeal to its authority because it has already been proved to be a corrupt actor. This constrains the available number of communication moves the university can make. By framing the relationship in this way, HU Resist employed a sound tactic to imply that Howard was a bad-faith negotiator and already stealing from the students and violating their obligations for care.

Occupying the A Building

The students were days into their occupation when Philip Lewis, a reporter for the *Huffington Post*, caught a spontaneous moment of joy. He tweeted a twelve-second clip of activists collectively singing Rihanna's track "Bitch Better Have My Money" ("BBHMM"). Lewis captioned the tweet "Howard students found out employees stole over $1M in financial aid so they took over their Administration building and started singing 'Bitch Better Have My Money.'"[53] Like a DJ selecting the proper sample, the students repurposed another bit of culture to fit their needs, positioning the administration as "Bitch" and explicitly demanding repayment of their stolen funds—a brilliant heckle at a sputtering administration that owed students money. Almost as soon as the post went online, several influencers shared it. When Rihanna retweeted the video, it went viral with more than 7.8 million views. HU Resist responded to Rihanna with a list of their demands, which did not get the same attention as their twelve-second clip. Nevertheless, through the vehicle of a pop hit, HU Resist's demands were quickly recognized, and their intensity was expressed in a way the public could feel. The substance of their claim happened to have a very catchy hook.

The video shot provides an intimate view of the group as if the viewer were immersed with the students in the A building. Students sing together: "Don't act like you forgot; I call the shots, shots, shots, like bra, bra, bra." The students' voices reverberate as they call for their cash back. The song brings up complicated associations among race, gender, and money by pointing to "the image of propertied black women in general, of black women recouping historical debts."[54] The snappy earworm would get caught in your head, refusing to let you forget. When the song was invoked in this specific context, it vent viral. The pithy sentiment perfectly encapsulated the students' grievance. The different media vectors distributed the Black sonic body and spatialized it.

The widespread sharing of "BBHMM" increased the visibility and urgency of the students' demands. The song's virality brought to light the extraordinary measures the students had taken—occupying a building to reclaim their funds after conventional methods failed. This reinterpretation of the song in the context of the protest emphasized the legitimacy of the students' claims for owed money. As the narrative spread across various platforms, it not only intensified the call for accountability but also put Howard University in a tight spot; removing the students would potentially damage the institution's reputation. While Frederick wanted the conversation to be about the university's proposal to fix corruption, HU Resist's heckle shifted the conversation to broader problems about the institution. This strategic heckling placed Howard University under a public microscope, compelling it to confront its actions or risk its moral and institutional credibility.

News coverage used the financial scandal as the motive for the sit-in. Much of the range named it in the headlines, like the *Seattle Times* with "Howard University Students Occupy Administration Building Amid Financial Aid Scandal," or ABC News with "'This Building Is Closed': Howard U Students Take Over Admin Building Financial Aid Scandal." Beyond the headlines, the ledes featured the financial aid scandal as the primary motivation for the protest. Examples include CNN explaining that the occupiers in the building "are protesting after university workers were accused of 'double-dipping' on financial aid," and *Time* magazine calling it a "protest fueled by outrage over a financial aid scandal."[55] In these articles, the students peacefully held their ground. ABC News said that in the protest, the students were "calling for further transparency and additional accountability after the years-long incident" and willing "to hold the building until university officials [met] a list of nine demands released by student protestors."[56] In this account and many others, students were painted as holding their ground, awaiting peaceful resolution for accountability.

In the context of this coverage, the students' violation of procedure—their unwillingness to move from the A building—became increasingly justified because the school had robbed them. In the new prevailing media narrative, their moves became understood within the border context of an administration that was understood as corrupt, willing to steal from students, and could not be trusted to work under ordinary means or use the usual channels to resolve the dispute. For much of the public, "BBHMM" stood in for their demand. While HU Resist might have several other issues, the capacity for the song to flicker across the public screen and accrue force increased the intensity of the sonic body. The power of "BBHMM" and the intensity with which the protest image spread gave their claim substance and moral valence, as national magazines anointed them the future of student protest. *The Atlantic* postulated, "How the Howard University Protests Hint at the Future of Campus Politics." Similarly, the *Chronicle of Higher Education* said, "Howard U. Sit-In Could Be the Start of Something Bigger."[57] At this point, it was too tricky for Frederick to remove the students from the building because the optics of ending the protest without addressing the financial scandal would only make the situation worse.[58] The intensity and relatability of the demand, coupled with HU Resist's virality, generated an excess of pressure.

As HU Resist waited for the board of trustees to accept their demands, the news coverage increased, validating their demands. The intensity for the administration to act ratcheted up. The students occupied the building for ten more days, representing the longest occupation in the university's history. The *Washington Post* proclaimed that "Echoes of the Past Reverberated in Howard University Student Occupation,"[59] and CNN declared that "Howard University Students' Win with Deal on Demands Continues Legacy of Protests."[60] As perhaps HU Resist already knew, selecting a meaningful protest date naturally lent itself to historical comparisons. This, in turn, increased the intensity of the sonic body, allowing it to stretch backward through time even as it expanded outward across space.

When the administration and HU Resist finally reached an agreement, the students exited the building singing, "Beep, beep! Bang, bang! Ungawa! Black power!"[61] Frederick responded, "I appreciate what they have done to unite this community. There's no university without its students, and the students must be the primary focus of the university."[62] If HU Resist's demand was anchored in the claim that the university failed to live up to its obligation to care for the students, it appears that Frederick recognized that he must listen to them. The only demand not accepted was Frederick's resignation, which HU Resist was willing to concede. Instead, Howard promised to start several initiatives and include students on many issues, freeze housing deposits, redress problems, and address other demands. Although the more than three hundred students represented only a fraction of the stakeholders, they generated enough pressure for the administration to accept eight of their nine demands.

Improvisation

The #HUResist movement gained significant attention on social media and garnered support from students, faculty, alumni, and activists. The presence of the sonic body ratcheted up the intensity as the subjectivity of who the students were, the nature of Howard, and the reason for their group's existence was post-hoc explained through the narrative of corruption. HU Resist's sound body occupied the public screen for a moment in "BBHMM," enough to pressure the board of trustees to shape the deliberations. After nine days of occupying the administration building, the students reached an agreement with the university administration, which led to the end of the occupation. While not all demands were met, the movement did result in some changes, such as the resignation of several board members, the allocation of additional funds for student housing and financial aid, and the establishment of a task force to address student concerns.

As HU Resist weighed their choice of sound and when to deploy it for maximum impact, they adapted to an evolving situation by adjusting the intensity to send a powerful signal that could not be mistaken for just noise. A critical aspect of their decision was a concept of kairos, a sense of appropriateness of time, to adduce their demands against the Howard University administration. The students recognized that the conditions were met for a "demand," and as events evolved, the conditions became even more favorable—in this manner, they utilized karotic timing. Furthermore, HU Resist found the potential to generate intensity through improvisation: inspiration, historical anniversaries, a financial scandal, and a little serendipity (Rihanna retweeting) came together in a viral moment to generate national attention on students leveraging demands against a school. In this collective improvisation arises the potential for cocreating new realities that "make 'a way' out of 'no way' by cultivating the capacity to discern hidden elements of possibility, hope, and promise in even the most discouraging circumstances."[63] This created a national presence for their sonic body, enabling them to exert more pressure on the school. From this narrative perspective, the initial conversation with Frederick, which failed to deliver their demands, led to a moment when they could fully enact a sound tactic.[64]

Improvisation is crucial for activists and those trying to subvert power structures. In contrast with a planned tactic that assumes set parameters, improvisation draws from the local histories tied to the situating presence at the moment—the energy and ideas of the moment construct a path forward. Improvisation requires taking in your surroundings, cataloging your resources, and applying the right intensity to make immediate meaning. Consider a DJ using a record player as an opportunity to scratch, a graffiti artist using a can of spray paint to create art with meaning, or using a product against its intended purposes. In circumstances where following rigid structures and rules has yet to afford success, the ability to improvise and restructure the playing field is essential to progress. When the constructs of the moment aren't enough to make your demand audible, improvisation is a resource that allows you to leverage whatever you *do* have. HU Resist balanced improvisation with strategic planning, ultimately forming an identity, an assertion of rights claims, and an ethic of cocreation.

Conclusion

While HU Resist occupied the A building, they did more than move the social sentiment and pressure the administration; they also cocreated a community, a move that ultimately expanded the sound body, catapulting it onto the national stage. Improvisation constantly trades between the individual and the community, much like *soundness*. Both of these can enable communities to emerge and cocreate. Consider the perspective of Jared Ware, an embedded journalist who helped document what it was like in the A building:

> During the occupation, students renamed the Administration building the Kwame Ture Student Center, a living embodiment of their dream to bring an actual student center to campus, which was one of their initial

demands. One that Frederick said he was most on board with over a year ago when the students first demanded it but which he has repeatedly ignored in practice. Students who spent time at the Kwame Ture Center frequently remarked about how inclusive it was, how it met their needs that the campus never had, how good the food was, etc. They had healthcare available, an impromptu barbershop/salon, and legal advice at all times.[65]

In Ware's recollection, we can see how the ethics of improvisation led to the emergence of not only the sound body to assert their rights through the demand but also a dynamic community.[66] The body's soundness fed the community dynamism, which further fed the soundness of the tactics in a self-feeding, self-intensifying cycle of pressure. To accomplish this, the students' knew that it was key to create an inclusive and welcoming space where everyone's needs were met, the ultimate goal of inclusivity and diversity. The Kwame Ture Center provided a range of services and resources that catered to the diverse needs of the students. The fact that the center could offer various services, such as healthcare, a barbershop/salon, and legal advice, required collaboration and the distribution of benefits. As Ware notes, there was an atmosphere of mutual respect and trust within the group. The students' collective decision to rename the administration building and demand an open student center indicates that shared responsibility and decision-making were central to their efforts. This approach challenges hierarchical power structures and promotes a more equitable distribution of authority and influence.

As the HU Resist students said in their interviews, they were inspired by previous protests at the university, just as journalistic documentation provided a bit of memory to the event that others could draw on for future inspiration. The different concepts offer fertile ground for populating an imagination with different potential futures from unrealized pasts and other presents. The present future becomes essential for sound tactics when we consider how a proper tactic draws from the history and the energy that previous sound bodies have created. The future is at stake not "only about the history, but in addressing the place and space of the African American presence in the past and present," and it points to the necessity of "counter-histories of searching for legible traces of black history, to be able to imagine possible futures."[67] Much like the anniversary of the occupation of the A building provided HU Resist with resources, this event enfolded the potential for future movements on the campus. Now the history of the A building has its memory covered, both as a campaign to realize goals against a corrupt administration and as a training ground for forms of Black relationality and living in communion, as it does in Ware's recollection.

The HU Resist protest at Howard University shares resonance with the 2012 Québec Casseroles' protest because both emerged as grassroots movements with specific goals, employing creative and improvisational tactics to engage supporters and gain attention. Both HU Resist and the Québec Casseroles were student-led movements. HU Resist addressed various issues at Howard University, including financial mismanagement, lack of transparency, and inadequate student resources. The Québec protests first started in response to the government's proposed tuition hikes, but with the passage of Bill 78, which restricted the right to protest, things changed. However, unlike HU Resist, the scope of the Québec Casseroles' protests extended beyond a single institution, encompassing students and citizens from various universities and regions across Québec.

The focus of the next chapter, the Casseroles movement presents another use of sound as a tactic. While HU Resist employed targeted heckling and occupied specific spaces on campus, the Casseroles expanded their sonic presence to encompass entire cities, creating an immersive auditory experience that blurred the lines between protesters and bystanders. This shift from localized to widespread sound demonstrates how different contexts can shape the deployment of sonic tactics. Moreover, the Casseroles drew from a rich historical tradition of charivari, explicitly linking their actions to a long-standing practice of using noise to challenge authority. This historical grounding, combined with the nightly rhythm of the protests and their integration into everyday life, created a unique form of sustained, participatory dissent that differs significantly from the more episodic nature of HU Resist's actions. As I delve into the Casseroles movement, I'll explore how the immersive quality of sound can be harnessed to create a sense of collective identity and mobilize "the people" in ways that transcend traditional protest boundaries.

4

The Charivari and the Casseroles

In Québec, the introduction of Bill 78 in May 2012 was a direct response to the escalating student protests over tuition hikes. Aimed to maintain public order, this legislation imposed significant restrictions on the right to protest. It specifically outlawed student picket lines near university premises and mandated that any group larger than forty people must notify the police about their protest plans, including the intended route and duration, at least eight hours in advance. Noncompliance was met with the threat of hefty fines or even jail time. The enactment of Bill 78 presented numerous challenges for protest movements, fundamentally impacting their strategy, operational dynamics, and broader engagement with the public. Among these challenges, the most significant was its potential to dissuade participation due to the fear of legal and financial repercussions. This chilling effect on would-be demonstrators posed a critical threat to the essence of social movements, which rely heavily on mass mobilization to effect change. The diminished participation risked reducing the visibility and impact of protests, undermining their capacity to challenge and instigate reform on the pressing issues at hand.

The rigid regulations introduced by Bill 78 highlighted the government's heavy-handed approach to dealing with dissent, prompting a broader debate on the right to protest and the role of governance in a democratic society. What do you do when the government makes it impossible for bodies to gather in the city? People took to the streets to bang pots and pans, a sonic demonstration against the unjust government that earned them the moniker "the Casseroles." Through this nightly banging of saucepans to signal a rally, the protest grew beyond the simple waveforms of each vibration as the sentiment and sound spread throughout the city. In his famous essay on the social purpose of why people make music, Christopher Small tells researchers to explore what it means that performance takes place at a specific time and location and with a particular person. This chapter explores what it means when the same people come out every night at eight o'clock to act as community members and forge an expansive, immersive, sound body. I wish to account for how this tapped into the people's lore, made them feel salient, and used that feeling to structure a space for deliberations about an antidemocratic law.

As a broader reason the government should act, the Casseroles provide an example of an appeal to the people. Michael C. McGee presents "the people" as an ideological construct that legitimizes democratic governance, shifting sovereignty from a divine right to the liberal notion of collective will. He argues that the people are not a tangible entity in nature but rather a rhetorical fiction, collectively agreed on to justify political systems like Whig, Fascist, and Communist. He writes that "the people" is "an attempt to describe an indescribable kind of power—the power of a collectivity, of ungoverned, undisciplined human beings whose behavior is totally variable in every direction and hence unpredictable. We can shoot at them, and we don't know whether they will run away or tear us limb from limb. We can talk to them, and we don't know whether they are going to cheer us or tear us limb from limb."[1] This concept, while abstract, wields considerable rhetorical power, suggesting that government authority stems from the people's will. McGee highlights the unpredictable nature of this collective power, noting its potential for violence and its role as a potent rhetorical force. Even if you do not accept the legitimacy of the people, there is a lingering argumentum ad baculum that threatens violence at every turn.

There are cultural variants as to who counts as the people (something covered in the introduction and conclusion), but the call to define the people is a nationalist choice. The argument made in this chapter is that the Casseroles used sound's capacity for immersion to give a sense of how the people feel. The group harnessed the vibrations that reflected off different surfaces to create dense networks of transductors, using their tactic to propagate a feeling of salience and proximity. This was a movement of the people as a collective against its government because the signal could be heard all around; everyone was drawn into the fray and invited to become part of the sound body. For the people of Montreal, the Casseroles manifested to tell the government what the people wanted. They felt their proper tactic in the physical waveform reverberation on the street and the echoes of those reverberations through various media. The democratic carnival became the talk of the town as the ordinary paper documented its experience of the event. Tweets, Facebook posts, and blogs emerged covering the Casseroles. The nightly flaunting of the rules set the tone for how the people felt about power and conditions for the discussion of the government. The Casseroles' presence was paired with their audible demand to repeal Bill 78.

To understand the Casseroles' power, we first examine how sound's immersive property provides a unique rhetorical resource—the waveform modulates to situate the audience in a particular place and time. I will argue that this mechanism is how a listener discerns signal from noise using the sound waves that bounce off different materials and how the ultimate coordination of sounds is modulated to envelop the listener. Sound's capacity to cover a space enables and disables certain social behaviors that give feeling to the people's demand for change. Like improvisation and cut-outs, these are unique articulations of rituals brought together to confer meaning onto the duration of sounds. I will cover the context of the event to outline the environment that helped emplace the immersive Casseroles in the street, the legacy media, and everywhere in between.

Emplacement

Sound emplaces people in an unfolding drama, situating them in an intersubjective, temporal space and defining others and objects through its immersive capacity. For auditors, the sounds, instruments, and agents in these narratives are situated in imagery that puts them within the purview of history. This includes both cultural considerations and material relationships. The key here is how sound creates an intersubjective, temporal space between people that defines relationships within particular times and places. Emplacement, in other words, uses listening to put the body in place.[2] Sound is profoundly relational and entwined within an acoustic ecology. Each unique ecology becomes mapped into the body, providing a sense of self. Steven Feld writes that sound vibrates the chest, head, and feet, "bringing a durative, emotional world of time and space simultaneously to front and back, top and bottom, and left and right, an alignment suffuses the entire fixed or moving body. This is why hearing and voicing link the felt sensation of sound and balance to those of physical and emotional presence."[3] The experience of sensing space and time is wed to sonorous dimensions as waves stretch or become ensnared in space, attack, and fade in time.

Feld's work demonstrates a vast wealth of vibration that can be perceived through the immersive world of sound. He draws from ethnographic work that describes a feeling of acoustic presence with visual absence, an internalized habitus that affects how people move through time and space. His primary example comes from the people who live in the dense tropical forest of Papua New Guinea, the Kaluli. Through ritual, the Kaluli link sounds with a profound cosmology of meaning, building connections between vibration and cultural myth and using these connections to navigate everyday life. The Kaluli say sounds provide important information about the coordinates of the forest, like "time, season, environmental conditions, forest height, and depth."[4] But sounds do more than give a sense of place; they also can convey the existence of presences in the forest—how close they are, where they might be located, and their significance.

Birds, for example, are central to the experience of everyday life for the Kaluli. Feld explains that they provide a semblance of the presence of spiritual ancestors, "ane mama," or "what humans become by achieving death."[5] When birds manifest sonically, their presence "instantly stimulates fleeting memories," conjuring "the trace of audio memory, fragmentary sonic remembrances."[6] The attack and fade of a waveform shape the unfolding in real time of a presence as it ebbs and flows over the forest. The different reverberations echolocate and guide. Feld notes, "Presence and absence of sounds or changes in direction and dimension coordinate space as intersecting upward and outward."[7] The birds and their presence grow and change, in practice "lift[ing] up over sounding," and this "evokes the way all sounds necessarily co-exist in fields of prior and contiguous sounds."[8] The birds are sonic bodies whose presence emerges to speak to the people. Since sound always coexists in the cacophony of all other activity, the lift-up speaks of how a sound is individuated from the other, how an entity can lift upward and onward over the noise to announce its presence. Different birds represent different spirits, and their sounds describe growth, proximity, and salience—a central way the Kaluli know the world.

The notion can also be translated to a cacophonous environment that removes the origin from the sound, like any urban environment where hard, flat surfaces dislocate the source of a sound from its signal. The tempos and rhythms of different parts of the city can be used to describe various sorts of premises. Yet the desire to attach the sound to its cause prompts searching for potential meanings. Like the Kaluli infuse their dense environment with rituals and mythology to give their environment meaning, the Casseroles felt both diffuse and salient, propagating their mythology through Twitter, blogs, YouTube, and traditional outlets. The banging of pots and pans vibrated off the buildings, their reverberations generating immediate recognition, but this noise was also transduced into texts to friends, images to a blog, and a video for future auditors. The environment emplaced the potential for the people's sonic bodies to grow and demand the restoration of their rights. This ubiquity created different temporalities, speeds, and notions of relationality. Newspaper articles are written, op-eds are published, new conversations circulate, and the carnival constitutes its temporality resonating throughout the day. The same sounds produced in a different context would not have the same immersive effect. When the sound of the Casseroles coming out every night became associated with a democratic movement, the people of Québec had the momentum they needed to demand change.

Everything, a Cymbal

In the 1960s and 1970s, Québec's Quiet Revolution brought with it a promise of accessible education. This is one of the distinguishing features of the province because it had a proud political tradition of free university education. However, in March 2011, Jean Charest, the premier of Québec, proposed a 75 percent tuition hike to be phased in over three years. Students immediately went on strike, aiming to shut down the public education system until the proposed tuition hike was thwarted. At first, the strike was localized to just a couple of student organizations. In the following months, labeled the Maple Spring, the protests intensified as student groups joined from across Québec. While the students' strike sparked several conflicts, things became more violent when the protests attracted other activist networks such as Convergence des Luttes Anti-capitalistes and Le Front D'Action Populaire en Réaménagement Urbain. The creation of the hashtag #ggi ("*Grève Générale Illimitée*," a French expression that can be translated to "Unlimited General Strike") allowed students to coordinate mass actions.[9] Some of these actions included students shutting down major urban bridges, occupying buildings, and blocking other students from entering classes. In some instances, the protests became violent when some students came with Molotov cocktails and rocks and met police equipped with pepper spray, batons, and loudspeakers.

The student-led protests paralyzed a number of the Collège d'Enseignement Général et Professional, the general and vocational colleges throughout the province. Local, national, and some international media covered the protests extensively, linking them to transnational movements like Occupy Wall Street. The ensuing turbulence provided a context for Charest to introduce Bill 78, restricting the ability for anyone to impede access to "education," including by blocking physical buildings. He represented this as a bill to protect the Canadian people from the unruly protesters. On May 18, 2012, the National Assembly of Québec adopted the controversial law.

Although Bill 78 offered education as the primary justification for the law, it was designed to curb student protests. *World Socialist* reporter Keith Jones notes, "Bill 78 effectively outlaws student picket lines. It will henceforth be illegal for strike supporters to picket or stage any 'form of gathering' within 50 meters of the 'outer limits' of the 'grounds' of any university."[10] The law meted significant fines and potential jail time for anyone striking *or potentially supporting attacking*. Bill 78's ramifications extended far beyond the student strikes to any form of activism. Jones continued, "Bill 78 makes it illegal for anyone to stage or participate in a demonstration of more than 40 people anywhere in Québec and *over any issue* unless the demonstration's organizers have informed police in writing at least 8 hours in advance of the precise route of the protest and the duration of the rally, and agree to abide by changes in the protest route made by police."[11]

Bill 78 created a dangerous presumption that all protest was illegal, not just the extreme actions of the few violent actors. Under the new law, demonstrations would have to be vetted and approved by the police. However, as Media Co-Op's Andrew Gavin Marshall notes, this type of resistance is effective precisely because it rejects the norms imposed by authorities; "This is no longer about tuition. Our very freedom is at stake."[12] The tuition hike originally implicated only students, but Bill 78 implicated liberal governance. The pivot in political discourse—from tuition to people—changed the nature of the argument, undermining the very legitimacy of the governing organization.

The May 18 passage of Bill 78 inaugurated entirely new rules (who can stand and where, procedures for approval), demarcated borders (appropriate and inappropriate space), segmented times (correct times and durations of protest), and defined subjects (who could speak). Within this territory, the denizens of Québec lost their capacity to enter a public disagreement unless they preplanned and met rigid requirements. Bill 78 gave the police the opportunity to deny protests or revise the sites, routes, or times on a whim. As Brian Massumi explains, Bill 78 "no longer waits for warning signs such as the stray rock thrown at police lines before criminalizing the entirety of an event in anticipation of more trouble. Now, the anticipation moves forward to become an a priori."[13] The presumption was so strong that it eliminated the chance to render the opposition audible, visible, or present in any embodied way. If the Maple Spring had been concerned earlier about the coming tuition hike, then the new bill would have had broader implications for the citizens' capacity to protest in the first place.

On May 19, a local political science teacher, François-Olivier Chené, sent out a Facebook invitation that encouraged the denizens of Québec to take to the streets of Montreal on May 22 at 8:00 p.m. and protest Bill 78. The invitation proclaimed, "Nos casseroles contre la loi spéciale!" or roughly translated, "Our saucepans against the special law." Using kitchen equipment to make noise bestowed the name "Casseroles" onto the protests. While the earlier fights might have been around access to education and the original promises made by the government, the Casseroles demanded that the Charest administration respect the democratic right to protest and repeal Bill 78.

The formulation of this claim is the most obvious in Chené's May 22 Facebook invitation for the first protest, in which he wrote, "The Chilean dictator [Augusto Pinochet] decided that all gatherings of more than four people was [sic] illegal. In response, the citizens used their casseroles to express their anger. Let's do like they did!" Chené likens Bill 78 to a law that the brutal and repressive Pinochet would pass. Both mandates moved power from the people and toward the state; as Pinochet usurped democratic authority by banning peaceful gatherings, the Charest government undermined citizens' fundamental rights. Even though Bill 78's regulation pertained to groups of forty or more (and not four), any incursion into the right to gather indicates a potential threat to democracy. The similarity in circumstance between Pinochet and Charest mandated a similar tactic in response: banging pots and pans. Many of those being hailed would be familiar with the lessons of Chile, so the reference situated what it might mean to participate in collective noise-making. This topos provided a powerful site to constitute the disparate noises into a coherent sense of the people.

For the Casseroles, citing the precedent of Chile situates the protest in a history of social movements challenging oppressive regimes. It will take the people's work to show them where the true power resides. The immersive sound becomes a metonymy for the people everywhere and nowhere at once, ubiquitous and all-encompassing, threatening to close in at any moment. The association between Charest and Pinochet works to inscribe the imaginary with a familiar, transcendent enemy. In Chile, the choice of pots and pans had more to do with symbolizing the food shortages during the Salvador Allende administration, where empty pans being banged represented an empty promise. The saucepans harkened back to an inspirational movement for the Casseroles and provided a mechanism for every ordinary citizen to join and create sound as a collective.

The Casseroles advanced a demand that was qualitatively different from that of the student protests. While the students were antagonistic, the Casseroles constituted a divide between all citizens and the government. A bargain of democracy is that if the people feel like the government is arbitrary in exercising its power over them, then they can replace the ruler. When the people rise and demand to repeal a law, the mobilization suggests the law falls outside the scope of reasonable exercise of power. This notion of proper scope is tricky to define and ultimately comes down to the people's will. It is not a concrete thing that can be measured but, as Michael C. McGee points out, "a fiction dreamed by an advocate and infused with an artificial, rhetorical reality by the agreement of an audience to participate in a collective fantasy."[14]

The shift from student protest to broader democratic movement enacted a sound tactic, a method of galvanizing a collective identified as the Casseroles but representative of a larger social position. Perhaps one of the best places to register this move from the initial protests as a student concern to the emergence of the people was in the classroom. Jonathan Sterne, teaching at a Canadian university in the middle of this, recalled the change in the disposition of his students with the passage of the bill. He wrote, "While the University du Québec Montréal and the University de Montréal lost a semester, at my university (McGill University) students were considerably more divided on whether—and how—to participate [in the earlier student protests]. The protests were eventually banned by the government, which had the effect of bringing even more people out into the streets, people who may not have supported the original student cause but who were offended by the ban on expression or who simply were excited to participate in what became a carnivalesque atmosphere."[15]

While few may have been interested in the "student strike," droves more were interested in protecting democracy. They would see images propagated online and hear the protests each night. A democratic carnival atmosphere was ideal as a sound tactic because it did not require a clear, specific message like a slogan; all it needed was the noise itself, which became inextricably entwined with public feeling. In short, it became a question about the people and no longer about repealing Bill 78. In recounting this movement, I have drawn from many different kinds of evidence, including the ongoing account of sound studies scholar Jonathan Sterne. Sterne played a prominent role in telling the story of the Casseroles; he appeared in the blogs, took part in the protests, wrote op-eds to help the public understand, participated in particular issues, and wrote book chapters. He took on this role, noting, "The texts I wrote were efforts to make sense of the strike, in the tradition of the left intellectuals I admired. They were also efforts to publicize the strike and notify international academic audiences that were not otherwise aware of what was happening in Québec."[16] However, as Sterne also notes, "Texts do not tell the whole story of the strike by any means"; the Casseroles were, instead, a dynamic, sensory experience that immersed the population in this particular sound tactic.[17]

"The people" results from an intersubjective reality that emerges between speaker and audience—a continually changing process that requires all group members to identify with the collectivity. Sometimes a group is formed and recognized based on visual cues, physical proximity, or other shared attributes. In the case of the Casseroles, sound played an essential role in creating a sense of a people rising against an unjust ruler. The process of performing the sound invited everyone to participate in the people, with their fellow citizens, and stand up against tyranny. The immersive sound of the people coming up and out gave a sense of the widespread sentiment. For those who objected to Bill 78, the vibration vectors propagated all over the province and spread from the original waveforms on the streets. Because you couldn't pinpoint *a* sound, you couldn't identify *a* protester or group and ignore it. Because the waveform became immersive, it was much harder to ignore.

On May 22, 2012, two hundred thousand people took to the streets and made their opposition audible. Some people marched down the street smacking pots and pans together, others played music and danced, and even more came out onto their patios and porches to slap their instruments together. The event was labeled the most significant act of civil disobedience in the history of Québec.[18] After the May 22 protest, the Casseroles continued each night at eight o'clock; the people were rhetorically constituted and sustained in and through the charivari, which made the people heard, felt, and sensed. Tweets and videos provided an electric experience of auditory feedback—a space where people could participate in an ecology of cultural, technological, and material unity propagated by the Casseroles. But what exactly were those sounds? How were they sensed and interpreted to make sense of the demand? On May 30, huge groups "in Toronto, Calgary, Halifax, and Vancouver made noise to show solidarity with Québec in what was called 'Casserole Night in Canada.'"[19] The events continued late into the summer, even if the Casseroles stopped their rapid proliferation throughout the region.

The History of the Casseroles

Canadians lucky enough to attend university might encounter a history of the Casseroles. The writings that formed this concept came from a social-cultural milieu of the early 1970s. Natalie Zemon Davis and Edward Thompson provided an essential set of texts to help understand what was going on; the term's language and cultural significance came from these two scholars' research and shared correspondence. As Alexandra Walsham notes when introducing a series of letters between the two authors as they were penning their respective works, "It is significant that it occurred in the aftermath of the student and worker's revolts of 1968. Their interests in forms of youth rebellion and customs that temporarily turned the world upside down must be seen against the backdrop of the social and civil rights movements with which Europe and the United States were awash in these years."[20] While Davis focused on sixteenth-century France, Thompson focused on the English crowd in the eighteenth century. Both of these cultural historians looked at rituals of the "youth" using loud sounds as a protest mechanism; both were interested in the production of the category of youth and its capacity to produce radical social change. They both found a commonality that created a special kind of "plebian street theater in publicizing scandal, compelling compliance with accepted norms, and criticizing unpopular authority figures."[21] Their respective research is among the most influential, cited, and taught since it is written for an accessible audience. As a result, the term charivari tied an image of justice, loud carnival music, and youth together.

As the protests started picking up, opinion editorials were written constituting the events as charivari. Vincent Raynauld, Mireille Lalancette, and Sofia Tourigny-Koné found that legacy media comprised the vast majority of a significant part of the ambient territory surrounding the protest. Davis returned and wrote an opinion editorial with Sterne for the *Globe and Mail*, a prominent periodical for Québec, to historicize the charivari. In their viral essay, Sterne and Davis explain that the charivari emerged for ordinary citizens as an alternative to violence to seek restorative justice against oppressive regimes that end in a party.[22] They give several examples in French traditions, like using noise against a King's Master of Forests for beating his wife and cutting down trees or royal tax collectors for oppressing families of peasants and artisans. They also locate the importance of Canadian independence, writing that "in the Rebellion of 1837, masked Patriots brought their pots, bells, and horns to the houses of government officials and demonstrated until they either resigned their office or shouted, 'Vive la liberte.'"[23] The charivari, in short, was a just tool of the people to restore the community's norms to the people. Citizens stepped onto their patios, walked on the sidewalks, and poured into the street while smacking kitchen utensils to make a hubbub. If Charest was a dictator, then the Casseroles historically situated themselves as something all Canadians could identify with: a transcendent agent that brings about just historical change with a bit of a party.

Sterne and Davis reconstitute that the casseroles and banging them emplaced the protesters in a fight against an oppressive ruler that wants to cut down trees or oppress artists. Like past tyrannical rulers such as Pinochet, Charest's decision to pass Bill 78 denied the people the ability to come together and demand redress. These new opinion editorials add more nuance and help flesh out how other leaders also attempted to thwart people's rights and how the just and right citizenry mobilized nonviolent instruments to realize justice. The practice of banging pots and pans renders audible the disapproval of these actions and demands leaders to account. But it does so in the democratic groove of a carnival. The modest instruments of pots, pans, and other objects around the house have begotten excellent results, from stopping domestic violence to helping with Canadian independence. This made it genuinely democratic since anything could be brought to make the noise, so anyone could participate. The people who take up these courageous acts are often youth who know what is right and are equipped with a sense of duty to act. In this imagination, sound is accorded the ultimate power of creating accountability and a festive environment. Now we have the people as the ones who are just, creating an open and welcoming environment that invites an unjust leader to a carnival to account for their actions through nonviolent and democratic means. The cultural and historical significance of such sound demonstrations adds energy and salience to the sounds of the Casseroles. By reminding the public of this history, media publications helped contextualize the sounds and galvanize the spread of the Casseroles movement.

A Growing Sound Body

Each night at eight o'clock, the Casseroles came together to make noise, challenging Bill 78's notion of territory. The city was divided, as violence had forced everything to become segmented and regulated; people were not allowed to congregate. The Casseroles' auditory context allowed anyone to speak in their capacity as a citizen on an issue of public concern—in this case, the state of democracy. A city is radiant, dense with reflexive bodies waiting to be constituted, and layered with different vectors that provide the conditions for action. Of course, the street is one of the first modalities offering regulations of what can go in which direction, at what speed, and where. Michel de Certeau wrote early on about the streets as one of the first places that the strategy of power inscribed its logic and made it an ideal place to locate an affordance of a tactic. While one night someone might not understand the meaning of the noise and never be emplaced, on another night they might be galvanized into action depending on the ambient conditions. The continued replay and reverberation of sound in the streets allowed more and more people to join the movement as they became emplaced.

Every night, eight o'clock became the effective moment citizens were called down, a moment of gathering and coming together to challenge the oppressive policies of the Charest regime. Nelson Wyatt remembered that the Casseroles "have acted like an alarm clock for regular evening marches by Québec student protesters, sounding at 8:00 p.m. on the nose."[24] The repetition of the Casseroles created a sense of timing, codifying and structuring the auditory context. The charivari upended those parameters if Bill 78 attempted to sequester protest to a specific space. In place of a segmented space regulated through force by the state, the entire city became immersed within a sonic environment. By trying to control the size and location of the protests, the government instead engendered a demonstration with no size or location limits; as far as the ear could hear were the Casseroles. The new auditory context came with a sonorous envelope energizing the crowd. Joseph Rosen, for example, described the Casseroles as "joyous and playful" with "an incredible effectivity" that "has fueled us for a week now: anarchic joy is a renewable resource!"[25] That sound carried a sense of comfort, joy, and positive affect required to propel the movement forward. Attunement describes the positive feedback loop between the arguers and the environment. The Casseroles' soundscape attuned and encouraged listeners to come out and alter the soundscape.

Anything could create a sound for those who wanted to participate. Since no specific note needed to be made, anything would do. They converted materials traditionally accorded to private spaces, such as wooden spoons, banks, and cookie sheets, into technologies of publicity. The banality of the tools made it truly democratic; since anything could be brought to make the noise, anyone could participate. Sterne, a recurring narrator of this tale, observed, "The percussion is overwhelming, beating a rhythm of phenomenal collectivity that is entirely immersive because it is so loud. The noise tickles neighborhoods at some distance, enticing some neighbors to join in while others, like Montreal's mayor, cringe at the protester's extended touch."[26] Sound went where bodies were forbidden, turning the entire city into a public space the city couldn't regulate. The groove of the protest became democratic with a free-form style, inviting texture that beckoned citizens onto the streets. The Casseroles grew each night as more people took to the streets to protest Bill 78, quickly reaching the public consciousness.

The sound attenuated the fears of many vulnerable populations that might otherwise have been averse to participating. The Casseroles attracted the elderly, young, and differently abled. For instance, Jeremy Stolow celebrated the kids, aged three to twelve, dancing in the streets with their parents.[27] Joseph Rosen applauded the "grandmothers, middle-class families, and neighborhood kids wearing capes and distributing cupcakes."[28] Carrie Rentschler noted a woman in her wheelchair on the street "to participate in the evening's activities."[29] In addition to attracting vulnerable populations, the police also became attuned to the sound. During the student protests, police were primed for violent encounters. However, their concerns diminished when they became enveloped in the dings of pots and pans. For instance, Stolow recounted feeling anxious when he saw the police, but "we were greeted by smiles from the cop car," and sometimes, "the police seemed even to be bouncing to our beat."[30] The Casseroles created an auditory environment where different generations and diverse population segments felt comfortable enough to advocate. In other words, the soundscape activated their convictions and motivated them to join. The external environment configured audience members' conviction, encouraging participation, amplifying the sounds, and expanding the protests. Because the waveforms became so immersive, people from all walks of life felt a sense of belonging when they joined the cacophony.

The public would take to the streets each night with a unifying ethos that welcomed everyone. This is a perfect example of what is called musicking. The familiar form of the 4/4 rhythm is contrasted by constantly evolving and fluctuating renditions, as each iteration is different depending on the composition of each group. One recognized rhythm often vernacularly goes by the name of the

"Let's go" cheer, with one measure being the chant, "Let's Go [insert local team]," followed by one measure of hand claps in a clap, clap, clap-clap-clap rhythm. This widely recognized and accessible cheer is often used in many sports contexts to unify disparate voices into one. The chant often brings the stands into the game to help the home team. Of course, depending on one's sports predilections, the group cheered on might be the Longhorns, Hawkeyes, or Trojans. The chant is taught to many people as they grow up rooting for sports teams. It provides an easy, democratic chant because it can synchronize entire groups. For the relationship between self and other, the charivari provides a democratic refrain that allows everyone to participate because it is a widely available cultural trope open to mass participation.

The Casseroles bloomed over the entire city and spread. Like other large metropolitan areas, Montreal is loud and large, filled with the concrete, metal, glass, and detritus that make up the urbane. It supplies protesters with an open, horizontal space for propagation where any emission must compete with so many other sounds—it is by its nature following the lines of a "ubiquity effect," which means its vectors are "diffused, unstable, omnidirectional."[31] The different spaces, buildings, and mixing of urban noises make it challenging to echolocate a sound. The propagation of the other sensual fragments coalesces around the rhetoric of "Casseroles" to create a sense of the people, where they were, and if they were growing. The people were not just an abstract idea but an enlivened grouping of nightly sounds, images, and videos ascribed to motives and demands.

Montreal operated as an exemplar of an ambient agora that was at once digitally diffuse, propagating through Twitter, blogs, YouTube, and traditional outlets, but also concentrated in person each night. The cityscape created different temporalities, speeds, and notions of relationality. As protesters came out each night, people tweeted, blogged, photographed, recorded, and disseminated their experiences, creating a positive-feedback loop. The amplification of the sound tactic helped it move beyond the material constraints of the city. While a speaker can only capture a specific vibration ratio, the protesters had a hashtag they used to organize: #manifencours (roughly French for demonstration happening now) and #casserole. These helped with preformed conversations, immersing the citizens in talks about the protests even when the streets were empty.

As the Casseroles transduced from analog into digital, their discourse grew and extended, propelling them farther into the territory. The shared sentiment of presence, of hearing it on the street, could now extend into homes and on screens. For someone just hearing the far-off sounds and uncertain about their meaning, the proliferation of digital content gave them a chance to experience the sound up close and personal. The acousmatic rhetoric constituted an emerging sound tactic growing salient for the repeal of Bill 78; the people were beginning to make meaning out of the sound, even without seeing the speaker or participating in the protest in the streets. Time, appearance, and sound are not merely instrumental but constitutive, providing sensual fragments that can be rhetorically constituted into a people. While one vector for the reverberation of the people was the concrete, another equally important one was how the sound-image vectors rapidly proliferated around all the different media. The acousmatic object was constituted as salient, ambient, and present.

Expanding the Casseroles' Sound Body

Pots, pans, cameras, talking, and news stories combined to form a people demanding repeal of Bill 78. The more people that heeded the call, the larger the Casseroles became. As the Casseroles grew, more people became aware, resulting in even louder protests. The recursive cue combined these sounds, images, and stories to form a template. People there were identified as sound bodies through this cyclical relationship between sound and social media. As one set the conditions for the other, they became entangled to produce an entire sensorium, transforming the Casseroles from an abstract idea to a felt, sensed presence.

Raynauld, Lalancette, and Tourigny-Koné, in exploring the digital components of activism, attend to how digital media's decentralized repertoire and technological affordances enabled the #ggi to generate a sense of "ambience," a metaphor for "understanding the highly reactive, decentralized, and personalized nature of social media–intensive dynamics of political protest."[32] For these scholars, Twitter exists beyond the purview of a tweet, extending to a distributed network of flows that surround and envelop citizens both online and offline. Functioning as a type of ambience, social media defines what is happening around us, allowing protesters to leverage participatory media as a strategy for self-presentation that can usurp the traditional role of legacy media. For the Casseroles, this was an important step. Raynauld, Lalancette, and Tourigny-Koné found that early coverage of the Casseroles was unfavorable due to journalistic norms; news sources favored institutional sources, cast protesters as deviant, and failed to interview Casseroles participants. The result was a rather pessimistic view of the movement.

The Casseroles often relied on social media to publish and republish the movement's limited favorable coverage to combat this negativity. In particular, #ggi tweeters cherry-picked news content to build and promote a positive narrative of the strike.[33] This countered mostly negative accounts of #ggi activists' actions and positions, as well as those of their allies, by Québec journalistic organizations.[34] For many, what made this ambient was that it became salient to every part of citizens' daily lives as the Casseroles flooded social media.[35]

Sharing positive news stories wasn't the only way the Casseroles used social media. By interviewing Casseroles participants, Lalancette and Raynauld found that protesters also circulated their content to spread the word.[36] Discussions, images, videos, and sounds ascribe a sense of the agents and their motives, who and what these people are about. In particular, a high percentage of positive newspaper articles were shared, discussing what it meant to be part of the Casseroles to when they will be meeting next. The propagation of this protester-created content played on the sensory nature of the Casseroles, with the fragments of media coalescing around the group to create feeling trajectories. These emplaced auditors in an unfolding narrative.

Some of the protesters used Facebook to coordinate action. For example, Patrick Québécois exclaimed, "Resistez! Demand elections! Get ready! Make yourself heard by the sounds of your pots!"[37] Protester Roxanna Turcotte shared an event that translates to, "Come and take a walk in Point-Claire. It's far but worth it. First, it's a beautiful corner, second, we don't bother anyone, and people ask many questions. They are often unaware of the news about pans, law 78, and student conflict. Also, we need to show that it's not only liberals in the west of the island. Clang clang!"[38]

Others wanted to ensure that auditors *knew* how and why the noise was being produced. Roosa OC, a protester who used Facebook for information gathering, requested help locating a flyer she'd seen. "I'm looking for a flyer already made," she wrote. "On one side, it has an invitation, and the other explains why.... I want to print it tomorrow, Wednesday, to spread it in my corner of the country (Bas-Saint-Laurent). I notice that those convinced are [are already on our side], and the others need information."[39] Roosa aimed to spread the word and recruit supporters to the cause by reposting the flyer she'd seen. Other posters participated in threads, posted photos, argued with one another, and engaged in content.

Much of this content was created by observers. People attended the protests and captured the movement on audiovisual devices, using the camera to share images of the moments as they happened. These images were often shared with hashtags to contextualize the protest sounds. Because the sounds came from everywhere and potentially anyone, the photos and videos propagated online humanized the protesters, giving a clear image of the sound's source and allowing listeners to imagine the cause for the clamor more accurately. For instance, "Manifestation de casseroles, 27 mai 2012, St-Denis/Villeray, Montréal," a post on *Un Vent Du Nord*, shows an image of a diverse crowd moving through a bustling intersection. The woman in the middle of the frame is wearing a hijab and an abaya. The hijab is a polarizing symbol that often sits at the fault line of liberal pluralism. Yet in the Casseroles, the woman is assimilated into the citizenship as she smiles, looking off to the left. The woman to her right wears a Sikh turban, another symbol with a turbulent history in Western liberal democracy.[40] In the image, these women blend into the larger protest body, surrounded by others with pots, pans, sticks, maracas, and a bottle of wine.

Another image in the series shows a woman holding her child, who wears a *lucha libre* mask, as they hit a mug with a wooden spoon. Another young child in the frame stares into the camera, bashing two metal measuring cups together, as a herd of people behind him march and make noise. A final image depicts an older woman alone on a balcony, smiling broadly as she smacks a wooden spoon against a pot.[41] The images, like many others, foreground what it means to be a Canadian citizen, emphasizing the label as inclusive. *Anyone is welcome to join*, the collective images seem to say. These brief snapshots provide an entirely different way of knowing the Casseroles than the disinterested gaze of the mainstream media. The visual tableau provides an anchor that gives meaning to the sounds. While an auditor might not *see* the source of the cacophony, the images propagating online provide context and, thus, a site of identification. The sound waves on the street drew people in, and the vibrations circulating online enveloped the city.

The exponential growth and intensity of the Casseroles eventually garnered legacy media attention. Newspaper articles and op-eds were published, sparking the circulation of new conversations and reconstituting the carnival, allowing it to resonate during nightly events and throughout the day. These articles, along with the social media posts, encouraged people to talk about the protests, thus continuing the reverberations from the previous night's activity while providing the context for why the protests happened. For instance, Rentschler recounted:

At the corner grocer, the young woman at the cash register checks in with me most days to see if I'll be at the *manifs* that night. Conversing in French, the owner of the dry-cleaning business I use asks if I beat on my pot. I tell him I most certainly do and that it's an actual civil act, to which he agrees. In practice, *les manifs* are not primarily about dialogue; they are about co-presence in taking over the streets. But as a result, I am talking more about the state of public culture and political engagement with my local shop merchants, store employees, and neighbors as mutually engaged, as participants and witnesses, in public action larger than ourselves.[42]

In Rentschler's account, the Casseroles transformed people from private strangers and shopkeepers into public citizens discussing an issue of public concern. People felt comfortable commenting on the Casseroles, Bill 78, and the tuition hike. Citizens argued about the merits of the Casseroles and the reasonableness of Bill 78 and the Charest government. Perhaps more importantly, they identified as existing and sharing a commonality, recognizing a shared imagination.

Rentschler's account is not isolated. When Bill 78 sought to silence dissent, the Casseroles sparked debate. It did not matter if citizens were for or against the measure; the Casseroles ensured Bill 78 was a topic of deliberation. The cacophony of pots and pans ringing out through the streets propelled the conversation into every corner of the public. It provided an entry point for debate, even for those who might not usually participate in civic dialogue. From bystanders to the police to the protesters, everyone was unified as citizens participating in an issue of public concern. The Casseroles, in short, created great conversations that allowed their demand to be audible even when the banging stopped for the night.

A Refrain

In September 2012, Jean Charest lost his seat to Pauline Marois. Marois and the Parti Québécois (PQ) immediately gutted Bill 78 and froze tuition hikes.[43] While the marches continued for a short time, the protests eventually ebbed. Perhaps the Casseroles alone were insufficient to prompt such change, but they were necessary. Rendering the people displeased enabled a robust debate and conversation that allowed for a new regime. But the win was short-lived. Not long after the election, the PQ government slashed university budgets, proposed tuition increases, and suggested a "Charter of Values" that fanned the flames of nationalist voters. Interestingly, nothing resembling the Casseroles returned; whatever had catalyzed, the initial tactic was no longer present.

While most of this chapter took the perspective of the emergence of the Casseroles over only a portion of their duration, the impact of their actions as a sound tactic is straightforward. Through the immersive quality of sound and its reverberation through media, the Casseroles rendered their demand audible: repeal Bill 78. The debates they encouraged showed both that right makes might and there are no other avenues that can be used to achieve this goal.

While the Casseroles did not immediately respond to the PQ government's conservative turn, they did appear as hope on the horizon. We can trace how the Casseroles linger as a sound body waiting to awaken. In "A Groove We Can Move To," Sterne notes that something like a charivari might appear again. He says, "As I wrote in August 2015, the largest unions in the province are organizing a general strike against the liberal's widely unpopular austerity measures.... [W]hat it will bring to the province is anyone's guess."[44] He was writing about the anti-austerity protests happening in Québec in late March 2015, years after the Casseroles' protests first broke out.

Many students came out and declared a strike around several issues, including cuts to public service. On March 23, students, union organizers, community members, and people from several other sectors linked together and took to the streets to protest proposed austerity cuts. The group refused to list the services they represented or those involved in the protests. In the media, some ideas appeared that paralleled the Maple Spring: students concerned about public services, people taking to the streets, and a strike. Thus, the amorphous group, dubbed Printemps2015, was quickly compared to its predecessor: "Student groups in the province are planning several strike days and demonstrations over the next few weeks in a new wave of protests dubbed Printemps2015 or Spring2015. The names are reminiscent of 2012's Maple Spring when thousands of students held nightly marches in downtown Montreal."[45] The Maple Spring preceded the sound tactic and created the conditions for future implementation. However, the protest did not last long and ultimately packed up shop. On May Day that year, they considered the protest over and reconsidered and reflected on what might be done in the future.[46]

The difference between these two movements resides in the immersive experience. In his accounts about the Casseroles, Sterne registers the protests' capacity to rise and bloom over the city. When the people are constituted, they are *everywhere*. This is in sharp contrast to the relatively brief discussion of Printemps2015. Not only did they barely take up any of the conversation; they also did not occupy much space in legacy media, social media, or the auditory territory in general. This has significant implications because this immersive salience is essential in creating the normative terrain for any deliberative exchange. While a longer potential might have existed in 2015, it failed to materialize. Yet this tactic's recurrence suggests that the Casseroles exist as a lingering potentiality awaiting a future to actualize. Sterne's language of presence helps provide a concrete example of the topos of immersion and the capacity for a sound tactic to enact it.

Additionally, the Casseroles' prolonged impact carries on as a potential cultural resource. As Chile was the historical marker used by a professor to encourage citizens to take up their pots and pans, the Maple Spring has become political shorthand for a kind of protest. The carnival-like atmosphere of the charivari informed later demonstrations in Canada, including not only Printemps2015 but also an ill-fated occupation during the first year of the COVID-19 pandemic, the Freedom Convoy. The 2021 Freedom Convoy challenged pandemic restrictions, taking on a carnival-like atmosphere, occupying city streets, and drawing comparisons to Maple Spring's subversion of the rule of law. Yet while the Freedom Convoy carried the same potential as a sound tactic, one crucial difference emerged: the soundness of their action. In the concluding chapter, I will unpack the idea of an unsound tactic and offer thoughts surrounding the lessons that sound's immediate, intense, and immersive qualities can provide for future agents of change.

Conclusion | Unsound Tactics

In Québec, the passage of Bill 78 in 2012 set restrictions on protests, notably limiting the ability to picket near educational institutions and mandating that groups over forty notify police in advance, with threats of fines and jail time for noncompliance. This sparked widespread protests, as citizens saw the bill as an infringement on their rights, much like the Greek protests in 2009. There, in Syntagma Square, the Greek populace rose in opposition to austerity measures imposed by their government under pressure from the European Union and the International Monetary Fund. Both protests were characterized by a deep connection to cultural identity—the Québec protests were infused with the spirit of Québécois resilience, while the Greek protests pulsed with the rhythm of decapentasyllabic chants, a traditional Greek poetic meter, exemplifying their cultural heritage.

In both scenarios, the sound demanded change; chants in Syntagma Square echoed in Athens, and pots and pans ricocheted against the walls of Montreal, in defiance of perceived governmental overreach. In both, a sound body emerged that expanded through the immersion of people in the streets, as the protests echoed through vectors of cities, concrete, and media; the presence of "the people" (understood as the ideological warrant) covered in the last chapter extended far beyond the confines of the street. For instance, while the Greek protests employed the traditional rhythm of decapentasyllabic chants to unify against austerity measures, a misuse of this cultural expression was evident when the far-right group Golden Dawn adopted the same rhythmic pattern to disseminate xenophobic rhetoric, defining "Greekness" in exclusionary terms against immigrants. This contrast illustrates that while the power of speech and cultural elements can be catalysts for solidarity and change, as in the protests in Syntagma Square or against Bill 78, they can also be harnessed for divisive purposes. The ethical dimension of these powerful tools of expression is crucial; it's essential to weave wisdom into public discourse, aiming to use our communicative assets to foster inclusivity and unity rather than division and harm.

In this concluding chapter, I demonstrate what I mean by an unsound tactic. I will do this by introducing the example of another appeal to the people, the Freedom Convoy in Canada in 2021. I will only stop here to briefly illustrate that a sound tactic becomes unsound when the conversation moves from violating the institution's norms and legitimacy to questioning the motives of the organization. When an agent is trying to occupy the moral high ground, ceding attacks to character attenuates the intensity of the claim. In the context of the truckers, changing their stance opened up lines of discussion about sincerity and character that consumed the discourse and ended any debate about the COVID protocols that might have started.

Freedom Convoy

On March 11, 2020, the world was officially battling a pandemic. The World Health Organization declared that the coronavirus disease first discovered in 2019, or COVID-19, had reached pandemic proportions, with attempts to contain the virus proving unsuccessful. As the outbreak spread to every continent, the estimated global death toll reached 5.2 million people by the end of 2021.[1] Many governments worldwide were facing a public health crisis for the first time in almost one hundred years, and their responses varied widely. In many cases, the severity and suddenness of the pandemic persuaded governments to enact mandates and policies that tested the extent of their authority. Several countries, including the United States and Canada, implemented various restrictions on travel, commerce, and daily activities.

The COVID-19 pandemic created a "lockdown" regime, providing discursive context. This regime enabled and constrained the available subjects, institutions, and moves in the discursive state. Pandemics and health emergencies created a distinct biopolitical configuration that distributed rights and responsibilities. To reduce casualty, the biopolitical state prioritized the calculation of risk, curtailed rights, and mandated new ordinances to save lives. The harms and benefits of these policy proposals were not equally distributed, and the most significant risk of injury from the COVID-19 strain represented a specific demographic, including the elderly and those with concomitant complications. The Canadian system worked fairly efficiently in getting all constituencies to adopt stringent lockdown policies in response to the Omicron variant, resulting in the third-highest vaccination rate in the world (much higher than the United States, with a much lower death rate).

Within this biopolitical context, I examine a protest by Canadian truckers in response to a new quarantine policy. In January 2022, Canada enacted a policy that mandated a fourteen-day quarantine for all unvaccinated truckers who crossed into Canada from the United States. Like vaccine mandates in other places, this was unpopular with some in this sector because it affected a sizable chunk of the industry. Even though Canada boasted a significantly higher vaccination rate, Cole Schisler reported that this new policy potentially sidelined twenty-six thousand out of one hundred sixty thousand truckers who regularly made the international crossing.[2] While the Canadian Truckers Alliance supported the mandate, a group of renegade truckers did not. The emergence of a disgruntled group of truckers that resisted the mandate built up friction around its implementation. In this context, the "Freedom Convoy" emerged.

The Freedom Convoy brought together a broad coalition of people from across Canada. Identifying a movement leader is difficult, but it coalesces around the fatigue of the COVID protocols. The group, or agent, viewed it as an overreach of Canadian power even though many were vaccinated. The truckers planned to travel to Ottawa to hold organized events to demand changes to the vaccine laws. The first caravan of truckers departed from Vancouver on January 23, another left from Nova Scotia on January 27, and the Freedom Convoy called on others from across the country to join them.[3] Truck driver and business owner Harold Jonker told the BBC on his drive to Ottawa, "We want to be free, we want to have our choice again, and we want hope—and the government has taken that away."[4]

On January 28, many truckers descended on Ottawa, occupying Parliament Hill and overrunning Canada's capital city. According to local reporting, the truckers expressed that "people have freedom of choice" and "no medical treatment can be mandated on anybody."[5] The group initially was about the truckers, but they soon came to represent a growing frustration with COVID protocols in the country. During freezing weather, the Freedom Convoy flooded Ottawa with trucks and people; media reports for January 29 estimate between eight thousand and eighteen thousand people.[6] While the number of protests waned after the first couple of days, the streets filled with trucks adorned with banners and flags, blaring horns, launching fireworks, clogging significant arteries, and parking on the sidewalks for the next few weeks.[7] The trucker became a synecdoche for the plight of "the people." What started as a convoy about vaccine-specific policies for truckers grew into a broader condemnation of pandemic-related lockdowns.

The people came to Ottawa to demand change; they broke the lockdown rules—some entered the major shopping centers maskless, while others entered sacred sites and desecrated monuments. Per one report, "Trucks that have gathered along Wellington Street in front of the Parliament Buildings are adorned with banners denouncing public health measures."[8] All around Ottawa, protesters could be found dancing in the streets, lounging in hot tubs, watching their children play in bouncy castles, and barbequing with neighbors.[9] And there were the trucks—giant protesting machines—providing difficult-to-move reprieves from the cold. Businesses reported sudden drops in sales because the protest made it impossible to get around the city. Deeper in the encampments, John Paul Tasker found that "the many flags flown in the crowd reflected the divergent groups that [were] calling for an end to mandates"; he noted protesters with "Canadian flags," while others had "placards that urged people to 'Think for Yourself,' a slogan used in anti-vaccine circles." He noted a "Patriots flag," a nod to the Lower Canada rebellions of 1837–38 when French-speaking settlers from Québec fought against British Colonial rule, and also spotted the white supremacy and far right elements: "Indigenous demonstrators flew the Mohawk warrior flag and waved the flag of the Métis Nation."[10] The protests extended beyond Parliament Hill and into the US-Canadian border, shutting down a key land crossing between the countries.

Can we imagine the Freedom Convoy as a sound body? Can we imagine their protest as a sound tactic? For those in the city, the body of the Freedom Convoy could undoubtedly be felt. The air was dense with the echoes of revolt as trucks, transformed into colossal symbols of resistance, created a pulsating hum in the city's core, underpinned by the incessant rhythm of engines running to provide warmth against the biting cold. These metal leviathans, festooned with banners decrying public health measures, served as both imposing obstacles and rallying points. The metronome-like beat of dancing feet and children's laughter, amplified by the cacophony of bouncing castles, created an almost surreal counterpoint to the severe backdrop of protest. For those watching at home, the march commanded around-the-clock media attention.

The Freedom Convoy violated decorum because the protesters felt that their autonomy was being violated. Rejecting restrictions on their ability to work became the substance of their claim. The decision to break norms and engage in obnoxious and sometimes illegal protests flowed from their claim that their "might" came from being on the right side of history. These displays would only bolster their claims if they believed the government had significantly overreached in extending its powers and curbing autonomy.

These truckers needed more reasonable avenues to express their perspectives regarding the process condition. Because the vaccine mandate was enacted at a federal level, voting would be the codified process to define a desired change in federal leadership. However, because the national elections were recently held in September 2020, the truckers could argue that there was not a "reasonable process" alternative on the horizon to voicing their concerns. Put through the perspective of conservative Jonathan Kay, the trucker protest tapped into more of the electorate, especially regarding COVID-19. He reported that their honks became about freedom; one mantra indicated, "The honking will continue until freedom improves."[11] The resonant tones were of people ultimately excluded from the policy discourses for too long. They had to subvert usual democratic processes because they felt excluded. He would argue that even the most conservative leader, Doug Ford, fell along the lines of the COVID regime.

After weeks of ignoring the protesters, the government's ultimate response was a loud and clear declaration that the protest no longer reflected the people's will and instead posed a federal-level threat to the citizens. Prime Minister Justin Trudeau enacted the Emergencies Act (a piece of Canadian legislation only used in wartime and terrorist attacks) on February 14, 2022. The demonstrators were removed, and the protest was over. Using force might provide the prime conditions for a robust debate about the underwriting values, but that did not happen. While a state (or institution) coming forcefully and removing someone with less power is not unusual, it did not prompt debate but was instead welcomed by many.

Many reports suggested that the "trucker" protest lost its fight when the apparent source of protest moved from ordinary truckers to potentially far-right extremists. The meaning of the sound itself changed as the radiating honks and sounds moved from cries of freedom to potential associations of white nationalism (or, more commonly, a confusing mix of the two). How did the sound shift so dramatically that those listening to the protest—both the government and the people—could no longer find grounds for discourse? How and why did this sound tactic lose momentum and ultimately become unsound? Perhaps it has to do with their sound body.

Instead of what the protesters had hoped would occur—the government acceding to their demands about COVID protocols—the situation quickly became confused. Who was making this demand? Was it now "the people" asking for everything to change radically? Is the demand directly attached to a change in government leadership? Because the sound itself was doing much of the persuading, the listeners had to rely on their interpretation of those sounds to inform an understanding.

Disassociating the Sonic Body

If we pause our retelling of the Freedom Convoy here, we can examine whether it is also *sound* (adjective). If we think about sound as a noun, the inference was iconic. The performance of a loud, cacophonous environment that could not be escaped is meant to represent the kind of environment that COVID restrictions imposed on the people. The protest enacted a claim that the Canadian people were rising and demanding a change in the law. The volume of the horns propagating against the city's infrastructure, the cacophony of people moving, and the music from the encampments contributed to an ungovernable sonic body that felt proximate, salient, and large. This tactic traded on sound's capacity for an immersive experience to give the sonic body of the truckers a sense that it was around everywhere. The social media impressions added to this sense as people tweeted, Instagrammed, and live streamed their experience at protests. The claim became that the iconic trucker was voicing a concern of the people, demanding a change. Yet when the Canadian government applied force and shut it down, why did this not prompt more robust discussion and debate, a chance for real democratic change?

The trucker protest can be identified as an unsound tactic when our examination moves away from the sound (noun) toward the soundness (adjective) of the claim and approach. The move to adjective as a unit of analysis reminds the critic that the tactic is located in an unfolding, local normative terrain that will influence the ability of the tactic to take hold. Because this speech is happening in the civic realm, constituting a relationship between speaker and listener, it is essential to recognize that the audience's impression or knowledge of the speaker is evolving. As I have pointed out before, the practice of good judgment recognizes how to operate within a particular case. Yet it becomes hard to converse when locating whom you are engaging with is challenging. One of the underwriting conditions of a conversation is the assumption that everyone will keep to the commitments they offer. When another agent does not, it raises questions that may detract from the original discussion and prevent the moral debate needed.

In the context of an acousmatic situation where the transmission is obscured and the causes are infinitely reproduced, this confusion creates a perceptual vacuum that pivots the conversation away from the moral center of the demand and toward the agent making that demand in the first place. After all, the listeners attribute the feeling of the tactic to someone who wants something. In the ongoing conversation, to recognize what this person wants, we need to understand who they are. We need to tether the message to the agent's character in a way that makes sense in the communication environment. In an era of the public screen, the agent making the demand and their proximity (spatially, temporally, or otherwise) matters. Since the waveform of immersion is predicated on the presence of the sound body, it becomes concerning when questions about the speaker arise. Remember that thing about the metaphysical impulse? Indeed, a conversation becoming derailed amid uncertainty about an unknown part of an unseen speaker can amplify the anxiety, especially when concerns grow around the speaker's character and authenticity.

For the truckers, the difficulty of maintaining a consistent connection between speaker and listener was apparent when the nature of the demand shifted without explanation; the vocal segment of the group explicitly called for the adoption of a "Memorandum of Understanding" (MOU) to the General Governor of Canada and Senate of Canada to overthrow the government. The group withdrew the MOU ten days later, citing their lack of legal knowledge, but the damage to their message had been done.[12] A new ethos emerged and surrounded the protesters in noise and confusion. Although many protesters insisted that the intent was never to overthrow the government, other citizens took the call and introduced more extreme elements into the fray. In small corners of the protest, swastikas and Confederate flags appeared, prompting general confusion about who the protesters were. Even many protesters "seemed to have only a hazy idea about who [the] leaders were and what they believed."[13] This confusion in messaging and apparent unease increased. The withdrawal of the MOU only sowed more distrust in the organization, irreparably damaging the formerly sound body and rendering the sound tactic decidedly unsound.

CONCLUSION 135

When the situation changed from debate to contestation, a dissociative scheme and a new place to connect the sound body emerged. If the horns, honks, and social media posts constitute how we knew the truckers demanded a change to the laws, a shift in the understanding of the demand changed how the public knew the body. The transition into who might be demanding changed how they felt about the group's presence. This had corresponding implications for the public thinking about the state's subsequent actions; for example, one of the debate sites asked about the group's motives. Speculation focused on some of the individual members of the organization, its funding sources, and potential goals.

Consider the following just as an example. A Canadian television report talked about James Bauder, the first name listed on the roll of organizers under "Who Is Who: A Guide to the Major Players in the Trucker Convoy Protest." This is significant because he founded Canada Unity, the group that drafted the *new demand* for an election overthrowing the government. His December 2020 anti-Semitic accusations and COVID-19 origin story also make him a white nationalist. As someone who both started with the movement and authored the new demand, it is easy to see how his adjacent actions and beliefs raised suspicions about the original narrative. Indeed, one of the intelligence reports points out that since its founding, it was never just about the vaccine.[14]

The focus on who was responsible for sowing the discord opened up conceptual terrain that enabled the gap and the anxiety to be further exploited. Consider, for example, that the Nazi flag appeared at several rallies. Still, onlookers could not determine its meaning; it could mean that the people holding it identified with the Nazi regime and its ideals or that they were calling out the government for Nazi-like actions. The difference pivots on the intention of the speaker. Based on the listener's assumption of the flag's meaning, the horns could suddenly change, as well as the feeling and context of the entire protest, too. Added to this complicated interpretation process is that many listeners make this assumption separately and react accordingly.

This interpretation of Nazis became tangled with sensory data and rapidly changing conditions, which made it hard for listeners to adhere to who was driving the demand on the institution and thus to leverage an ethos to help provide context for interpretations; all the different sensations were polysemic. For those who saw the swastika as a sign of white supremacy, the image anchored an auditory landscape. For instance, one member of parliament, Ya'ara Sacks, heard it that way. The *Toronto Sun* reported that "'honk honk' is a 'dog whistle commonly used by neo-Nazis' that's essentially code for 'Heil Hitler,' [originating] from the 'right-wing side of the clown world movement,' with honk honk as the sound from a clown's nose."[15] Sacks explained that the honks, then, were meant as a new way to constitute a relationship between subject and government, organized around a new vision of white nationalism. Here the meaning of the immediate, immersive, and intense sound changed.

The shift in sensation amplified the signs and discourse of extremism and danger. The lack of any solid understanding of the protest and the lingering potential for violence created the conditions that undermined the force of the group's moral claim. The topoi of the debate shifted from the nature of their warrant to a discussion about the relationship of the effect and whose presence was being felt. For instance, much of the coverage became about constituting who was imposing on the everyday life of those in Canada. The government appeared justified in closing the conditions for discourse. The potential for a meta-debate about the government's activity was foreclosed because it seemed like a reasonable response, given the confusion. The result turned a claim for an unreasonable extension of state power into the total suspension of the ruler instead of a discourse about the COVID protocols. Here the debates moved the vector of danger from the virus to the crowd, and the truckers are seen as an intensifier threatening government rule.

The rapidly changing conditions on the ground ultimately made this an unsound tactic for the Freedom Convoy. For the truckers and the general public, when the definition of the agent making the demand could not be precisely understood, it undermined the entire process. The substance of the claim and the conditions of the deliberation changed. The truckers needed to adapt to these changes rapidly enough to avoid undermining their claim to the moral high ground, so their attempts at manipulating facets of their sound waveform went unheard through the noise. Although there was the potential to build support for some of the initial claims outlined in the above section, rendering one's intent audible is critical; it outlines who is speaking and the corresponding aesthetic. When there is confusion about who it might be, the listener cannot determine if they support the demand or even feel themselves as part of the sonic body.

The example of the Nazi flag at the Freedom Convoy protests illustrates a broader phenomenon in the context of the public screen: the dissembling and decontextualization of images and symbols. In this media landscape, even potent symbols like the swastika can become untethered from their historical meaning, leading to ambiguity and multiple interpretations. This ambiguity is not merely a matter of misunderstanding but a reflection of how the public screen fragments and recirculates information, often stripping it of crucial context. The inability to definitively interpret the intention behind the Nazi flag—whether it was a genuine expression of white supremacist solidarity or a provocative critique of government overreach—demonstrates how symbols can lose their fixed meanings in the swirling vortex of the public screen. This ambiguity then requires a normative force, a shared understanding or consensus, to hold the meaning together. Without this normative anchor, symbols and images become floating signifiers, open to wildly divergent interpretations that can drastically alter the perception of an entire movement or event.

Sound Demands

As we have seen, there is no universal sound definition but a constantly changing one. A rhetorical account of sound tactics recognizes that there is no universal audience on which to base a theory of sound; there are only contingent possibilities, situated within polyvalent histories. A tactic might not even register as something meaningful but just be heard as harsh noise. The purpose here is not to give a set of techniques that can be universally adapted but rather to provide a set of guides to think about how sound is used to change society. While culturally linked topoi can help bolster a movement, there are other times when the same event triggers divergent interpretations because agents and listeners have different cultural topoi.

This book is about what happens when a sound, as a noun, becomes understood as a process when sound is disseminated through the public screen soundly (adjective). We thought about what happens when you extend sound so that it can be divorced from its origin and infinitely repeated. For the potential of deliberation, I argued that it must satisfy three conditions: (1) the intent of the demand must be audible, (2) the substance must be a moral argument, and (3) the group must have exhausted the usual procedure. The soundness of the tactic is tied not to whether a demand is accepted or not but instead to the sort of communication environment that it designs. If the audience fully understands what is being demanded and from whom, it becomes easier for them to grapple with the underlying values, assumptions, and enthymemes that might underwrite a controversy.

The purpose of this book is a transdisciplinary exchange between sound studies and rhetoric to think about how sound can be used for resistance soundly. I have demonstrated in the previous chapters how immediacy, intensity, and immersion can help sound bodies manifest tactics to realize productive deliberations. The goal of sound tactics is not to develop a universalizable theory but to construct a practical account of how sound tactics might be used. I am interested in how real people might use these different tactics to hold those in power accountable. I drew from the discipline of speech, a history of cultivating speaking agents in public that foregrounds judgment and civic responsibility. At the most basic level, I have yet to start with a universalizable understanding of sound. The waveform provides a method for cultivating judgments at a level of abstraction that is just enough to give some insight into other potential cases in the future. It looks for some commonalities that come up across contexts. Still, it is not prescriptive, ultimately giving over to the agent's judgments to choose among the available means of persuasion.

Although the language comes from tech waveform, the ideas come from a core principle of nineteenth-century speech teachers that suggests that a conversation—public speaking—is a primary metaphor for social and civic life. In this framework, speech acts, such as making a demand, are a formative part of our interaction, exchanging ideas and structuring our social interactions. These different moves set expectations, distribute roles and responsibilities, and regulate the pace and flow of the exchange. This book focuses on one kind of speech act, demands, as a norming act that can set the expectations between an agent and an institution. Yet a waveform is different because the sound is separated from its source and infinitely repeated. Without visual cues, our interpretation of a tactic hinges heavily on the context of the conversation and our imaginative attributions, such as social media, television, and other forums.

Consequently, this larger discursive framework and cultural norms profoundly influence sound bodies. Adding the overlooked aspect akin to the "sonic body" in sound studies introduces another layer to this complex dynamic. The sonic body asserts the presence of an entity in the conversation without needing a physical, visible presence. It may occupy any place and time, giving it a panoptic power. These bodies can undertake duties and responsibilities, as well as confer them onto others. And, in real and pragmatic senses, they can distribute risks

CONCLUSION   139

differently among individuals. Yet this means we need to account for the sort of judgments that an audience may make about the constituted sound body.

Ultimately what makes a sound tactic sound is not whether the demands were met; although, of course, legislative wins are the goal of many social movements. But legislative wins are not indicative of a *sound* tactic. As we learned from the early speech teachers, argumentation is soundly based on the judgments made in a conversation. The idea is that the agent can make their intentions known and demonstrate both that they have met a process condition that satisfies the usual means and that the substance condition of right makes might. A good use would be one where it can satisfy the conditions as they are locally defined. But what about an unsound tactic? In those cases, how do particular decisions make it difficult for an audience to relate to the presence, create confusion, or raise questions of whether the conditions have been met?

As an adjective, the second meaning of sound raises concerns about how it can be used and taught—the secondary question of judgment. I reviewed several cases that questioned whether a tactic was sound and concluded that the audience's ability to hear it was crucial. A sound tactic, therefore, is one that not only addresses the immediate rhetorical situation but also lays the groundwork for ongoing dialogue and potential shifts in value hierarchies. It requires the rhetor to go beyond general principles and apply nuanced judgment to the specific context, considering not just the immediate persuasive impact but also the long-term implications for public discourse.

The magnitude of the risk taken by the agent making the demand determines the strength of the obligation imposed on both parties. In simpler terms, the bigger the norm violation, the more credible the demand, as the audience assumes the speaker wouldn't take such a risk without good reason. This creates a high-stakes situation that impacts reputations and emotions. The intense emotions give moral force to the demand, leading to discussions about values and what is right. The demand influences different value systems and drives discussions about actions to take.

In the example of the truckers in Canada, the difficulty in understanding a clear association between the cacophony and their plight created a strategic opening for others to step in and hijack the movement. When people are endowed with the capacity to make sense of sound, there must be communally accepted interpretations on which to base the claims. For the truckers, it became difficult for the public to understand exactly what they all gathered around, so it became easy for the message to be immersed in noise. As the different interpretations proliferated, it became hard for the public to know who made the claim. Thus, the movement lost its power. The shifting changes made it hard to know what they wanted, and thus the demand lost its potential power to compel an interlocutor. As a result, the ensuing debate had less to do with the current biopolitical rights regime and more with fears of grassroots extremism in Canada. But more than anything, the larger problem in the long term, the truckers, became a punch line and fodder.

We can see the contrast with the other cases examined in this book; Parkland, HU Resist, and the Casseroles all used elements of speech to deploy their sounds to send a message that their intended audience could hear and understand. In all the examples, the undetermined condition created a sound tactic attached to an unseen sound body (the social moment); the connection between the sonic body and their demands allowed them to retain the three conditions for advancing their objections and adjust as necessary to calibrate in response to the audience. Each chapter shows that when these two components stay connected, the result can shape the conversation around the values that underwrite the moral conflict. The goal of this transdisciplinary rhetorical analysis has always been the development of phronesis, or practical wisdom, that can help build a narrative to inform future actors in their fights for change. Each of these different case studies yields practical applications of how other groups used sound as a resource. What salient lessons are we left with as we identify how some groups made a demand that sparked a good conversation? Each chapter explains how sound tactics might take advantage of other resources for the invention to foment deliberations that could make things otherwise.

For the Parkland Kids, finding the moral high ground wasn't hard. Gun violence, especially in schools, had to stop. To move the discourse meaningfully, however, they needed a way to amplify their feelings and convey that sense of urgency to the rest of the country. They turned their definition of "right" into "might" using the cut-out technique to propel their voices to the masses. The cut-out comes from an affective structure of feeling grounded in a sudden drop. This helped shape their claim about the urgency of their argument to address gun violence. X González used this topos from music to convey what it felt like to experience the uncertainty of a school shooting. They used aesthetic tropes to achieve this immediacy effect; by modulating their pace and voice, they could build up and violate expectations to give a template of feeling.

A heavily advertised campaign, a well-funded march, headlining a movement, and a mass-mediated speech to amplify their voice worldwide all coalesced to give their moral message the might it needed. When they delivered their address, the commonality of the experience coupled with the massive media assemblage of being on the significant media network gave an apparent reason for the norm violation, making it easily understandable for their tactic. The viral speech and a memetic image provided shorthand templates to mobilize disparate listeners to their cause.

The March for Our Lives and their claim that parents violated their normative obligation to care for the youth pivoted on the number of murders the adults kept allowing with their lax gun laws. Something needed to happen immediately. González's cut-out was designed to put the audience in a place where they desired quick relief from the pain of unexpected silence. This feeling could not ever be put into words, but it is tied directly to the moral high ground the movement sought to occupy. The body of the Parkland Kid and the associated violence was in the living room of every American. This pain illustrated how seriously the parents failed in their obligation. The group reasoned that once people knew what it was like, then they might identify with the kids and realize that they needed to lead a new gun control movement.

In the example of HU Resist, the topoi came from disparate histories and created polysemic interpretations. An attempt to find the sound tactic that resonated with the cultural and political mindsets of the right audience was a big reason that HU Resist engaged in several different tactics along its sonic campaign around resisting white supremacy. As far as HU Resist was concerned, Howard University was violating its duty to care for Black students based on several concerns, the least of which involved its commitment to upholding white supremacist obligations. So, HU Resist wanted to pressure the administration to change its ways through an orchestrated campaign that drew attention to times when the administration made choices against the students' interests. They knew they were "right," but they needed the tactic to turn that conviction into "might."

The variety of HU Resist's efforts illustrates how many different sonic bodies can occupy space, feeling simultaneous. For many, the emergence of a Black tradition of resistance might be invisible. These still moved diachronic and synchronic temporalities. HU Resist traded on a network of Black student movements that did not reach the public screen but existed in the lower frequencies of podcasts and discussion among other historically Black institutions or less covered protests. For instance, the history of protest provided a critical keynote for HU Resist. But it also came up in the barbershop as a discussion of what was happening in other Black university spaces. The fact that, for many, their protest emerged and propagated through discourses of podcasts about Black radical thought is a prime example of acousmatic Blackness—or how Blackness bears at the *lower frequencies*. Here, different frequencies enabled HU Resist to express itself and propagate.

Sometimes topoi can come from a long cultural history that provides scaffolding to make sense of the present. In the context of the charivari, or rough music, there is a tradition of critique using a carnival atmosphere in response to misdeeds by someone with significantly more power. These provide examples of leaders failing to live up to their obligations to care for their people. Using culturally situated sound tactics can help advance the claim and give more power to the idea that the agent is "right." In the case of the Casseroles, the shift in the environment accompanying a callback to cultural sounds and actions was critical to the claim that it was okay to unseat people from power. When the citizens turned to charivari, they were evoking historical moments where the people gathered enough power to speak out against a government that failed to provide its obligatory care (like the events in Chile). But as time passed, Montreal provided its auditory context—its agora—as an emergent rhythm. Using sound tactics that link culturally embedded practices with the current environment offers topoi for the broader public and helps citizens interpret the nightly protests. The ultimate displays gave the diverse audience (some present but many not) a way to understand who made the sound and why it must mean something. It ascribes meaning and situates it within a larger narrative and story, helping to amplify the link between what's "right" and the tactics used to appeal to the government.

The Casseroles used charivari to claim that the state violated its foundational obligation to care for the needs of the citizens, which appeals to antecedent cultural mythologies about shaming the king. If the citizens felt their rights were being respected, they would not need to come out nightly to demonstrate loudly. Critical to its claim as a rising up of the people was that it enveloped the entire city to represent people everywhere, which served to both notify the leaders and tell fellow citizens that people were out. The recursive, growing back-and-forth of images, sounds, and discussions symbolized the increase in people participating. Here immersion—how large the protest spread—spoke directly to the breadth of the threat. Pots and pans rang against the entire city and grew nightly, underwriting the claim that it meant *everyone*, the people. The salience and ubiquity became a crucial part of their claim that if the government was serious about representing the people, they needed to redress the claim.

Throughout the other chapters, sound tactics illustrate how different topoi were deployed to render intent to persuade audibly. Each of these enabled the sonic body to be felt. The cut-out, improvisation, and charivari are all examples of different topoi that help create connections between speaker and audience to constitute structures of feeling and exert pressure to compel an institution to participate in the exchange. Each of these comes from patterns that audiences recognize and in which they fill in appropriate forms of emotion that help advance the tactics. Yet each operated in different ways that helped the unique groups amplify their message and structure the debates.

When groups constitute subjects to these institutions, they co-constitute with one another to conform to certain social norms or risk social sanction. These movements are reciprocal, and this expectation provides the force that enables the movement. I am interested in how sound expands and exists to change the tenure of the relationship. The goal is that a demand opens up the conversation for the transvaluation of values, potentially leading to policy changes and producing more discourse. Sound trades on a reciprocal relationship between the agent's idea that right makes might and the tools used to make that conviction heard. In other words, a moral high ground on its own may not be enough to capture an audience's attention, just as sound alone is not enough to effect a change in discourse. Working together, however, each amplifies the other.

The study of speech provides a way to make practical judgments about a tactic regarding how well it adhered to the conditions set forth throughout this book. It helps us situate and study the constrained choices and illuminate why and how a group like the truckers might not be able to generate any force. The speaker's shifting nature made the demand stoke concerns about the agent, derailing the conversation. Throughout each chapter of the book, I advance a theory of the market that anchored it in ordinary conversation. Making a demand leads to conflict as groups define themselves in opposition. It involves calling for an institution's attention and creating a subject, leading to a relationship where the gap between the agent and the institution influences the demands and obligates the recipient to comply.

Speech: Its History and Future

While we can ultimately give a template for how to design a demand for social movements, the best judgment of when the conditions are right is up to the agents. The idea that people needed to learn the judgment surrounding when to deploy different topoi under constraint became the foundation of a tradition of

US speech. In contrast to other perspectives, like English anchored in aesthetics, speakers stressed the relationship with the public. *Sound Tactics* brings various theories of sound studies together to advance an approach that brings us back to some of the underlying issues with speech analysis

As I have demonstrated, speech emerged in a historical conjuncture defined as a civic art. As public speaking became known as its own area of study, it became imbricated in a theory that replaced those of universal taste because it was an ordinary practice people used to navigate life. Even as there were segmented and increasingly distinct areas of knowledge in practical and working life, we sought to cultivate a judgment that could help navigate all competing contexts. The public became implicated in a democratic "conversation" to provide a way of knowing the speech rhetoric that underwrites a research agenda that helps with our duty toward developing phronesis. How we constitute this discipline offers another perspective on the transdisciplinary exchange and contextualizes new conversations. Combining new tools from different disciplines can give us a more robust and nuanced appreciation of an issue. Thus, it provides fodder for us to articulate fertile terrain for the further study of rhetoric grounded in speech. If this book promises to complicate a theory of rhetoric by replacing text with a waveform, then a return to address opens up even greater conceptual ground.

As I point out in the second chapter, in 1914, seventeen men formed the National Association of Academic Teachers of Public Speaking, which was significant because it was a national association. As rhetoric differentiated itself from English and composition (who claimed the term "rhetoric") and the elocutionists (who claimed the province of oral expression), speech teachers adopted a civic frame from the progressivists at the time. Drawing from the work of people like John Dewey, these teachers believed speech performed an essential democratic function that mediated the affairs of everyday life. It is these banal interactions that make up politics. We must move our understanding of politics outside the formal institutions of power, like the court, the church, or the legislator, and recognize how ordinary communication contexts provide important agency sites. As Keith explains, speech teachers advanced "a civic element in public speaking" by recognizing the "public" and celebrating "the democratic and populist aspects of American politics and life."[16] While these might feel like banal insights, they were revolutionary then.

While there might have been agreement on the centrality of the object, there were significant divisions early on regarding how to study it. The most famous division was between the Illinois school (people like Charles Woolbert), which championed "speech science," and the Cornell school, an idiom for a humanistic commitment to oratory.[17] Reading Woolbert's account of speech's founding and conception as a civic sonic space gives new purchase into the theoretical ground for Herbert Wichelns's oratorical criticism.[18] It is here amid new ways of knowing and speaking that we can identify terrain that can be instrumentalized and taught and made rich with resources. Research practice is guided toward practical judgment that can be implemented in the classroom. Several scholars point out that we should remember that these teachers' pedagogy was deeply intertwined with their scholarship. We should return to the earliest textbook as a paradigm case of an imagination that underwrites a place teeming with sonic civic potential.

The concept of a conversation underwrites the fundamental difference in composition between writing an essay and giving a public speech. A conversation is dynamic, transformative, and responds to a specific circumstance. Part of what happens is that speaking has its trajectory to address its audience in time. The critical book in the nascent discipline, *Public Speaking*, was written and published by James Albert Winans in 1915. Implicit in teaching public speaking was a vision of democratic order. This is in the tradition of the progressive philosophy of John Dewey and other pragmatists of the time. The frame of conversation underscored the idea that speech was an extension of ordinary conversation. It also understood the practical nature of conversation needed for navigating complex problems and how the immediate circumstance contains the potential for radical transformation. Although imperfect, it did convey a sense of the distribution of rules and responsibilities to prepare people for skills necessary in the public sphere.

While Winans was writing, the study of speech was important and timely; this work suffered the subsequent linguistic turn that over-determined the potential methods that could be used to make sense of this world. Like Winans's imagined audience of the democratic conversation, this discussion metaphor provides the scaffolding for how it might be able to progress and operate with different parties and groups moving forward. If we extend his understanding, we might consider how this project grew some of the initial insights around speech to move along the vectors of resistance. When we know this space only textually, it forecloses creative potential, shifting to the text form, force, and flow of the object of inquiry. If we understand technological development as providing new technology that changes our conversations, how might we think of the situated judgments of an evolving conversation? While we have had extended meditation on the nature of printing, something was lost when we didn't consider the public speaking classroom. Instead of thinking about the conversation as a circulation of letters, we begin thinking about the propagation of acousmatic objects.

Sound Tactics seeks to update our understanding of speech, situating it within the confines of acousmatics. It urges us to think about the propagation of acousmatic objects repeated along the public screen. The discipline of sound studies helps contribute to a robust discussion of a sound object and how it may move through different contexts. Through a rich grouping of interdisciplinary inputs from film, music, and sociology, the groups in these case studies thought about how sound might propagate on a public screen. Sound adds a temporal dimension to the public screen, emplacing it within a theater, where people might hear time's progression. This creates the tactic spaces for others to resist and exploit power differences. The opening up of dimensionality accompanies understanding the physical place where public speech happens. Sounds come from somewhere in the public; we use public categories to make sense of them.

Our theoretical imaginary is enriched in this transdisciplinary space if we reconsider how public speech occurs. If we consider it a public sensorium, this project extends some of the initial insights from sound studies to think about how speech can move along the vectors of resistance. The metaphors that come with the reproduction of sound and its removal from the source provide a contingent way to make sense of a massively disseminated moment. Here the sound is understood as an object that separates the head from the signal. When you might not know an object's origin but are forced to ascribe its meaning, sound opens up vast vistas for invention. These are not abstracted; instead, they are a set of vectors that help underwrite what might feel right. *Sound Tactics* thinks about what rhetoric might feel like in an intense, immediate, and immersive world that extends around the public screen. Each of these, I have argued, provides a unique site to advance a claim.

This metaphor gives us a language to start thinking about the speaker and the speech. The sonic body provides a way to think about collective agency, a resonant body not considered an abstract entity, which these agencies certainly can be. There exists a transcendental presence that can be felt. The Parkland Kids were immediately supposed, HU Resist ebbed and flowed, and the Casseroles' company persisted. For the truckers, the disruption around the nature of the body (and the corresponding danger) proved disastrous. When we separate the signal from the source, we apprehend a presence in transcendental spaces. The relationship between the perception of the speech and the body raises fascinating questions about how there might be different frequencies for other kinds of tactics, how an audience may perceive sonic bodies, and how a lecture presents essential questions for us to consider in the future of speech.

As I delve into the intricacies of sound bodies, I find myself revisiting the foundational principles laid out by the speech teachers, where the concept of a demand manifests quite profoundly. The beauty of this concept lies in its anchoring of moral arguments within the institution's sphere of legitimacy. When we examine how different agents utilize sound to shape the context and constitute the subject of address, it becomes apparent how these conditions pave the way for moral disagreements. Take, for instance, the case of the Parkland Kids. They leveraged the protective ethics that adults should bestow on children as the foundation for their demand for change. When the adults failed to uphold this duty, it sparked a moral urgency for transformation. The HU Resist case presents another intriguing perspective, showing how varying interpellations contour the substance of the argument. Terms like "hecklers," "nonviolent protesters," and "students" shift the agential institutions that define collective roles and responsibilities.

This dynamic interplay among agent, sound, and demand offers a fresh perspective on how we perceive and build relationships and intimacies. Even when we think of the most abstract institutions like corporations, they can cultivate relations of intimacy. While the political is intertwined with the moral, this observation carries crucial implications as we navigate contemporary debates and deliberations. However, the discourse doesn't end here. To broaden our perspective, we must acknowledge that the fabric of argument and deliberation is woven from diverse threads. While my exploration has mainly focused on moral arguments, such as the appealing cultural touchstones that resonate within a community, there's much more to consider. Immediacy, immersion, and intensity play pivotal roles in shaping the perception of agents operating within this auditory landscape. If we open the doors of rhetoric farther, we can imagine how facts might be reconfigured within this soundscape.

Suppose we return to the start of our story. In that case, the truckers bring out the tension when multiple epistemologies compete for prominence in ways that might represent an agora where there are clashes of values and different perspectives on what constitutes the good. Our problem is not to turn sound, as a kind of episteme, into a way of mediating the vastly different types of knowledge at play in the controversy unfolding in Canada (this would be the sonic episteme that Robin James warned us about). Instead, our goal is to consider how sound informed the practice of demand and how sound itself may reconfigure the local normative terrain and open up space for contestation. Different sounds render intelligible the presence of a kind of entity wanting rights and contesting ways of knowing the responsibilities associated with liberal governance. Who, what, and when were all thrown up for debate as a physical presence enacted its force and drew the appropriate governance limits into relief. This approach aligns with the early twentieth-century shift in speech studies toward understanding public speaking as a civic art and a form of democratic conversation. Just as the early speech teachers recognized the importance of the public sphere and everyday interactions in shaping political discourse, the acousmatic view acknowledges that in our current media environment, sounds (including speeches, protests, and other forms of public address) often circulate independently of their original contexts.

Sound, as both a physical presence and a tactic, has the potential to open new avenues of conversational ground for advocates in diverse social realms. Harnessing sound's immediacy, intensity, and immersive qualities to advance a position is almost a requirement now in an age where signal and source are so frequently separated. Returning to the fundamental idea of speech as a community act—a method of engaging in the everyday—we can see that sound holds the potential for agents to engage their audiences more directly and entirely than text alone. Speakers and advocates who want to harness the power of sound in advancing their claims should begin noticing its impact in the demonstrations and movements around us. As we continue to a more digital world, sound becomes more ubiquitous. Through studying the sound tactics used in everyday discourse, agents can develop new phronesis around sound and its immense power.

Notes

Introduction

1. Serafis, Kitis, and Archakis, "Graffiti Slogans," 779.
2. Serafis, Kitis, and Archakis, "Graffiti Slogans," 786.
3. Topintzi and Versace, "Linguistic Analysis," 236.
4. Chakrabortty, "Athens Protests."
5. Certeau, *Practice of Everyday Life*, xix.
6. Certeau, *Practice of Everyday Life*, xix.
7. DeNora, *Music in Everyday Life*, 53.
8. DeNora, *Music in Everyday Life*, 111.
9. DeNora, *Music in Everyday Life*, 121–22.
10. DeNora, *Music in Everyday Life*, 122.
11. Gunn, "On Recording Performance."
12. Gunn, "On Recording Performance," 6.
13. Validity (mainly formal) assumes a standard with a troubling, ahistorical logic. When we appeal to universal logic, we privilege some groups over others. Who gets to determine what is valid often reflects the logic of the ruling classes.
14. For more, see Eemeren and Grootendorst, *Systematic Theory*.
15. I am of course talking about the European models such as Pragma-Dialectics.
16. See Jacobs, "Rhetoric and Dialectic"; Jacobs, "Nonfallacious Rhetorical Strategies"; Kauffeld, "Presumptions and the Distribution"; Goodwin, "Comments"; Goodwin and Innocenti, "Pragmatic Force"; Goodwin, "Should Climate Scientists Fly?"; Jackson and Jacobs, "Structure of Conversational Argument."
17. This is a loose school of thought called "normative pragmatics," which can be grouped by a loose set of principles that are in the process of being elaborated. Such a perspective locates the ordinary object of argumentation starting from the social act of speaking and theorizes up. This could be seen as participating in that conversation here. Also read Goodwin, "Argument Has No Function"; Kauffeld, "Presumptions and the Distribution"; Jackson, "Reason-Giving"; and Innocenti, "Normative Pragmatic Model."
18. Goodwin, "Conception of Speech Acts," 82–83.
19. Goodwin, "Conception of Speech Acts," 82–83.
20. Beth Innocenti has done much work in the normative pragmatic tradition theorizing the demand and presentational force. In addition to what I will cite, please see Innocenti (Manolescu), "Norms of Presentational Force"; Innocenti, "Countering Questionable Tactics"; and Innocenti, "Demanding a Halt."
21. The hypothetical example of a worker requesting versus demanding time off work from a boss illustrates the point. When a worker requests maternity leave through the appropriate channels, it recognizes a boss's prerogative to deny or accept the request. If a worker is making a demand, it suggests that the normal channels are unfair (perhaps maternity leave is only three weeks) and challenges the boss's capacity to make the right decision. The charged nature of this interaction constrains the decisions available to both the worker and the audience. For

the hypothetical worker, the morally correct side is the idea that a family should be paid to be home with a newborn for at least six weeks. The side making the demands believes they will be vindicated because they are on the right side of history. But the nature of the moral claim itself can be polarizing and result in controversy. This particular culture does not value the life of the worker; for example, some might believe in the values of a right-to-work state. This mentality might suggest that workers should allow employers to compete with one another to give more attractive contractor terms. Such a position might place the employee who demands leave as "entitled."

22. Of course, these two issues are blunt instruments, and if you try hard enough to differentiate the two, they fold into each other because a procedure is a substance. An order of something represents a principle of something. But maintaining some separation between the two opens up terrain for a conversation, demonstrating how a demand operates to draw speaker and institution into relation and impose and distribute duties and obligations on both.

23. Innocenti and Kathol, "Persuasive Force," 62.

24. The term *citizenship* will appear throughout this text. Sometimes it means being included as a member of a community; other times, it delineates the meeting of perlocutionary conditions for other rights and duties.

Chapter 1

1. In the early 2000s, Michael Leff, William O. Keith, and Steven Mailloux debated in the Rhetoric Society of America's journal, discussing whether rhetoric should have a porous, ubiquitous understanding or be framed through specific disciplinary histories, focusing on the practical pros and cons of globalizing rhetoric. See Keith, "Identity, Rhetoric and Myth"; Leff, "Rhetorical Disciplines"; Mailloux, "Disciplinary Identities."

2. For instance, Robin James points out how much of new materialism (from people like Karen Barad, Jane Bennett, and Elizabeth Groz) comes from speculations about music that naturalizes the entire music industry (from the studio to listening practices). But music cannot be assumed to be "matter in the wild" because each genre has its history.

3. James, *Sonic Episteme*, 21.

4. Burke, *Rhetoric of Motives*, 22.

5. Burke, *Rhetoric of Motives*, 22–23.

6. Sterne, "Sonic Imaginations."

7. Byron Hawk's recent exploration positions sound as a "quasi-object"—an emergent, constantly changing event shaped by material relations and encounters. This move, coming from composition studies, has been collectively known as "sonic rhetoric." Hawk, *Resounding the Rhetorical*.

8. The famous story of the arrival of acousmatics, like many other "arrival on the academic scene" narratives, is notably only top of mind thanks to the history of systematically crediting men for contributions that were not born in a vacuum but appeared to spring into existence due to a cultural preference for their esteemed academic standing.

9. Schaeffer, "Acousmatics," 77.

10. Schaeffer, "Acousmatics," 77.

11. Schaeffer, "Acousmatics," 77.

12. Kane, *Sound Unseen*, 52.

13. Schaeffer, "Acousmatics," 77.

14. For example, we might even look at a speaker and think that we know the voice comes from that speaker. But where in that speaker did the voice come from? Where is the source?

Is it their brain? What is the source of their thoughts? But, as Friedrich Nietzsche reminds us, "The 'inner world' is full of phantoms . . . : [T]he will is one of them. The choice no longer moves anything; hence, it does not explain anything either—it merely accompanies events." For more, see Nietzsche, *Twight of the Idols*.

15. Ultimately, Pierre Schaeffer's chart of sound objects has a few problems. Michel Chion notes that Schaeffer had two biases: First, since the language and ear he used while composing the chart reflect his sensibilities, it produced neat forms that reflected musical form. After all, he was trying to make a symphony and build units that could be composed for music. He often had elegant objects and did not create space for things that might exist outside the Western musical canon. Second, the naturalistic assumption of only a couple seconds on the tape recorder constituted his domain of study and thus delimited his forms in time. A third problem, flagged by Brian Kane, is that Schaeffer naturalizes technology when the kind of auditory technology making the audio should not matter; he misses how there might be different force qualities of sound.

16. Chion, *Audio-Vision*, 90.

17. Kane, *Sound Unseen*, 9.

18. As explored in Nicholas S. Paliewicz's work on corporate personhood (*Extraction Politics*), entities without physical form can exert significant influence through legal and market strategies. Similarly, sound bodies possess a metaphysical power that can impact sovereignty and market dynamics. In my article "Belarus's Sound Body," I argue that these unseen presences shape our understanding of authority and control in ways that parallel corporate influence. The ability of sound bodies to affect sovereign power via markets demonstrates their profound, yet often overlooked, role in shaping our societal framework. This intersection of sonic presence, political sovereignty, and market forces reveals new dimensions in how we conceptualize and experience power structures in contemporary society.

19. Dyson, *Sounding New Media*, 9.

20. Edgar, *Culturally Speaking*.

21. Winans, *Public Speaking*, 188.

22. Winans's 1914 keynote quoted in Keith, *Democracy as Discussion*, 250.

23. Winans, *Public Speaking*, xi.

24. Schudson, "Why Conversation."

25. Winans, *Public Speaking*, 22.

26. As contrasted with James Winans, who thinks of the conversation as a dynamic system of speech and feedback, Michael Schudson argues that conversation is polite nothing, and in the public sphere if we are not debating, then we have failed. Schudson assumes that conversation stands in for a *kind of interaction* rather than the notion of interaction itself. A more complex and nuanced definition of conversation is taken up in this book, but the critique is noteworthy. Schudson, "Why Conversation."

27. Winans, *Public Speaking*, 31.

28. Keith, *Democracy as Discussion*.

29. Winans quoted in Keith, *Democracy as Discussion*, 22.

30. Winans quoted in Keith, *Democracy as Discussion*, 22.

31. Keith, *Democracy as Discussion*.

32. Keith, "Identity, Rhetoric and Myth," 99–100.

33. Winans, *Public Speaking*, 21.

34. Woolbert, "Teaching of Speech," 1.

35. Keith, *Democracy as Discussion*, 49.

36. Woolbert, "Organization of Departments," 65.

37. Woolbert, "Organization of Departments," 67.

38. Keith, *Democracy as Discussion*, 96.
39. Keith, "We Are the Speech Teachers," 241.
40. Wichelns, "Literary Criticism of Oratory," 2.
41. I see this as a move that eventually takes people from outside formal institutions, like voting, into the everyday acts that people use to engage questions of power, sovereignty, and so on. Rob Asen outlines a discourse theory of citizenship in "Discourse Theory."
42. Wichelns, "Literary Criticism of Oratory," 2.
43. Wichelns, "Literary Criticism of Oratory," 2.
44. Wichelns, "Literary Criticism of Oratory," 2.
45. Gunn and Rice, "About Face"; emphasis added.
46. Philipsen, "Paying Lip Service."
47. Philipsen, "Paying Lip Service," 52.
48. Gunn and Dance, "Silencing of Speech."
49. Eadie, "Stories We Tell," 169.
50. Redding, "Extrinsic and Intrinsic," 102.
51. Redding, "Extrinsic and Intrinsic," 102.
52. Joshua Gunn draws a similar conclusion in his essay "On Speech and Public Release."
53. Medhurst, "Public Address," 35.
54. Leff and Sachs, "Words the Most Like Things," 255.
55. Leff, "Things Made by Words," 298.
56. Leff and Kauffeld, "Preface," ix.
57. Leff and Kauffeld, "Preface," ix.
58. Enck-Wanzer, "Trashing the System," 185; emphasis added.
59. Brian Kane has done extensive work on the relationship between acoustics and the phenomenological reduction and bracket.
60. DeNora, *Music in Everyday Life*, 53.

Chapter 2

1. Harris, "Media's Week-Long Attention Span."
2. Ihde, *Listening and Voice*, 85.
3. Chion, *Sound*, 33.
4. Chion, *Audio-Vision*, 19.
5. Chion, *Sound*, 36.
6. Chion, *Sound*, 37.
7. Segarra et al., "Sheriff's Office."
8. Eckstein, "(Parkland) Kids."
9. Witt, "How the Survivors of Parkland."
10. Eckstein, "Sensing School Schoolings."
11. Miller and Kudacki, "On the Ground."
12. Oppenheim, "Emma González."
13. Witt, "Urgency and Frustration."
14. Miller and Kudacki, "On the Ground."
15. Miller and Kudacki, "On the Ground."
16. Miller and Kudacki, "On the Ground."
17. Witt, "Urgency and Frustration."
18. Liebelson and Wing, "Behind Millions of Dollars."
19. Pullum, "Social Movement Theory."

20. Stuart, "Gun Control."
21. Georgantopoulos and Sacks, "Parkland Teens."
22. "March for Our Lives Highlights."
23. "March for Our Lives Highlights."
24. Quoted in Witt, "March for Our Lives Presents."
25. Weismann, "Emma González."
26. Garber, "Powerful Silence."
27. Simón, "Emma González Going Silent."
28. Jamieson, "Emma González Stood."
29. Tognotti, "Emma González's Powerful Words."
30. Sathish-Van Atta, "This One Moment."
31. Berman, "Loudest Silence."
32. Berman, "Loudest Silence."
33. Lopez, "Watch: Emma González's Incredible Moment."
34. Amatulli, "Emma González Stands."
35. Menza, "Emma González Explained."
36. Bowden, "Parkland Student."
37. Garber, "Powerful Silence."
38. Weismann, "Emma González."
39. Lopez, "Watch: Emma González's Incredible Moment."
40. Jamieson, "Emma González Stood."
41. Berman, "Loudest Silence."
42. Kember and Zylinska, *Life After New Media*, 84.
43. West, "Lean In Collection," 433.
44. West, "Lean In Collection."
45. West, "Lean In Collection," 431.
46. Miranda, "Recent Mass Shootings."
47. Harris, "Year the Gun Conversation Changed"; Watts, "2018 Was the Year."
48. Pane, "Parkland Attack."
49. Colias-Pete, "One Year After Parkland."
50. Thunberg, "Remarks at United Nations."
51. Aronoff, "How Greta Thunberg's."
52. Jarvie, "Girl Thrown from Desk."

Chapter 3

1. McIlvenny, "Heckling in Hyde Park," 32.
2. McIlvenny, "Heckling in Hyde Park," 33.
3. One key example is the number of violent audiovisual images confronting the culture. Images are removed from their context all the time, allowing for context collapse and making it more challenging to exercise sound judgment. In a video, a shooting can look like self-defense or intentional first-degree murder depending on the context ascribed to the fragment.
4. Daughtry, *Listening to War*, 200.
5. Daughtry, *Listening to War*, 187.
6. Schweitzer, "As Howard University Turns 150."
7. "HU Resists Shuts Down Comey," episode 1 of *Millennials Are Killing Capitalism* (podcast), October 4, 2017, https://millennialsarekillingcapitalism.libsyn.com/episode-1-hu-resist-shuts-down-comey.

8. "HU Resists Shuts Down Comey."
9. HU Resist (@HUResist), Twitter, February 12, 2017, https://pbs.twimg.com/media/C4g_itRW8AE2G6r.jpg.
10. HU Resist (@HUResist), Twitter, February 15, 2017, https://twitter.com/HUResist/status/831872211728334848?s=20.
11. Concerned Students HU, Periscope Post (no longer available). See "HU Resists Shuts Down Comey."
12. Devyn Springer, *Off Tha Record* (blog), https://www.patreon.com/posts/huresist-shuts-14803363.
13. Steele, "Digital Barbershop," 1.
14. Jarrett and Maake, "Former FBI Director Spoke."
15. Abdul-Alim, "Howard University Appoints Comey."
16. For his work fighting civil rights, Kwame Ture was to be awarded the senior class humanity award. Yet Howard divulged sensitive information to a government organization, the FBI. HU Resist posted an image of a Howard document demonstrating the linkages between Howard, Ture, and the FBI.
17. Sanger, "Functions of Freedom."
18. Powell, "Protest Chants."
19. Steinskog, *Afrofuturism and Black Sound*, 11.
20. For a longer list, see Keith and Whittenberger-Keith, "Conversational Call"; and Boone, "When the 'Amen Corner.'"
21. Sanger, "Slave Resistance."
22. Brown, "Protesters Silence."
23. Brown, "Protesters Silence."
24. "Comey Listens."
25. Brown, "Protesters Silence."
26. Brown, "Protesters Silence."
27. Roll, "Rejecting a Speaker."
28. Hudson, "Controversial Speakers."
29. Hudson, "Controversial Speakers."
30. Horley, "Rethinking the Heckler's Veto."
31. Greenberg, "Rejecting the 'Heckler's Veto.'"
32. Greenberg, "Rejecting the 'Heckler's Veto.'"
33. Meads, "Howard University Students."
34. Goldman, "James Comey Is Interrupted."
35. Nzanga, "Protesters Jeer."
36. Jarrett and Maake, "Former FBI Director Spoke."
37. Kurtz, "Campus Free-Speech Crisis."
38. Turley, "Protesters Disrupt Comey Speech."
39. Roll, "Rejecting a Speaker."
40. Chamseddine, "#HUResist Is Anti-Racist."
41. Stoever, *Sonic Color Line*.
42. Stoever, *Sonic Color Line*, 13.
43. Steele, "Digital Barbershop," 43.
44. Steele, "Digital Barbershop."
45. Weheliye, *Phonographies*, 19.
46. For example, in the *Sonic Episteme*, Robin James talks about how some Rihanna music exists "in the red," a place for the Black body to exist, but it is often considered excess.
47. Steele, "Digital Barbershop," 18.

48. Chamseddine, "#HUResist Is Anti-Racist."
49. Chamseddine, "#HUResist Is Anti-Racist."
50. HU Resist, *Medium* (blog), https://medium.com/@HUResist?p=e4dbdb6fff65.
51. Veritas 1867, "President Frederick."
52. HU Resist (@HUResist), Twitter, March 28, 2018, https://twitter.com/HUResist/status/979029614952681473.
53. Philip Lewis (@Phil_Lewis_), Twitter, March 29, 2018, https://twitter.com/Phil_Lewis_/status/979456564221399042.
54. St. Felix, "Prosperity Gospel."
55. Reilly, "Howard Students Take Over"; Hanna, Kelly, and Brocchetto, "Protesting Howard University Students."
56. Clemens, "'This Building Is Closed.'"
57. Harris, "How the Howard University Protests"; Kerr, "Howard U. Sit-In."
58. Jared Ware, in my interview with him on September 17, 2021, made a compelling argument that we must consider race, too. He argues that the optics of a Black president calling the police on a Black student body might also have been a factor.
59. Heim, "Echoes of the Past."
60. CNN Wire, "Howard University Students' Win."
61. Heim, "Echoes of the Past."
62. Vera, "9-Day Sit-In."
63. Fischlin, Heble, and Lipsitz, *Fierce Urgency*, xii.
64. From my extensive interview with Jared Ware on September 17, 2021, some might speculate that underwriting the dissipation is an administration slowly cracking down on the protesters, the eventual onset of COVID, or perhaps some combination of these factors.
65. Ware, "Community, Joy and Understanding Power Lessons."
66. HU Resist propagated in the barbershop. In his podcast, Jared Ware tells the stories of ordinary people in the long, important history of Black activists on college campuses, playing an important role in securing the public memory around HU Resist. Ware interviewed HU Resist twice, covering the year 2018 as an opportunity to reflect on what #studentpower was able to accomplish. While most of the public might have been aware of HU Resist as they flickered across the public screen, Ware was interviewing the members of the organization, providing on-the-ground details of what was happening at Howard, not reducing it to the bits on the public screen. But his podcast provides the kind of performative, narrativizing, and humanizing heroes required, as well as a granularity to and memory of the event that help us understand the contingent circumstances that gave rise to their project. As an important vector for propagating these stories and ensuring they can keep going, the podcast operates as a kind of oral history of the movement and provides networks to inspire future movements.
67. Steinskog, *Afrofuturism and Black Sound*, 6.

Chapter 4

A version of this chapter was previously published as Justin Eckstein, "Designing Soundscapes for Argumentation," *Philosophy and Rhetoric* 51, no. 3 (2018): 269–92, https://doi.org/10.5325/philrhet.51.3.0269.

1. McGee, "People," 12.
2. The combination of the acoustic configurations of the material conditions and the different vibrating matter moving through space gives each place a unique sound.
3. Feld, "Places Sensed, Senses Placed," 184.

4. Feld, "Acoustemology," 16.
5. Feld, "Acoustemology," 16.
6. Feld, "Places Sensed, Senses Placed," 187.
7. Feld, "Places Sensed, Senses Placed," 187–88.
8. Feld, "Places Sensed, Senses Placed," 187.
9. Raynauld, Lalancette, and Tourigny-Koné, "Political Protest 2.0."
10. Jones, "Quebec Law."
11. Jones, "Quebec Law."
12. Marshall, "Quebec Steps Closer."
13. Massumi, "Buying Out."
14. McGee, "In Search," 238.
15. Sterne, "Groove We Can Move To," 61.
16. Sterne, "Groove We Can Move To," 61.
17. Sterne, "Groove We Can Move To," 61.
18. Hallward, "Student Mobilization."
19. Masis, "Quebec Bangs."
20. Walsham, "Rough Music," 247.
21. Walsham, "Rough Music," 243.
22. In my interview with Jonathan Sterne, he noted the viral nature of the article, how often it was shared, and how popular it became.
23. Sterne and Davis, "Quebec's *Manifs*."
24. Wyatt, "Student Protests."
25. Rosen, "Multigenerational Casserole Orchestras," para. 6–7.
26. Sterne, "Bodies-Streets," para. 4.
27. Stolow, "Revolution on the Corner."
28. Rosen, "Multigenerational Casserole Orchestras," para. 1.
29. Rentschler, "On s'en câlisse."
30. Stolow, "Revolution on the Corner," para. 2.
31. Augoyard and Torgue, *Sonic Experience*, 130.
32. Raynauld, Lalancette, and Tourigny-Koné, "Rethinking Digital Activism," 46.
33. Raynauld, Lalancette, and Tourigny-Koné, "Rethinking Digital Activism," 46.
34. Lalancette and Raynauld, "Under-the-Hood Look."
35. Lalancette and Raynauld, "Under-the-Hood Look."
36. Lalancette and Raynauld, "Under-the-Hood Look."
37. Facebook translation of "Resistez! Exigez des élections! Défoulez-vous! Faites-vous entendre par le son de vos chaudrons!" May 31, 2012, https://www.facebook.com/events/384615538257665/?active_tab=discussion.
38. Facebook translation of "Venez faire un prit tour à Pointe-claire. C'est loin mais ça en vaut la peine. Premièrement c'est un beau coin, deuxièmement . . . on dérange pas mal et les gens questionnent beaucoup. Souvent, ils ne sont pas même au courant de l'actualité au sujet des casseroles, de la loi 78 et du conflit étudiant. . . . Aussi, il faut montrer qu'il n'y a pas que des libéraux dans l'ouest de l'Ile. Cling clang cloc kling." May 30, 2012, https://www.facebook.com/events/384615538257665/?active_tab=discussion.
39. Facebook translation of "Je cherche un tract déjà fait d'un côté invitation et de l'autre explication du pourquoi. . . . Je veux l'imprimer demain mercredi pour en passer dans mon coin de pays (Bas-Saint-Laurent) Je remarque que les convaincu le sont et les autres ont besoin d'informations . . . y'm'semble que j'en vu passer une affiche ou un tract??? MERCI." 2018, https://www.facebook.com/events/384615538257665/?active_tab=discussion.

40. Quebec has a particular issue with the hijab (for instance, after the protests, there were issues with bans on religious clothing); see Maimona, "Quebec's Ban."
41. "Manifestation de casseroles, 27 mai 2012, St-Denis/Villeray, Montréal," *Un Vent Du Nord* (blog), http://unventdunord.blogspot.com/2012/06/manifestation-de-casseroles-27-mai-2012.html.
42. Rentschler, "On s'en câlisse."
43. "Quebec Student Associations."
44. Sterne, "Groove We Can Move To," 62.
45. "Police Swiftly."
46. Mehreen and Gray-Donald, "Spring 2015."

Conclusion

1. "COVID-19 Pandemic Deaths."
2. Schisler, "Unvaccinated Truckers."
3. Schisler, "Unvaccinated Truckers."
4. Murphy, "Freedom Convoy."
5. Meissner, "Video: Crowd of Supporters."
6. Hwang, "Vulnerable Downtown Residents."
7. Hwang, "Vulnerable Downtown Residents."
8. Tasker, "Thousands Opposed."
9. Kay, "Ottawa Trucker Protest."
10. Tasker, "Thousands Opposed."
11. Kay, "Canada's Truck Convoy."
12. Parent, "'We're Not Lawyers.'"
13. Kay, "Ottawa Trucker Protest."
14. Parkhill, "Who Is Who?"
15. "Toronto MP."
16. Keith, "On the Origins of Speech," 241.
17. Benson, "Cornell School."
18. Benson, "Cornell School."

Bibliography

Abdul-Alim, Jamaal. "Howard University Appoints Comey to Endowed Chair." *Diverse*, August 23, 2017. https://www.diverseeducation.com/leadership-policy/article/15101139/howard-university-appoints-comey-to-endowed-chair.

Amatulli, Jenna. "Emma González Stands on Stage in Total Silence to Remember Parkland Shooting." *Huffington Post*, March 24, 2018. https://www.huffpost.com/entry/emma-gonzalez-spends-6-minutes-20-seconds-in-silence-to-remember-shooting_n_5ab69b82e4b0decad04a7a32.

Aronoff, Kate. "How Greta Thunberg's Lone Strike Against Climate Change Became a Global Movement." *Rolling Stone*, March 5, 2019. https://www.rollingstone.com/politics/politics-features/greta-thunberg-fridays-for-future-climate-change-800675/.

Asen, Robert. "A Discourse Theory of Citizenship." *Quarterly Journal of Speech* 90, no. 2 (2004): 189–211.

Augoyard, Jean Francois, and Henry Torgue. *Sonic Experience: A Guide to Everyday Sounds*. Montreal: McGill University Press, 2009.

Benson, Thomas W. "The Cornell School of Rhetoric: Idiom and Institution." *Communication Quarterly* 51, no. 1 (2003): 1–56.

Berman, Ari. "Emma González Is Responsible for the Loudest Silence in the History of US Social Protest." *Mother Jones*, March 24, 2018. https://www.motherjones.com/politics/2018/03/emma-gonzalez-is-responsible-for-the-loudest-silence-in-the-history-of-us-social-protest/.

Boone, Patrice R. "When the 'Amen Corner' Comes to Class: An Examination of the Pedagogical and Cultural Impact of Call–Response Communication in the Black College Classroom." *Communication Education* 52, nos. 3–4 (2003): 212–29.

Bouie, Jamelle. "Show the Carnage." *Slate*, February 15, 2018. https://slate.com/news-and-politics/2018/02/its-time-to-show-the-carnage-of-mass-shootings.html.

Bowden, John. "Parkland Student Holds Six Minutes of Silence for Slain Classmates." *The Hill*, March 24, 2018. https://thehill.com/blogs/blog-briefing-room/news/380108-parkland-student-holds-six-minutes-of-silence-for-slain.

Brown, A. B. "Protesters Silence James Comey at Howard University." *Hilltop Online*, February 28, 2017. https://thehilltoponline.com/2017/09/28/protesters-silence-james-comey-at-howard-university/.

Burke, Kenneth. *A Rhetoric of Motives*. Berkeley: University of California Press, 1969.

Certeau, Michel de. *The Practice of Everyday Life*. Vol. 1. Translated by Steven Rendall. Berkeley: University of California Press, 1984.

Chakrabortty, Aditya. "Athens Protests: Syntagma Square on Frontline of European Austerity Protests." *The Guardian*, June 19, 2011. https://www.theguardian.com/world/2011/jun/19/athens-protests-syntagma-austerity-protests.

Chamseddine, Roqayah. "#HUResist Is Anti-Racist Student Activism That Goes Beyond Trump." Shadowproof.com, November 27, 2017. https://shadowproof.com/2017/11/27/huresist-anti-racist-student-activism-goes-beyond-trump/.

BIBLIOGRAPHY

Chion, Michel. *Audio-Vision: Sound on Screen*. 2nd ed. New York: Columbia University Press, 2019.

———. *Sound: An Acoulogical Treatise*. Durham, NC: Duke University Press, 2016.

Clemens, Danny. "'This Building Is Closed': Howard U Students Take Over Admin Building Amid Financial Scandal." ABC News, March 31, 2018. https://abc7ny.com/howard-university-wayne-frederick-tyrone-hankerson-financial-aid/3286794/.

CNN Wire. "Howard University Students' Win with a Deal on Demands Continues Legacy of Protests." wreg.com, April 7, 2018. https://www.wreg.com/news/howard-university-students-win-with-deal-on-demands-continues-legacy-of-protests/.

Colias-Pete, Meredith. "One Year After Parkland, Crown Point Student Says the Need for Change Continues: 'It Doesn't Mean That You Stop.'" *Chicago Tribune*, February 13, 2019. https://www.chicagotribune.com/suburbs/post-tribune/ct-ptb-guns-students-parkland-anniversary-st-20190208-story.html.

"Comey Listens, Responds as Howard U. Protesters Drown out Speech." Video. NBC News, September 22, 2017. https://www.nbcnews.com/video/comey-interrupted-by-protesters-at-howard-university-convocation-1052721219751.

"COVID-19 Pandemic Deaths." Wikipedia. https://en.wikipedia.org/wiki/COVID-19_pandemic_deaths#2021._2nd_half.

Daughtry, J. Martin. *Listening to War: Sound, Music, Trauma, and Survival in Wartime Iraq*. Oxford: Oxford University Press, 2015.

DeNora, Tia. *Music in Everyday Life*. Cambridge: Cambridge University Press, 2000.

Dyson, Frances. *Sounding New Media: Immersion and Embodiment in the Arts and Culture*. Berkeley: University of California Press, 2009.

Eadie, William F. "Stories We Tell: Fragmentation and Convergence in Communication Disciplinary History." *Review of Communication* 11, no. 3 (2011): 116–76.

Eckstein, Justin. "Belarus's Sound Body." *Philosophies* 9, no. 5 (2024): 141. https://doi.org/10.3390/philosophies9050141.

———. "The (Parkland) Kids Are Alright." *Communication and the Public* 5, nos. 1–2 (2020): 26–34.

———. "Sensing School Shootings." *Critical Studies in Media Communication* 37, no. 2 (2020): 161–73.

Eckstein, Justin, and Sarah Partlow Lefevre. "Since Sandy Hook: Strategic Maneuvering in the Gun Control Debate." *Western Journal of Communication* 81, no. 2 (2017): 225–42.

Edgar, Amanda Nell. *Culturally Speaking: The Rhetoric of Voice and Identity in a Mediated Culture*. Columbus: Ohio State University Press, 2019.

Eemeren, Frans H. van, and Rob Grootendorst. *A Systematic Theory of Argumentation: The Pragma-Dialectical Approach*. Cambridge: Cambridge University Press, 2004.

Enck-Wanzer, Darrel. "Trashing the System: Social Movement, Intersectional Rhetoric, and Collective Agency in the Young Lords Organization's Garbage Offensive." *Quarterly Journal of Speech* 92, no. 2 (2006): 174–201.

Feld, Steven. "Acoustemology." In *Keywords in Sound*, edited by David Novak and Matt Sakakeeny, 12–21. Durham, NC: Duke University Press, 2015.

———. "Places Sensed, Senses Placed: Toward A Sensuous Epistemology of the Environment." In *Empire of the Senses: The Sensual Culture Reader*, edited by David Howes, 179–91. Oxford: Berg, 2005.

Fischlin, Daniel, Ajay Heble, and George Lipsitz. *The Fierce Urgency of Now: Improvisation, Rights, and the Ethics of Cocreation*. Durham, NC: Duke University Press, 2013.

Garber, Megan. "The Powerful Silence of the March for Our Lives." *The Atlantic*, March 24, 2018. https://www.theatlantic.com/entertainment/archive/2018/03/the-powerful-silence-of-the-march-for-our-lives/556469/.

Georgantopoulos, Mary Ann, and Brianna Sacks. "The Parkland Teens for Gun Control Have the Backing of These Huge Organizing Groups." *Buzzfeed News*, February 27, 2018. https://www.buzzfeednews.com/article/maryanngeorgantopoulos/parkland-teens-organization.

Goldman, Adam. "James Comey Is Interrupted by Protesters During Speech at Howard." *New York Times*, September 9, 2017. https://www.nytimes.com/2017/09/22/us/politics/james-comey-protesters-howard.html.

Goodwin, Jean. "Argument Has No Function." *Informal Logic* 27, no. 1 (2007): 69–90.

———. "Comments on 'Rhetoric and Dialectic from the Standpoint of Normative Pragmatics.'" *Argumentation* 14, no. 3 (2000): 287–92.

———. "Conception of Speech Acts in the Theory and Practice of Argumentation: A Case Study of a Debate About Advocacy." *Studies in Logic, Grammar and Rhetoric* 36, no. 49 (2014): 79–98.

———. "Should Climate Scientists Fly? A Case Study of Arguments at the System Level." *Informal Logic* 40, no. 2 (2020): 157–203.

Goodwin, Jean, and Beth Innocenti. "The Pragmatic Force of Making an Argument." *Topoi* 38, no. 4 (2019): 669–80.

Greenberg, Zach. "Rejecting the 'Heckler's Veto.'" TheFire.org, June 14, 2017. https://www.thefire.org/rejecting-the-hecklers-veto/.

Gunn, Joshua. "On Recording Performance or Speech, the Cry, and the Anxiety of the Fix." *Liminalities: A Journal of Performance Studies* 7, no. 3 (2011): 1–30.

———. "On Speech and Public Release." *Rhetoric and Public Affairs* 13, no. 2 (2010): 175–215.

Gunn, Joshua, and Frank E. X. Dance. "The Silencing of Speech in the Late Twentieth Century." In *A Century of Communication Studies: The Unfinished Conversations*, edited by Pat J. Gehrke and William M. Keith, 64–81. New York: Routledge, 2015.

Gunn, Joshua, Greg Goodale, Mirko M. Hall, and Rosa A. Eberly. "Auscultating Again: Rhetoric and Sound Studies." *Rhetoric Society Quarterly* 43, no. 5 (2013): 475–89.

Gunn, Joshua, and Jenny Rice. "About Face/Stuttering Discipline." *Communication and Critical/Cultural Studies* 6, no. 2 (2009): 215–19. https://www.doi.org/10.1080/147914 20902868029.

Hallward, Peter. "The Student Mobilization in Quebec: The Most Significant Act of Civil Disobedience in Canadian History." Centre for Research on Globalization, June 6, 2012. https://www.globalresearch.ca/the-student-mobilization-in-quebec-the-most-significant-act-of-civil-disobedience-in-canadian-history/31278.

Hanna, Jason, Liv Kelly, and Marilia Brocchetto. "Protesting Howard University Students Take Over Administration Building." CNN, March 30, 2018. https://www.cnn.com/2018/03/30/us/protests-financial-aid-scandal-howard-university/index.html.

Harris, Adam. "How the Howard University Protests Hint at the Future of Campus Politics." *The Atlantic*, April 4, 2018. https://www.theatlantic.com/education/archive/2018/04/protest-howard-university/557270/.

———. "The Media's Week-Long Attention Span for a Mass Shooting." *The Atlantic*, November 15, 2018. https://www.theatlantic.com/education/archive/2018/11/how-long-does-media-cover-mass-shootings/575926/.

———. "The Year the Gun Conversation Changed." *The Atlantic*, December 27, 2018. https://www.theatlantic.com/education/archive/2018/12/2018-year-gun-conversation-changed/579067/.

Hawk, Byron. *Resounding the Rhetorical: Composition as a Quasi-Object*. Pittsburgh: University of Pittsburgh Press, 2018.

Heim, Joe. "Echoes of the Past Reverberated in Howard University Student Occupation." *Washington Post*, April 7, 2018. https://www.washingtonpost.com/local/education/echoes-of-the-past-reverberated-in-howard-university-student-occupation/2018/04/07/17e438be-38e0-11e8-acd5-35eac230e514_story.html.

Horley, Timothy E. D. "Rethinking the Heckler's Veto After Charlottesville." *Virginia Law Review* 104, no. 8 (2018). https://www.virginialawreview.org/articles/rethinking-hecklers-veto-after-charlottesville/.

Hudson, David L., Jr., "Controversial Speakers and the Problem of the Heckler's Veto." Freedom Forum Institute, April 26, 2017.

Hwang, Priscilla Ki Sun. "Vulnerable Downtown Residents Hit Breaking Point as Convoy Enters 5th Day." CBC News, February 1, 2022. https://www.cbc.ca/news/canada/ottawa/truck-convoy-downtown-ottawa-residents-mental-health-1.6333674.

Ihde, Don. *Listening and Voice: Phenomenologies of Sound*. 2nd ed. Albany: State University of New York Press, 2007.

Innocenti, Beth. "Countering Questionable Tactics by Crying Foul." *Argumentation and Advocacy* 47, no. 3 (2011): 178–88.

———. "Demanding a Halt to Metadiscussions." *Argumentation* 36, no. 3 (2022): 345–64.

———. "A Normative Pragmatic Model of Making Fear Appeals." *Philosophy and Rhetoric* 44, no. 3 (2001): 273–90.

Innocenti (Manolescu), Beth. "Norms of Presentational Force." *Argumentation and Advocacy* 41 (2005): 139–51.

Innocenti, Beth, and Nichole Kathol. "The Persuasive Force of Demanding." *Philosophy and Rhetoric* 51, no. 1 (2018): 50–72.

Jackson, Sally. "Reason-Giving and the Natural Normativity of Argumentation." *Topoi* 38 (2019): 631–43. https://doi.org/10.1007/s11245-018-9553-5.

Jackson, Sally, and Scott Jacobs. "Structure of Conversational Argument: Pragmatic Bases for the Enthymeme." *Quarterly Journal of Speech* 66, no. 3 (1980): 251–64. https://doi.org/10.1080/00335638009383524.

Jacobs, Scott. "Nonfallacious Rhetorical Strategies: Lyndon Johnson's Daisy Ad." *Argumentation* 20, no. 4 (2006): 421–42.

———. "Rhetoric and Dialectic from the Standpoint of Normative Pragmatics." *Argumentation* 14, no. 3 (2000): 261–86.

James, Robin. *The Sonic Episteme: Acoustic Resonance, Neoliberalism, and Biopolitics*. Durham, NC: Duke University Press, 2019.

Jamieson, Amber. "Emma González Stood Silently on Stage for Minutes in a Powerful Protest." *Buzzfeed News*, March 24, 2018. https://www.buzzfeednews.com/article/amberjamieson/emma-gonzalez-march-for-our-lives-protest-dc.

Jarrett, Laura, and Katishi Maake. "The Former FBI Director Spoke at Howard University. It Did Not Go Well." CNN, September 22, 2017. https://www.cnn.com/2017/09/22/politics/james-comey-howard-speech/index.html.

Jarvie, Jenny. "Girl Thrown from Desk Didn't Obey Because the Punishment Was Unfair, Attorney Says." *Los Angeles Times*, October 29, 2015. https://www.latimes.com/nation/la-na-girl-thrown-punishment-unfair-20151029-story.html.

Jones, Keith. "Quebec Law Criminalizing Student Strike Threatens Basic Rights of All." *World Socialist*, May 19, 2012. https://www.wsws.org/en/articles/2012/05/queb-m19.html.

Kane, Brian. *Sound Unseen: Acousmatic Sound in Theory and Practice*. Oxford: Oxford University Press, 2014.

Kauffeld, Fred J. "Presumptions and the Distribution of Argumentative Burdens in Acts of Proposing and Accusing." *Argumentation* 12 (1998): 245–66. https://doi.org/10.1023/A:1007704116379.

Kay, Jonathan. "Canada's Truck Convoy Is Just a Stunt in a Country Where Populism Is Still Taboo." *Washington Post*, February 7, 2022. https://www.washingtonpost.com/outlook/2022/02/07/canada-truck-convoy-ottawa/.

———. "The Ottawa Trucker Protest Was Disruptive. The Hysterical Reaction to It Was Worse." *Quillette*, February 21, 2022. https://quillette.com/2022/02/21/the-ottawa-trucker-protest-was-disruptive-the-hysterical-reaction-to-it-was-worse/.

Keith, William. *Democracy as Discussion: Civic Education and the American Forum Movement*. Lanham, MD: Lexington Books, 2007.

———. "Identity, Rhetoric and Myth: A Response to Mailloux and Leff." *Rhetoric Society Quarterly* 30, no. 4 (2000): 95–106. https://www.jstor.org/stable/3886119.

———. "On the Origins of Speech as a Discipline: James A. Winans and Public Speaking as Practical Democracy." *Rhetoric Society Quarterly* 38, no. 3 (2008): 239–58.

———. "We Are the Speech Teachers." *Review of Communication* 11, no. 2 (2011): 83–92.

Keith, William M., and Kari Whittenberger-Keith. "The Conversational Call: An Analysis of Conversational Aspects of Public Oratory." *Research on Language and Social Interaction* 22 (1988/89): 115–56.

Kember, Sarah, and Joanna Zylinska. *Life After New Media: Mediation as a Vital Process*. Cambridge: MIT Press, 2012.

Kerr, Emma. "Howard U. Sit-In Could Be the Start of Something Bigger." *Chronicle of Higher Education*, April 2, 2018. https://www.chronicle.com/article/howard-u-sit-in-could-be-the-start-of-something-bigger/.

Kurtz, Stanley. "The Campus Free-Speech Crisis Deepens." *National Review*, September 27, 2017. https://www.nationalreview.com/corner/campus-free-speech-crisis-deepens/.

Lalancette, Mireille, and Vincent Raynauld. "An Under-the-Hood Look at Social Media-Fueled Protest: Defining Interactions Between News Media Organizations, Activists, and Citizens on Twitter During the 2012 Quebec Student Strike." *Communication and Culture Review* 2, nos. 1–2 (2019): 4–21.

Leff, Michael. "Rhetorical Disciplines and Rhetorical Disciplinarity: A Response to Mailloux." *Rhetoric Society Quarterly* 30, no. 4 (2000): 83–93. https://www.jstor.org/stable/3886118.

———. "Things Made by Words: Reflections on Textual Criticism." In *Rethinking Rhetorical Theory, Criticism, and Pedagogy: The Living Art of Michael C. Leff*, edited by Antonio de Velasco, John Angus Campbell, and David Henry, 291–306. East Lansing: Michigan State University, 2016.

Leff, Michael, and Fred Kauffeld. "Preface." In *Texts in Context Critical Dialogues on Significant Episodes in American Political Rhetoric*, edited by Michael C. Leff and Fred J. Kauffeld, vii–xix. Davis, CA: Hermagoras Press, 1989.

Leff, Michael, and Andrew Sachs. "Words the Most Like Things: Iconicity and the Rhetorical Text." *Western Journal of Speech Communication* 54, no. 3 (1990): 252–73.

Liebelson, Dana, and Nick Wing. "Behind Millions of Dollars Raised by Parkland Students, an Adult Board of Directors." *Huffington Post*, March 19, 2018. https://www.huffpost.com/entry/march-for-our-lives-action-fund_n_5ab02dbbe4b0697dfe19a488.

Lopez, German. "Watch: Emma González's Incredible Moment of Silence at March for Our Lives." *Vox*, March 25, 2018. https://www.vox.com/policy-and-politics/2018/3/24/17159916/march-for-our-lives-emma-gonzalez-silence.

Mailloux, Steven. "Disciplinary Identities: On the Rhetorical Paths Between English and Communication Studies." *Rhetoric Society Quarterly* 30, no. 2 (2000): 5–29. https://www.jstor.org/stable/3886158.

Maimona, Mashoka. "Quebec's Ban on Religious Clothing Is Chilling: To Be Like Us, You Must Dress Like Us." *Los Angeles Times*, June 24, 2019. https://www.hrw.org/news/2019/06/24/quebecs-ban-religious-clothing-chilling-be-us-you-must-dress-us.

"March for Our Lives Highlights: Students Protesting Guns Say 'Enough Is Enough.'" *New York Times*, March 24, 2018. https://www.nytimes.com/2018/03/24/us/march-for-our-lives.html.

Marshall, Andrew Gavin. "Quebec Steps Closer to Martial Law to Repress Students." *Media Co-op*, May 18, 2012. https://www.mediacoop.ca/story/quebec-steps-closer-martial-law-repress-student-movement/10960.

Masis, Julie. "Quebec Bangs Pots and Pans in Growing Protests." *The World*, July 31, 2016. https://www.pri.org/stories/2012-06-03/quebec-bangs-pots-and-pans-growing-protests.

Massumi, Brian. "Buying Out: Of Capitulation and Contestation." *Theory and Event* 15, no. 3 (2012). https://muse.jhu.edu/article/484453.

McGee, Michael C. "In Search of 'the People': A Rhetorical Alternative." *Quarterly Journal of Speech* 61, no. 3 (1975): 235–49.

———. "The People." In *Rhetoric in Postmodern America: Conversations with Michael Calvin McGee*, edited by Carol Corbin, 115–36. New York: Guilford Press, 1998.

McIlvenny, Paul. "Heckling in Hyde Park: Verbal Audience Participation in Popular Public Discourse." *Language in Society* 25, no. 1 (1996): 27–60.

Meads, Timothy. "Howard University Students Chant 'F**k James Comey' During His Convocation Speech." Townhall.com, September 22, 2017. https://townhall.com/tipsheet/timothymeads/2017/09/22/howard-university-students-shout-down-james-comey-n2385261.

Medhurst, Martin J. "Public Address and Significant Scholarship: Four Challenges to the Rhetorical Renaissance." In *Texts in Context: Critical Dialogues on Significant Episodes in American Political Rhetoric*, edited by Michael C. Leff and Fred J. Kauffeld, 29–42. Davis, CA: Hermagoras Press, 1989.

Mehreen, Rushdia, and David Gray-Donald. "Spring 2015 Anti-Austerity Movement in Québec: A Critical Retrospective of the Organizing." *Canadian Dimension*, October 21, 2015. https://canadiandimension.com/articles/view/spring-2015-anti-austerity-movement-in-quebec-a-critical-perspective.

Meissner, Deb. "Video: Crowd of Supporters Greets Anti-Vaccine-Mandate Truck Convoy as It Leaves Vancouver for Ottawa." *Interior News*, January 23, 2022. https://www.interior-news.com/news/video-crowd-of-supporters-greets-anti-vaccine-mandate-truck-convoy-as-it-leaves-vancouver-for-ottawa-2-6500330.

Menza, Kaitlin. "Emma González Explained How She Finds Strength During Those Tough Speeches." *Cosmopolitan*, April 12, 2018. https://www.cosmopolitan.com/politics/a19755629/emma-gonzalez-speeches/.

Miller, Lisa, and Andres Kudacki. "On the Ground with the Parkland Teens as They Plot a Revolution." *New York Magazine*, March 5, 2018. https://nymag.com/intelligencer/2018/03/on-the-ground-with-parkland-teens-as-they-plot-a-revolution.html.

Miranda, Carolina A. "Recent Mass Shootings in the US: A Timeline." *Los Angeles Times*, September 1, 2019. https://www.latimes.com/world-nation/story/2019-08-03/united-states-mass-shootings.
Murphy, Jessica. "Freedom Convoy: Why Canadian Truckers Are Protesting in Ottawa." BBC News, January 29, 2022. https://www.bbc.com/news/world-us-canada-60164561.
Nietzsche, Friedrich. *Twilight of the Idols*. New York: Modern Library, 1968. Accessed at https://www.handprint.com/SC/NIE/GotDamer.html.
Nzanga, Merdie. "Protesters Jeer, Disrupt James Comey Speech at Howard University." NBC News, September 22, 2017. https://www.nbcnews.com/politics/white-house/protesters-jeer-james-comey-howard-university-n803756.
Oppenheim, M. "Emma González: Student Who Survived Florida Shooting Hailed as Hero for Her Impassioned Speech at Gun Control Rally." *The Independent*, February 18, 2018. https://www.independent.co.uk/news/world/americas/emma-gonzales-speech-gun-control-hero-florida-shooting-a8216746.html.
Paliewicz, Nicholas S. *Extraction Politics: Rio Tinto and the Corporate Persona*. University Park: Penn State University Press, 2024.
Pane, Lisa Marie. "Parkland Attack Fueled Big Shift in America's Gun Politics." *Spokesman-Review*, February 7, 2019. https://www.spokesman.com/stories/2019/feb/07/parkland-attack-fueled-big-shift-in-americas-gun-p/.
Parent, Rachel. "'We're Not Lawyers': Ottawa Protest Organizer Says MOU Not Meant to Endorse Toppling the Canadian Government." *Saltwire*, February 10, 2022. https://www.saltwire.com/atlantic-canada/news/were-not-lawyers-ottawa-protest-organizer-says-mou-not-meant-to-endorse-toppling-the-canadian-government-100691492/.
Parkhill, Maggie. "Who Is Who? A Guide to the Major Players in the Trucker Convoy Protest." CTV News, February 22, 2022. https://www.ctvnews.ca/canada/who-is-who-a-guide-to-the-major-players-in-the-trucker-convoy-protest-1.5776441.
Philipsen, Gerry. "Paying Lip Service to 'Speech' in Disciplinary Naming, 1914–1954." In *A Century of Communication Studies: The Unfinished Conversations*, edited by Pat J. Gehrke and William M. Keith, 46–63. New York: Routledge, 2015.
"Police Swiftly Shut Down Student Protest About Quebec Spending Cuts." CTV News, March 23, 2015. https://www.ctvnews.ca/canada/police-swiftly-shut-down-student-protest-about-quebec-spending-cuts-1.2293027.
Powell, Aziz. "Protest Chants During Former FBI Director James Comey's Convocation Address at Howard University." *Pancocojams*, September 23, 2017. https://pancocojams.blogspot.com/2017/09/protest-chants-during-former-fbi.html.
Pullum, Amanda. "Social Movement Theory and the 'Modern Day Tea Party.'" *Sociology Compass* 8, no. 12 (2014): 1377–87.
"Quebec Student Associations Cheer PQ Tuition Freeze." *CBC / Radio Canada*, September 20, 2012. https://www.cbc.ca/news/canada/montreal/quebec-student-associations-cheer-pq-tuition-freeze-1.1176860.
Raynauld, Vincent, Mireille Lalancette, and Sofia Tourigny-Koné. "Political Protest 2.0: Social Media and the 2012 Student Strike in the Province of Quebec, Canada." *French Politics* 14, no. 1 (2016): 1–29.
———. "Rethinking Digital Activism as It Unfolds: Ambient Political Engagement on Twitter During the 2012 Quebec Student Strike." In *What's Trending in Canadian Politics? Understanding Transformations in Power, Media, and the Public Sphere*, edited by

Mireille Lalancette, Vincent Raynauld, and Erin Crandall, 44–62. Vancouver: University of British Columbia, 2019.

Redding, W. Charles. "Extrinsic and Intrinsic Criticism." *Western Speech* 21 (1957): 96–102.

Reilly, Katie. "Howard Students Take Over Administration Building in Protest Amid Financial Aid Scandal." *Time*, March 30, 2018. https://time.com/5222906/howard-university-financial-aid-scandal-protest/.

Rentschler, Carrie. "On s'en câlisse, La loi spéciale: The Music Festival That Wasn't." *Wi: Journal of Mobile Media* 6, no. 2 (2012). https://web.archive.org/web/20151104011918/http://wi.mobilities.ca/on-sen-calisse-la-loi-special-the-music-festival-that-wasnt/.

Roll, Nick. "Rejecting a Speaker." *Inside Higher Ed*, September 24, 2017. https://www.insidehighered.com/news/2017/09/25/howard-university-students-shout-throughout-james-comey-speech.

Rosen, Joseph. "Multigenerational Casserole Orchestras: The New Face of Anarchist Insurgency." *Wi: Journal of Mobile Media* 6, no. 2 (2012). https://web.archive.org/web/20160414102330/http://wi.mobilities.ca/multigenerational-casserole-orchestras-the-new-face-of-anarchist-insurgency/.

Sanger, Kerran L. "Functions of Freedom Signing in the Civil Rights Movement: The Activists' Implicit Rhetorical Theory." *Howard Journal of Communications* 8, no. 2 (1997): 179–95.

———. "Slave Resistance and Rhetorical Self-Definition: Spirituals as a Strategy." *Western Journal of Communication* 59, no. 3 (1995): 177–92.

Sathish-Van Atta, Madhuri. "This One Moment from March for Our Lives Will Make You Feel the Parkland Students' Grief." *Bustle*, March 24, 2018. https://www.bustle.com/p/emma-gonzalez-did-a-moment-of-silence-at-march-for-our-lives-that-will-stick-with-you-forever-8596763.

Schaeffer, Pierre. "Acousmatics." In *Audio Culture: Readings in Modern Music*, edited by Christoph Cox and Daniel Warner, 76–81. New York: Continuum, 2004.

Schisler, Cole. "Unvaccinated Truckers Plan 'Freedom Convoy' to Protest Cross-Border Vaccine Mandate." *Langley Advance Times*, January 22, 2022. https://www.langleyadvancetimes.com/news/unvaccinated-truckers-plan-freedom-convoy-to-protest-cross-border-vaccine-mandate/.

Schudson, Michael. "Why Conversation Is Not the Soul of Democracy." *Critical Studies in Media Communication* 14, no. 4 (1997): 297–309.

Schweitzer, Ally. "As Howard University Turns 150, Students Question Its Commitment to Social Justice." *WAMU 88.5 American University Radio*, October 21, 2017. https://wamu.org/story/17/10/21/howard-university-turns-150-students-question-commitment-social-justice/.

Segarra, Lisa Marie, Katie Reilly, Eli Meixler, and Jennifer Calfas. "Sheriff's Office Had Received About 20 Calls Regarding Suspect: The Latest on the Florida School Shooting." *Time*, February 18, 2018. https://time.com/5158678/what-to-know-about-the-active-shooter-situation-at-florida-high-school/.

Serafis, Dimitris, E. Dimitris Kitis, and Ariris Archakis. "Graffiti Slogans and the Construction of Collective Identity: Evidence from the Anti-Austerity Protests in Greece." *Text and Talk* 38, no. 6 (2018). https://dx.doi.org/10.1515/text-2018-0023.

Simón, Yara. "Emma González Going Silent Is the Most Powerful Moment from March for Our Lives Protest." *Remezcla*, March 24, 2018. https://remezcla.com/culture/emma-gonzalez-march-for-our-lives-moment-of-silence/.

Steele, Catherine Knight. "The Digital Barbershop: Blogs and Online Oral Culture Within the African American Community." *Social Media and Society* 2, no. 4 (2016). https://doi.org/10.1177/2056305116683205.

Steinskog, Erik. *Afrofuturism and Black Sound Studies: Culture, Technology, and Things to Come*. New York: Palgrave Macmillan, 2018.

Sterne, Jonathan. "Bodies-Streets." *Wi: Journal of Mobile Media* 6, no. 2 (2012). https://web.archive.org/web/20160416104204/http://wi.mobilities.ca/bodies-streets/.

———. "A Groove We Can Move To: The Sound and Senses of Quebec's *Manifs Casseroles*, Spring 2012." In *Unruly Rhetorics: Protest, Persuasion, and Publics*, edited by Jonathan Alexander, Susan C. Jarratt, and Nancy Welch, 60–71. Pittsburgh: University of Pittsburgh Press, 2018.

———. "Sonic Imaginations." In *The Sound Studies Reader*, edited by Jonathan Sterne, 1–18. London: Routledge, 2012.

Sterne, Jonathan, and Natalie Zemon Davis. "Quebec's *Manifs Casseroles* Are a Call for Order." *Globe and Mail*, May 31, 2012. https://www.theglobeandmail.com/opinion/quebecs-manifs-casseroles-are-a-call-for-order/article4217621/.

St. Felix, Doreen. "The Prosperity Gospel of Rihanna." *Pitchfork*, April 1, 2015. https://pitchfork.com/thepitch/724-the-prosperity-gospel-of-rihanna/.

Stoever, Jennifer Lynn. *The Sonic Color Line: Race and the Cultural Politics of Listening*. New York: New York University Press, 2016.

Stolow, Jeremy. "A Revolution on the Corner of St-Hurbert and Marie-Anne." *Wi: Journal of Mobile Media* 6, no. 2 (2012). https://web.archive.org/web/20160416104126/http://wi.mobilities.ca/a-revolution-on-the-corner-of-st-hubert-and-marie-anne/.

Stuart, Tessa. "Gun Control: Why the Response to Parkland Was Different." *Rolling Stone*, March 23, 2018. https://www.rollingstone.com/politics/politics-features/gun-control-why-the-response-to-parkland-was-different-202219/.

Tasker, John Paul. "Thousands Opposed to COVID-19 Rules Converge on Parliament Hill." CBC News, January 29, 2022. https://www.cbc.ca/news/politics/truck-convoy-protest-some-key-players-1.6332312.

Thunberg, Greta. "Remarks at United Nations." NBC News, September 23, 2019. https://www.nbcnews.com/news/world/read-greta-thunberg-s-full-speech-united-nations-climate-action-n1057861.

Tognotti, Chris. "Emma González's Powerful Words at March for Our Lives Are Necessary Reading." *Bustle*, March 24, 2018. https://www.bustle.com/p/transcript-of-emma-gonzalezs-march-for-our-lives-speech-will-absolutely-crush-you-8596656.

Topintzi, Nina, and Stefano Versace. "A Linguistic Analysis of the Modern Greek *Dekapentasyllavo* Meter." *Journal of Greek Linguistics* 15, no. 2 (2015): 235–69.

"Toronto MP Thinks a Freedom Convoy Term Is a Call for Hitler." *Toronto Sun*, February 22, 2022. https://torontosun.com/news/national/toronto-mp-thinks-a-freedom-convoy-term-is-call-for-hitler.

Turley, Jonathan. "Protesters Disrupt Comey Speech at Howard University." JonathanTurley.org, September 26, 2017. https://jonathanturley.org/2017/09/26/protesters-disrupt-comey-speech-at-howard-university/.

Vera, Amir. "9-Day Sit-In at Howard University Ends." CNN, April 6, 2018. https://www.cnn.com/2018/04/06/us/howard-university-protest-ends/index.html.

Veritas 1867. "President Frederick, Staff Exposed Student Whistleblower in Financial Aid Fraud, Targeted Protestors." Medium (blog), March 27, 2018. https://medium.com/@veritas1867/president-frederick-staff-exposed-student-whistleblower-in-financial-aid-fraud-targeted-60ba3e81d0c9.

Walsham, Alexandra. "Rough Music and Charivari: Letters Between Natalie Zemon Davis and Edward Thompson, 1970–1972." *Past and Present* 235, no. 1 (2017): 243–62.

Ware, Jared. "Community, Joy and Understanding Power Lessons from HUResist." *Millennials Are Killing Capitalism* (podcast). https://www.patreon.com/posts/community-joy-18075176.

Watts, Shannon. "2018 Was The Year We Turned the Tide on Ending Gun Violence." *Huffington Post*, December 27, 2018. https://m.huffpost.com/us/entry/us_5c23d58ae4b08aaf7a8d4380/amp?ec_carp=7198207910443105795.

Weheliye, Alexander G. *Phonographies: Grooves in Sonic Afro-Modernity*. Durham, NC: Duke University Press, 2005.

Weismann, Jerry. "Emma González: Sound of Silence." *Forbes*, March 26, 2018. https://www.forbes.com/sites/jerryweissman/2018/03/26/emma-gonzalez-sound-of-silence/#46a43c2060b8.

West, Caroline. "The Lean In Collection: Women, Work, and the Will to Represent." *Open Cultural Studies* 2, no. 1 (2018): 430–39.

Wichelns, Herbert A. "The Literary Criticism of Oratory [1925]." In *Landmark Essays on Rhetorical Criticism*, edited by Thomas A. Benson, 5:1–35. Davis, CA: Hermagoras Press, 1993.

Winans, James Albert. *Public Speaking: Principles and Practice*. Ithaca, NY: Sewell, 1915.

Witt, Emily. "How the Survivors of Parkland Began the Never Again Movement." *New Yorker*, February 19, 2018. https://www.newyorker.com/news/news-desk/how-the-survivors-of-parkland-began-the-never-again-movement.

———. "The March for Our Lives Presents a Radical New Model for Youth Protest." *New Yorker*, March 25, 2018. https://www.newyorker.com/news/dispatch/the-march-for-our-lives-presents-a-radical-new-model-for-youth-protest.

———. "Urgency and Frustration: The Never Again Movement Gathers Momentum." *New Yorker*, February 23, 2018. https://www.newyorker.com/news/news-desk/urgency-and-frustration-the-never-again-movement-gathers-momentum.

Wolfe, Sean. "Instagram Just Surpassed Snapchat as the Most Used App Among American Teens, According to a New Wall Street Survey." *Business Insider*, October 22, 2018. https://www.businessinsider.com/instagram-snapchat-popularity-teens-piper-jaffray-2018-10.

Woolbert, Charles H. "The Organization of Departments of Speech Science in Universities." *Quarterly Journal of Public Speaking* 2, no. 1 (1916): 64–77.

———. "The Teaching of Speech as an Academic Discipline." *Quarterly Journal of Speech* 9, no. 1 (1923): 1–18. https://doi.org/10.1080/00335632309379407.

Wyatt, Nelson. "Student Protests: Pots-and-Pans Tactic Spreads Through Quebec." *Toronto Star*, May 25, 2012. https://www.thestar.com/news/canada/2012/05/25/student_protests_potsandpans_tactic_spreads_through_quebec.html

Index

accountability
  demands for, 3, 17, 79, 118
  heckling as driver of, 81
  at Howard University, 86, 101–3
  power and, 5, 17, 26, 29–30, 138
  of Québec government, 24
acousmatics
  Blackness and, 142
  cut-outs and, 59
  defined, 32
  history of, 31–33, 150n8
  HU Resist and, 98
  in media environment, 9, 12, 16, 22, 33, 148
  point of audition and, 34–35
  presence affects and, 11
  public screen and, 55, 146
  Pythagorean curtain/veil and, 22, 32–34
  rhetoric and, 27, 29–30, 35, 50, 55, 122
  sound bodies and, 35–37, 84
  sound studies and, 21, 28
  sound tactics and, 16, 122
  waveforms and, 53–54
advocacy. *See* social movements
African Americans. *See* Black Americans
Ajiake, Jason, 85
Allende, Salvador, 114
Amsterdam School of Argumentation, 14
Aquinas, Thomas, 36
Archakis, Argiris, 3
argument, 7, 13–16, 139–47
arguments
  dialectical approach to, 14
  first cause argument, 36
  heckling in undermining of, 80
  moral, 137, 147
  power of sound in, 37
  rhetoric compared to, 7
  as social acts, 13, 15
  soundness of, 14–16, 139
  speech acts and, 15, 17
  of Syntagma Square protesters, 3–4
  validity of, 14, 98, 149n13
Aristotle, 5, 21

artificial intelligence, 37
Asen, Rob, 152n41
audiovisual materials, 34, 62, 81–82, 84, 98, 124, 153n3
augmentation, 68, 70–71

Bain, Alexander, 41–42
Barad, Karen, 150n2
barbershops, 87, 97–99, 106, 141, 155n66
Barge, Alexis, 92
Bauder, James, 135
Bennett, Jane, 150n2
Bernstein, Robin, 78
Bill 78 (Québec, 2012), 24, 107–22, 125–26, 128
Black, Hugo, 93
Black Americans
  barbershops and, 87, 97–99, 106, 141, 155n66
  civil rights activism by, 79, 82, 87–90, 93, 97–98, 100, 117
  class consciousness among, 80
  HBCUs and, 79, 86, 100, 141
  oral tradition among, 79, 90, 98
  racism experienced by, 78, 79, 98
  visual features associated with, 89
  See also Howard University
Black Liberation, 24, 85–88, 98
Black Lives Matter movement, 5
Black Power, 82, 103
Brandon, Alex, 75
Broad, Eli, 67
Burke, Kenneth, 29

call-and-response, 79, 88–93, 95
capitalism, 5, 19–20, 76, 80, 85
Carmichael, Stokely (Kwame Ture), 88–89, 154n16
Casseroles, the, 108–27
  charivari and, 24, 107, 116–19, 121, 126–27, 142
  as cultural resource, 127
  demands of, 25, 110, 112, 114, 115, 126
  history of, 117–18
  immersion and, 25, 53, 107, 109, 114, 116, 120, 121, 142

Casseroles, the (*continued*)
  improvisation used by, 107
  media coverage of, 25, 109, 122–24
  musicking used by, 25, 120–22
  power of, 110, 114, 142
  on social media, 25, 53, 109, 111, 121–24
  sound body of, 53, 109, 111–12, 118–26
  sound tactics and, 115–16, 122, 126, 142
Certeau, Michel de, 6, 119
Charest, Jean, 112–14, 118, 119, 125
charivari, 24, 107, 116–19, 121, 126–27, 142, 143
Chavez, Edna, 67
Chené, François-Olivier, 114
Chion, Michel, 34, 60–61, 151n15
citizenship, 25, 45, 124, 150n24, 152n41
civil rights activism, 79, 82, 87–90, 93, 97–98, 100, 117
climate activism, 78
close textual analysis, 47–49
Columbine High School shooting (1999), 57
Comey, James, 81, 87–92, 94–98
communication
  channels of, 2
  environment for, 4, 17, 19, 134, 137
  as field of study, 46
  models of, 15–16, 27
  political, 42
  See also conversation; listening; speech
conversation
  democratic, 43, 145, 148
  interdisciplinary, 38
  as metaphor for discourse, 20
  preformed, 121
  public speaking as, 40–41, 43, 138, 145
  rules and norms for, 17, 91–92, 134
  Schudson on, 151n26
  sound in structuring of, 5
  Winans on, 40–41, 43, 151n26
Corin, Kalyn, 66
Cornell school of speech, 44, 145
COVID-19 pandemic, 25, 127, 129–33, 135, 136, 155n64
cut-outs
  acousmatics and, 59
  augmentation and, 68, 70–71
  diminution and, 68, 71–72
  expectations violated by, 23, 58, 62, 68
  immediacy and, 23, 51–52, 58, 67–68, 140
  at March for Our Lives, 23, 58, 59, 67–77, 141
  in music, 59, 140
  performance and, 52, 58

  photography of, 75–77
  power of, 74
  release from, 58, 68, 73
  sound bodies and, 23, 69, 143
  time and, 58, 68–69

Daughtry, J. Martin, 83–84
Davis, Natalie Zemon, 117–18
dekapentasyllavos (Greek poetic meter), 1, 3–5, 128
demand, 3–17, 137–43
demands
  for accountability, 3, 17, 79, 118
  amplification of, 5
  of the Casseroles, 25, 110, 112, 114, 115, 126
  credibility of, 17–18, 139
  efficacy of, 18, 19
  feelings and, 17, 18, 20, 110
  of Freedom Convoy, 25, 130–36, 140
  of HU Resist, 24, 85–87, 93, 100–106
  immersion and, 25
  intensity of, 85
  moral nature of, 4, 6, 18–19, 80, 137, 139, 150n21
  of Parkland Kids, 23, 58, 63, 65, 67–68, 73, 147
  performance of, 21
  presentational force of, 149n20
  procedural condition for, 18, 150n22
  protest chants as, 1–4
  requests versus, 2, 17, 149–50n21
  sound bodies and, 12, 54, 140
  soundness of, 137–43
  substantive condition for, 18–19, 150n22
  tactical, 16–20
  transparency of, 15, 18
  See also social movements
democracy
  bargain of, 115
  in everyday life, 44
  feelings of, 25
  governance in, 108, 109
  judgment for, 28
  liberal, 24, 124
  rhetoric and, 21
  threats to, 94, 114
DeNora, Tia, 8, 51
Derrida, Jacques, 10–11
DeVos, Betsy, 80, 82, 86
Dewey, John, 144, 145
dialectical approach, 14
digital environment
  acousmatics in, 22
  Black orality in, 97

credibility of sources in, 37
engagement in social movements, 30
fragmentation within, 16
replicative nature of media in, 54
sound bodies and, 12, 55
See also public screen; social media
diminution, 68, 71–72
Douglass, Frederick, 100
Dyson, Frances, 37

Eadie, William, 46
echolocation, 53, 111, 121
Electronic Voice Phenomena (EVP), 11
elocutionists, 39, 42, 43, 144
emotions. *See* feelings
emplacement, 35, 110–12, 118, 119, 123, 155n2
ethical considerations, 5, 105, 106, 128, 147
European Union, 1, 128
Everytown for Gun Safety, 67
EVP (Electronic Voice Phenomena), 11

Facebook, 109, 114, 123
feelings
    amplification of, 3, 20, 140
    in call-and-response, 90
    collective, 71, 73, 74
    demands and, 17, 18, 20, 110
    of democracy, 25
    embodied, 30, 68
    intensity and, 51, 52, 102
    point of audition and, 34
    public, 4, 50, 115
    of salience, 4, 20, 25, 109
    sound and, 2–4, 8, 11, 13, 30, 32
    speech and, 39, 45
    of urgency, 20, 52, 77
Feiner, Irving, 93
Feiner v. New York (1951), 93–94
Feld, Steven, 110–11
Ferguson effect, 88
Ford, Doug, 132
Frederick, Wayne A. I., 86–88, 99–106
Freedom Convoy, 25, 127, 129–36, 139–40
free speech, 93–94, 96

Getty Images, 76–78
Gifford, Gabrielle, 67
Goldman, Adam, 95
González, X
    cut-out utilized by, 23, 58, 59, 62, 67–77, 140–41

March for Our Lives speech by, 23, 58, 59, 67–75
    photographic images of, 75–78
    strategic use of immediacy by, 52, 56, 67
    "We Call BS" speech by, 64–66
Goodwin, Jean, 17
Greece
    austerity measures in, 1–2, 4, 128
    Colonel's Junta in (1967–74), 2, 15
    dekapentasyllavos used in, 1, 3–5, 128
    Golden Dawn extremists in, 5, 128
    Syntagma Square protests in, 1–5, 13, 19–20, 128
Groz, Elizabeth, 150n2
Gunn, Joshua, 11, 45–47
gun violence, 22–23, 52, 56–58, 61–72, 76–79, 140

Hawk, Byron, 150n7
HBCUs (historically Black colleges and universities), 79, 86, 100, 141
heckler's veto, 87, 93–96
heckling
    arguments undermined by, 80
    Comey protests and, 90–91, 94–98
    music and, 82, 101–2
    power of, 52, 80–81, 93
    soundness of, 97
    strategic, 24, 79, 102
    timing of, 81, 82, 87
hijab, 124, 157n40
historically Black colleges and universities (HBCUs), 79, 86, 100, 141
Hogg, David, 66
Horley, Timothy E. D., 93
Howard University
    accountability at, 86, 101–3
    assistance with FBI investigation of Ture, 88, 154n16
    Comey's speaking engagement at, 81, 88–92, 94–98
    federal money received by, 80, 86
    financial aid scandal at, 24, 82, 99–103
    in perpetuation of inequality, 80, 85–86
    See also HU Resist
humanism, 30, 44, 145
HU Resist, 85–107
    acousmatics and, 98
    administration building occupation, 82, 100–106
    call-and-response used by, 79, 88–93, 95
    Comey protests by, 81, 87–92, 94–98

HU Resist *(continued)*
   demands of, 24, 85–87, 93, 100–106
   formation of, 23, 80, 85–86
   heckler's veto and, 93–96
   identity of, 82, 85, 88, 105
   improvisation by, 24, 82, 85–86, 90–91, 104–7
   intensity of, 82, 85–87, 96, 102–4
   media coverage of, 92, 95–96, 101–3
   protest songs used by, 24, 52, 79, 89, 101–3
   public screen and, 82, 86, 87, 92, 103, 104, 155n66
   recruitment by, 82, 86, 87, 92
   on social media, 82, 86–88, 98–100, 104
   sound body of, 82, 85, 92, 99, 103–6, 141
   See also heckling

identity
   collective, 3–5, 12, 90, 107, 116
   creation by protesters, 16, 24–25
   cultural, 1, 3, 128
   of HU Resist, 82, 85, 88, 105
   politics of, 77
Ihde, Don, 59
Illinois school of speech, 44, 145
immediacy
   acousmatics and, 30
   cut-outs and, 23, 51–52, 58, 67–68, 140
   description of, 22, 51
   durational, 61
   of March for Our Lives, 23, 54–56
   point of audition and, 35, 60
   power of, 55–56
   public speaking and, 44
   of Snapchat, 62
   of sound, 59–62, 78–79
   vibrations and, 51
immersion
   acousmatics and, 30
   the Casseroles and, 25, 53, 107, 109, 114, 116, 120, 121, 142
   demands and, 25
   description of, 22, 51
   point of audition and, 35
   power of, 24
   sound and, 25, 109, 110, 114, 116, 126, 133
   vibrations and, 22, 51–53, 109–11
improvisation, 24, 82, 85–86, 90–91, 104–7, 143
Innocenti, Beth, 19, 149n20
intensity
   acousmatics and, 30
   of demands, 85
   description of, 22, 51

   feelings and, 51, 52, 102
   of HU Resist, 82, 85–87, 96, 102–4
   improvisation and, 105
   point of audition and, 34, 35
   of sound, 81–84
   vibrations and, 52, 83
International Monetary Fund, 1, 128
Iraq War, 83, 84

James, Robin, 29, 148, 150n2, 154n46
Jarrett, Laura, 96
Jones, Keith, 113
Jonker, Harold, 130
Journal of Communication, The, 46
judgment
   civic, 43
   contextual, 13
   critical, 49, 51
   for democracy, 28
   ethical, 5
   norms of, 38
   practical, 7, 14, 16, 143, 145
   rhetorical, 28, 38, 48–50
   situated, 40, 146
   soundness of, 6–7, 14–16, 28, 82, 153n3
   in warfare, 83
   See also phronesis
justice, 5, 13, 82, 88–89, 91, 95, 98, 117–18

kairos, 104
Kaluli people, 111
Kalven, Harry, Jr., 93
Kane, Brian, 10, 35, 151n15, 152n59
Kasky, Cameron, 66
Kathol, Nichole, 19
Katz, Deena, 66
Kauffeld, Fred, 48
Kay, Jonathan, 132
Keith, William O., 44, 144, 150n1
Kember, Sarah, 75
King, Yolanda Renee, 67
Kitis, E. Dimitris, 3
Kudacki, Andres, 65, 66

Lalancette, Mireille, 117, 122–23
Leff, Michael, 47, 48, 150n1
"Let's go" chant, 121
Lewis, Philip, 101
listening
   acousmatics and, 11, 31, 35
   to amplification, 61

Comey on, 91–92
to demands, 13
emplacement and, 110
experience of, 59–61
to sound tactics, 20
logic, 4, 14, 68, 70, 88, 119, 149n13

Maake, Katishi, 96
Mailloux, Steven, 150n1
Maple Spring protests (Québec), 112–14, 126, 127
March for Our Lives (2018)
context of, 52, 57
cut-out at, 23, 58, 59, 67–77, 141
González's speech at, 23, 58, 59, 67–75
immediacy of, 23, 54–56
media coverage of, 67, 73–78
organization of, 66–67
turnout for, 67
Marjory Stoneman Douglas (MSD) High School shooting (2018), 22–23, 57, 62–64
Marois, Pauline, 125
Marshall, Andrew Gavin, 113
mass shootings. *See* gun violence
Massumi, Brian, 113
McGee, Michael C., 12, 109, 115
McIlvenny, Paul, 80
McKenney, Alexis, 85–87
Meads, Timothy, 94–95
media environment
acousmatics in, 9, 12, 16, 22, 33, 148
the Casseroles in, 25, 109, 122–24
Freedom Convoy in, 130, 131, 135
HU Resist in, 92, 95–96, 101–3
Maple Spring protests in, 112
March for Our Lives in, 67, 73–78
school shootings in, 56, 57, 62–64
sound bodies and, 12, 13, 36, 55
transnational networks, 13
warfare and, 83, 84
See also digital environment
memories
audio, 111
of civil rights activism, 88, 89
embodied, 11
mobilization of, 56, 59
presence affects and, 11
public, 15, 75, 155n66
Midwest/Illinois school of speech, 44, 145
Miller, Lisa, 65, 66
Moms Demand Action, 66, 67
Moodus village (East Haddam, Connecticut), 10

MoveOn, 66, 67
MSD (Marjory Stoneman Douglas) High School shooting (2018), 22–23, 57, 62–64
Murray, Elwood, 46
music
ambience created by, 8–9
augmentation in, 68, 70
carnival, 117
classical, 70
contemporary, 8–9
cut-outs in, 59, 140
electronic, 31
experimental (*musique concrete*), 7, 31
heckling and, 82, 101–2
new materialism and, 150n2
protest songs, 24, 52, 79, 89, 101–3
time conveyed through, 51
See also sound
musicking, 25, 120–22

National Association of Academic Teachers of Public Speaking (NAATPS), 42, 43, 144
National Society for the Study of Communication (NSSC), 46
Nazi flag, 135–37
Nietzsche, Friedrich, 151n14
normative pragmatics, 149n17, 149n20
Nzanga, Merdie, 95

oral traditions, 3, 79, 90, 98
oratorical texts, 41, 47–49

Paliewicz, Nicholas S., 151n18
Pangalos, Theodoros, 2
Panhellenic Socialist Movement (PASOK), 1–2, 4
Parkland Kids
demands of, 23, 58, 63, 65, 67–68, 73, 147
immediacy of sound used by, 78–79
as inspiration for Thunberg's climate activism, 78
March for Our Lives and, 23, 52, 54–59, 66–78, 141
MSD shooting and, 22–23, 57, 62–64
public screen and, 64, 69
as sound bodies, 56, 63–64, 69
Parti Québécois (PQ), 125–26
PASOK (Panhellenic Socialist Movement), 1–2, 4
performance
by the Casseroles, 116
cut-outs and, 52, 58
of demands, 21

performance *(continued)*
    by Freedom Convoy, 133
    by HU Resist, 87, 91, 92, 99
    of sound tactics, 4
    specificity of, 108
    of speech, 42, 43, 69
Periscope, 82, 86, 87
persuasion
    power of, 94
    rhetoric and, 7, 45
    sound reasoning and, 14, 15, 53
    speech and, 39, 43, 46
Philipsen, Gerry, 46
photography, 75–78, 124
phronesis
    conversation and, 40
    cultural history of, 16
    rhetoric and, 28, 45, 140
    sonic, 30, 148
    speech and, 38, 43, 144
    unsound tactics and, 25
    waveforms and, 54
Pinochet, Augusto, 114, 118
Pittsburgh synagogue shooting (2018), 77
point of audition (POA), 34–35, 55, 60
point of view (POV), 34, 98
politics
    agonistic, 15, 19
    biopolitics, 129–30, 140
    in everyday life, 5, 42, 144
    generational, 59
    of identity, 77
    racialized, 96
    rhetoric and, 29, 42, 45
    warfare and, 83
POV (point of view), 34, 98
power
    accountability and, 5, 17, 26, 29–30, 138
    in agent–institution relationships, 6–7
    of Black community, 97
    of the Casseroles, 110, 114, 142
    coercive, 19
    collective, 109
    of cut-outs, 74
    of heckling, 52, 80–81, 93
    hegemonic, 80
    of immediacy, 55–56
    immersive, 24
    metaphysical, 36, 151n18
    of persuasion, 94
    of photography, 77
    rhetorical, 11, 109

of social movements, 37, 55
of sound, 34, 37, 118, 148
of sound bodies, 12, 13, 36, 37, 138, 151n18
of speech, 5, 128
structures of, 79, 85, 105, 106, 151n18
of students, 100
transdisciplinary, 41
PQ (Parti Québécois), 125–26
presence affects, 10, 11, 28, 35–37
protest songs, 24, 52, 79, 89, 101–3
public screen
    acousmatics and, 55, 146
    in decontextualization of symbols, 136–37
    HU Resist and, 82, 86, 87, 92, 103, 104, 155n66
    noises of everyday life and, 9
    Parkland Kids and, 64, 69
    Pythagorean curtain/veil as, 34
    sound bodies and, 12, 13, 53, 134
    Syntagma Square protests on, 5, 13, 20
    war sounds and, 84
    See also media environment
public speaking, 16–17, 20–21, 27, 38–44, 138, 144–46, 148
Pythagorean curtain/veil, 22, 32–34

Quarterly Journal of Public Speaking, 43–44
Québec
    anti-austerity protests in, 126–27
    Bill 78 in, 24, 107–22, 125–26, 128
    government accountability in, 24
    hijab wearing in, 124, 157n40
    Maple Spring protests in, 112–14, 126, 127
    public education system in, 112, 125–26
    Quiet Revolution in, 112
    See also Casseroles, the
Québécois, Patrick, 123

race and racism
    HU Resist sit-in and, 155n58
    sound tactics and, 78, 95, 96
    systemic racism, 98
    white supremacy, 80, 88, 92, 131, 135, 137, 141
    youth-led movements and, 79
    See also Black Americans
Raynauld, Vincent, 117, 122–23
Redding, W. Charles, 46
Rentschler, Carrie, 120, 124–25
rhetoric
    acousmatic, 27, 29–30, 35, 50, 55, 122
    arguments compared to, 7
    Aristotle's treatise on, 5
    civic conception of, 42–43

INDEX   175

debates regarding study of, 27, 150n1
democracy and, 21
judgment and, 28, 38, 48–50
phronetic approach to, 28, 45, 140
politics and, 29, 42, 45
power of, 11, 109
social movements and, 12, 42, 51
sound and, 6–7, 45, 137–38, 150n7
speech and, 21, 27, 28, 38, 42–46, 144
textual analysis and, 41, 47–49
xenophobic, 128
Rice, Jenny, 45
Rihanna, 82, 101, 104, 154n46
Rosen, Joseph, 119, 120

Sacks, Ya'ara, 135–36
Schaeffer, Pierre, 31–33, 151n15
Schisler, Cole, 130
school shootings, 22–23, 52, 56–58, 61–69, 76, 78–79, 140
Schudson, Michael, 151n26
Serafis, Dimitris, 3
Shaw, Noelle, 92
signification, 11, 33, 51, 53
Small, Christopher, 108
Snapchat, 56, 62–63
social media
  the Casseroles on, 25, 53, 109, 111, 121–24
  Freedom Convoy and, 133, 135
  HU Resist on, 82, 86–88, 98–100, 104
  March for Our Lives on, 67, 74
  MSD shooting on, 56, 62–64
  See also public screen; specific platforms
social movements
  abstract nature of, 12
  change resulting from, 6
  digital engagement in, 30
  diversification of, 5
  institutionalized, 66–67
  legislative wins for, 139
  mass mobilization by, 108
  power of, 37, 55
  rhetoric and, 12, 42, 51
  transnational, 55
  waveforms and, 23
  See also demands; specific movements
Solomon, Mikayli, 92
sonic imagination, 29
sound
  civic role of, 27, 28, 145
  color line and, 95, 96
  defining, 6, 7, 29–31, 137, 150n7

echolocation, 53, 111, 121
emplacement and, 35, 110–12, 118, 119, 123, 155n2
feelings and, 2–4, 8, 11, 13, 30, 32
immediacy of, 59–62, 78–79
immersive, 25, 109, 110, 114, 116, 126, 133
intensity of, 81–84
mechanics of, 22
phenomenology of, 59
power of, 34, 37, 118, 148
recorded, 9, 11, 50
reproduction of, 9, 10, 22
rhetoric and, 6–7, 45, 137–38, 150n7
temporal shape of, 60–61
transcendent qualities of, 12
tripartite ontology of, 33
warfare and, 83–84
See also acousmatics; music; vibrations; waveforms
sound bodies
  acousmatics and, 35–37, 84
  agency of, 12, 35–36, 54, 146
  Black barbershops and, 97
  of the Casseroles, 53, 109, 111–12, 118–26
  cut-outs and, 23, 69, 143
  demands made by, 12, 54, 140
  Freedom Convoy and, 131–36
  of HU Resist, 82, 85, 92, 99, 103–6, 141
  imaginative nature of, 9–10, 35
  media environment and, 12, 13, 36, 55
  Parkland Kids as, 56, 63–64, 69
  power of, 12, 13, 36, 37, 138, 151n18
  presence affects and, 10, 11, 35–37
  public screen and, 12, 13, 53, 134
  sound tactics produced by, 13, 20, 140
  warfare and, 84
  waveforms and, 54–55, 134
soundness
  of arguments, 14–16, 139
  of demands, 137–43
  of heckling, 97
  of judgment, 6–7, 14–16, 28, 82, 153n3
  of reasoning, 7, 13–16, 40, 53
sound objects, 7, 32, 33, 146, 151n15
sound studies, 7, 21, 28–31, 50, 138, 144, 146
sound tactics
  acousmatic, 16, 122
  amplification of, 121
  call-and-response, 79, 88–93, 95
  the Casseroles and, 115–16, 122, 126, 142
  civic use of, 28
  defined, 2, 6

sound tactics *(continued)*
   dekapentasyllavos, 1, 3–5, 128
   extension of influence, 54
   "Let's go" chant, 121
   musicking, 25, 120–22
   performance of, 4
   protest songs, 24, 52, 79, 89, 101–3
   race and, 78, 95, 96
   sound body production of, 13, 20, 140
   See also cut-outs; heckling
speech
   arguments and, 15, 17
   civic role of, 28, 40, 144–45, 148
   Cornell school of, 44, 145
   decline as object of inquiry, 46–47
   English studies compared to, 42, 44
   feelings and, 39, 45
   free, 93–94, 96
   future of, 147
   mechanics of, 22, 42
   Midwest/Illinois school of, 44, 145
   norms of judgment required for, 38
   performance of, 42, 43, 69
   phronesis and, 38, 43, 144
   power of, 5, 128
   presence affects and, 28
   professionalization of, 38, 43–45
   rhetoric and, 21, 27, 28, 38, 42–46, 144
   teaching, 20–21, 28, 38–44, 138–39, 144–45, 147–48
   textual analysis of, 41, 46–49
   See also conversation; demands; public speaking
Steele, Catherine Knight, 97, 98
Sterne, Jonathan, 29, 30, 115–18, 120, 126–27, 156n22
Stolow, Jeremy, 120
Syntagma Square protests (Athens), 1–5, 13, 19–20, 128

tactics
   defined, 6–7, 85
   demands and, 16–20
   unsound, 25, 129, 132–34, 136, 139
   See also sound tactics
Tarr, Delaney, 66
Tasker, John Paul, 131
textual analysis, 41, 46–49
Thompson, Edward, 117
Thousand Oaks bar shooting (2018), 77

Thunberg, Greta, 78
time
   augmentation and, 68, 70–71
   cut-outs and, 58, 68–69
   diachronic, 14, 141
   digital media and, 37, 55
   diminution and, 68, 71–72
   kairos and, 104
   photography and, 75–76
   shape of sound in, 60–61
   shared sense of, 3, 15, 21
   sound bodies and, 36
   waveforms and, 50–51
   See also immediacy
Topintzi, Nina, 3
Tourigny-Koné, Sofia, 117, 122–23
transparency, 15, 18, 81, 100, 102, 107
Trudeau, Justin, 132
Trump, Donald J., 5, 23, 80, 85–88
Turcotte, Roxanna, 123
Ture, Kwame (Stokely Carmichael), 88–89, 154n16
Turley, Jonathan, 96
Twitter, 74, 82, 86, 88, 98, 100, 111, 121–23

ubiquity effect, 121
unsound tactics, 25, 129, 132–34, 136, 139

vaccine mandates, 25, 130–32
validity, 14, 98, 149n13
value hierarchies, 18, 19, 139
Versace, Stefano, 3
vibrations
   emplacement and, 110, 155n2
   immediacy and, 51
   immersion and, 22, 51–53, 109–11
   intensity and, 52, 83
   materially produced, 9
   measurement of, 50
   as narrative wholes, 8
   subterranean, 10
   waveforms of, 108, 116
   See also sound
violence
   of audiovisual images, 153n3
   in Black communities, 88, 93
   charivari as alternative to, 117
   collective power and, 109
   domestic, 117, 118
   Freedom Convoy and, 136

gun-related, 22–23, 52, 56–58, 61–72, 76–79, 140
HU Resist and, 95, 96
in Maple Spring protests, 112
in Syntagma Square protests, 3

Walsham, Alexandra, 117
Ware, Jared, 105–7, 155n58, 155n64, 155n66
warfare, role of sound in, 83–84
Watson, Jim, 75
waveforms
    acousmatics and, 53–54
    amplification of, 54
    cut-outs as, 59
    defined, 50–51
    metaphorical function of, 29–30, 50
    social movements and, 23
    sound bodies and, 54–55, 134
    Syntagma Square protests and, 3
    of vibrations, 108, 116
    See also immediacy; immersion; intensity
Weismann, Jerry, 74
white nationalism, 132, 135–36
white supremacy, 80, 88, 92, 131, 135, 137, 141
Wichelns, Herbert, 44–45, 145
Williams, Brianna, 92
Winans, James Albert, 21, 39–41, 43, 44, 145, 151n26
wisdom, 5, 45, 48, 49, 128, 140
Women's March LA, 66
Woolbert, Charles, 43–44, 145
World Health Organization, 129
Wyatt, Nelson, 119

YouTube, 74, 111, 121

Zylinska, Joanna, 75

THE RSA SERIES IN TRANSDISCIPLINARY RHETORIC

Other titles in this series:

Nathan Stormer, *Sign of Pathology: U.S. Medical Rhetoric on Abortion, 1800s–1960s*

Mark Longaker, *Rhetorical Style and Bourgeois Virtue: Capitalism and Civil Society in the British Enlightenment*

Robin E. Jensen, *Infertility: A Rhetorical History*

Steven Mailloux, *Rhetoric's Pragmatism: Essays in Rhetorical Hermeneutics*

M. Elizabeth Weiser, *Museum Rhetoric: Building Civic Identity in National Spaces*

Chris Mays, Nathaniel A. Rivers and Kellie Sharp-Hoskins, eds., *Kenneth Burke + The Posthuman*

Amy Koerber, *From Hysteria to Hormones: A Rhetorical History*

Elizabeth C. Britt, *Reimagining Advocacy: Rhetorical Education in the Legal Clinic*

Ian E. J. Hill, *Advocating Weapons, War, and Terrorism: Technological and Rhetorical Paradox*

Kelly Pender, *Being at Genetic Risk: Toward a Rhetoric of Care*

James L. Cherney, *Ableist Rhetoric: How We Know, Value, and See Disability*

Susan Wells, *Robert Burton's Rhetoric: An Anatomy of Early Modern Knowledge*

Ralph Cintron, *Democracy as Fetish*

Maggie M. Werner, *Stripped: Reading the Erotic Body*

Timothy Johnson, *Rhetoric, Inc: Ford's Filmmaking and the Rise of Corporatism*

James Wynn and G. Mitchell Reyes, eds., *Arguing with Numbers: The Intersections of Rhetoric and Mathematics*

Ashely Rose Mehlenbacher, *On Expertise: Cultivating Character, Goodwill, and Practical Wisdom*

Stuart J. Murray, *The Living from the Dead: Disaffirming Biopolitics*

G. Mitchell Reyes, *The Evolution of Mathematics: A Rhetorical Approach*

Jenell Johnson, *Every Living Thing: The Politics of Life in Common*

Kellie Sharp-Hoskins, *Rhetoric in Debt*

Jennifer Clary-Lemon, *Nestwork: New Material Rhetorics for Precarious Species*

Nicholas S. Paliewicz, *Extraction Politics: Rio Tinto and the Corporate Persona*

Paul Lynch, *Persuasions of God: Inventing the Rhetoric of René Girard*

Loretta Victoria Ramirez, *The Wound and the Stitch: A Genealogy of the Female Body from Medieval Iberia to SoCal Chicanx Art*

Barbara A. Biesecker, *Reinventing World War II: Popular Memory in the Rise of the Ethnonationalist State*